ECONOMICS AND SOCIETY SERIES: No. 1

Economics in Society:

A Basic Course

ECONOMICS AND SOCIETY SERIES No. 1

General Editor: Professor C. D. Harbury

Economics in Society: A Basic Course

by

D. T. KING

Principal Lecturer in Public Sector Economics,
City of London Polytechnic

and

G. D. HAMILTON

Senior Lecturer in Economics
City of London Polytechnic

London George Allen & Unwin Ltd
Ruskin House Museum Street

First published in 1976

ISBN 0 04 330261 0 Hardback
      0 04 330262 9 Paperback

© George Allen & Unwin Ltd 1976

Printed in Great Britain
in 10pt. Times Roman
by Clarke, Doble, & Brendon Ltd
Burrington Way, Honicknowle
Plymouth, Devon

Preface

This book arose from the need to design a course to provide one of the launching platforms for the series of course units which make up the Modular Degree Scheme (CNAA) operated by the City of London Polytechnic since September 1973. The course evolved and taught by us for this purpose has provided the general framework for this book and we have therefore had the benefit of the reactions and suggestions of our students, most of whom were complete newcomers to economics and were not intending to specialise in the subject. It was our intention to develop a course that was clearly relevant to everyday life and which was rooted in the observation of economic, social and political behaviour, both past and present. This meant that where it seemed helpful, social and political aspects of economic relationships have been dealt with explicitly. This in turn helped to make the course more acceptable to students intending to specialise in sociology, politics or law rather than in economics.

It is impossible to avoid simplification in an introductory text on economics, but we have tried to avoid the over-simplification that can come from assuming away all the complexities and irregularities of the real world. Hence there is little in the way of abstract theorising in the book except in Chapter 4 which is intended to give the flavour of the kind of analysis that students must expect if they proceed to a further and deeper study of economics.

We hope that the book will be of use in a variety of introductory courses in economics taught in colleges and universities, although it is most likely to suit courses run by the polytechnics and leading to first degrees awarded by the Council for National Academic Awards. The book could be used as the first step towards more advanced economics courses or as a complete support course for other disciplines. We feel that it could be useful for courses in economics run as minority time studies in school sixth forms. The treatment in the book is meant to encourage classroom discussion and could be used as the basis for a teacher's own individually designed course. We like to think that the general reader will find the approach interesting and relevant.

Our thanks are due to Professor C. D. Harbury of the City University for his many helpful and pertinent comments and suggestions at all stages of the writing of this book; to our colleagues at the City of

London Polytechnic, Barbara Allison, Alan Burford and Len Stafford who advised and assisted on the taught course; to our modular degree students for their classroom contributions; to Dorothy Lay for her assistance with typing; and of course to our wives and families in general for their encouragement and support and on whom so much of the burden inevitably fell. Figure 11.2 on p. 200 comes from *The Limits to Growth: A Report for The Club of Rome's Project on the Predicament of Mankind,* by Donella H. Meadows, Dennis L. Meadows, Jørgen Randers, William W. Behrens III (a Potomac Associates book published by Universe Books, New York, 1972), graphics by Potomac Associates.

Don King and Duncan Hamilton

January 1975

Contents

Chapter 1

Man and Motoring

INTRODUCTORY REMARKS

A chapter about man's relationships with the motor-car may seem to
be an odd way to begin a book about such an all-embracing subject as
economics in society. There is quite a practical reason. We can hardly
be expected to draw a rough sketch of the entire world of economic
relationships in the space of a few introductory paragraphs, let alone
point out in addition all the links with the other social sciences such as
politics, history and sociology. This book is an attempt to encourage
students to look at the world about them, to observe patterns of
economic behaviour, and also to note when other disciplines have
something useful to say or when the 'economics' of a situation alone
give an adequate picture.

We are not so concerned with building up a body of 'received'
theory concerning economic relationships as with trying to open (or
keep open) the student's eyes to the complexities of the real world.
We want him to recognise both the rationalities and irrationalities of
human behaviour, the development of habits and trends as well as
sudden change and confusion. There is no shortage of 'experts' and
'specialists' in the field of social science, but few of the problems facing us have uni-disciplinary solutions, neither is the grouping together
of a mixed bag of specialists likely to give us the highest possible level
of overall competence. We are putting the emphasis on man in society
because we feel that the economist who is sensitive to the wider environment of man than that epitomised by statistics and the predictions of abstract theory will probably be a more useful economist. (In
our experience, nothing discourages a student more than his being
told that such-and-such a theory is of no practical use after he has
spent much time and effort in mastering it!)

In looking at the behaviour patterns associated with the motor-car,
we shall be outlining the content of the rest of this book. What will
emerge, we hope, is a realisation of how dependent we are on each
other, that economic man can exist in a meaningful sense only in a
society of men.

THE NEED FOR TRANSPORT

What is the significance of the car for most people today? Most would accept that its primary purpose is to enable the owner to change location. All forms of transport have evolved as solutions to the general need for people and goods to change their location. The primordial cave-man leaving the shelter of his den in search of game followed the same instinct for survival as the suburban commuter fighting his way on to the 8.10 to Waterloo — both have to move to new locations in order to get access to their necessary life-support systems! The role of transport will vary considerably between socio-economic systems. One has only to compare the way of life of a nomadic people dependent on herds and flocks on the hoof and forced into a continuous search for new and lusher pastures, with the more stable life-style of an agricultural peasantry living and working on the few hectares round their homes, to see that a study of transport patterns will reveal a great deal about a society and its economy. Transport has a vital role in developed industrial economies, and the various modes of transport interact with economic, social and environmental factors in a complex way.

The car, then, is one of many modern forms of transport. For many it is a more comfortable and convenient means of transport for short and medium distances than any other means available. For some purposes the car is also cheaper than alternatives, but we must remember that most drivers are not aware of the true running costs of their car and usually only consider fuel costs. Even if the driver does his sums properly we should also note that the cost to the driver is not likely to be the same as the cost to society. The driver will be comparing his fuel, maintenance, depreciation and other costs with, say, the fares on a nationalised railway system. In terms of money cost to the driver, the rail trip might well be more expensive. But note that the driver does not pay directly to use public roads, even though he does pay licence fees and petrol tax; rail fares may be set at an overall 'break-even' non-profit-making level so that profit-earning routes can subsidise loss-makers; or perhaps rail passengers find themselves surcharged for travelling at peak times. There are other costs too that should be considered, but enough has been said to indicate caution in equating money costs with society costs. A glance at the average advertisement for a new car will convince one, however, that the car is not simply a means of changing location. Car ownership carries prestige, it confirms the owner's belief about his assumed status in society, it can convey a sense of adventure and erotic expectation — or so the advertising executive would have us believe. In the Western-style industrial economy of today, it is not enough for the car to be a reliable form of transport: the marketing men have made it into a way of life in itself. The car is portrayed as a magical vehicle in which distances are ever more rapidly diminished (in spite of speed limits), in which personal freedom is maximised, in which a sense of power over the environment is increased and freedom from danger guaranteed. While the car owner revels in his feeling of personal well-being, the non-owners look on enviously, and it seems clear that the growing problem of car stealing and joyriding by juveniles in our big cities is a reflection of a craving for the status that car ownership grants. Clergymen can be heard to mutter about the usurpation of their Sunday services by the weekly washing rite afforded to this metallic deity. We have become ensnared by what one writer has called 'the car-libido mystique',[1] or perhaps by one powerful form of what Marx called 'commodity fetishism'.

How far should the economist concern himself with these human manifestations of potentially irrational behaviour? The traditional elementary economics textbook will simply argue that the good or service to be consumed will yield 'utility' or 'satisfaction' to the consumer and we do not need to explore how or why this 'satisfaction' is generated since this is the proper realm of the philosopher or psychologist, and in any case it is enough to know that 'satisfaction' is produced. As far as we are concerned, we feel that the particular bundle of pleasures and satisfactions generated by car ownership should be of real interest to an economist anxious to understand and predict consumer behaviour. Part of the reason why foreign cars have penetrated the UK market so successfully in the late sixties and early seventies might well be that 'buying foreign' carries a social cachet for a particular class of people which is strong enough to overcome the increased costs involved — the higher prices may even enhance the effect. This sort of behaviour would make it more difficult for a government to discourage imports in an effort to handle a balance of payments problem. We should also remember that at Budget time the powerful 'car lobby' (as represented by the AA, RAC, and the big car firms) will be watching for any tax change that would adversely affect the motorist and his ability to enjoy the freedom of the road, and that many a Chancellor of the Exchequer may think twice before arousing their wrath. There is an interesting tendency for economists to equate the exercise of such economic power with inefficiency and irrationality.

[1] Ralph Glasser, *The New High Priesthood* (Macmillan, 1967).

THE CAR AND THE PRODUCTION PROCESS

Having explored some aspects of what the car means to those who buy and use it, we now turn to consider that car as a 'product'. A visit to a modern car plant will quickly demonstrate the complexity of the organisation required to bring together and assemble the many thousand bits and pieces that make up a car. The continually moving assembly line emphasises the need to arrange for the right parts to arrive at the right place at the right time. Economists have in the past labelled the collecton of inputs necessary for production processes as 'factors of production'. This rather antiquated title will include fixed capital, in the form of large building, machine tools, conveyor systems, metal presses and welding equipment; working capital, illustrated by stacks of raw materials and bins of components; land to carry the buildings and to provide storage and handling space; labour to operate the machinery and to supervise and plan the operations.

Shop-floor supervision is only one part of the organisational effort required. In offices, warehouses and showrooms, other vital activities are going on. Accountants keep track of movements in costings and prices, designers work on future models, marketing men work at the sales potential of the product, and engineers sort out problems of technology. This total organisational effort is carried on within a unit of management usually referred to as a 'firm'. In terms of numbers, the typical firm is a small business run by one man or by a few partners. In terms of volume of sales, number of employees and value of capital employed, however, UK industry is dominated by a few hundred firms. Car manufacture is an activity in which it is increasingly difficult for small operations to survive. Production of the medium-sized family car is firmly in the hands of a limited number of very large international companies such as the Ford, British Leyland, General Motors and Chrysler motor companies. In order to keep costs and therefore prices down to a level where mass sales are possible, all the economies of large-scale production have to exploited. As the small firms are swallowed up by the big firms, so the range of available models declines even though the old brand names survive in an effort to retain goodwill. One problem that goes with mass production is the need to maintain mass sales levels. Now the car is a moderately durable good. Many of the coach-built models of sixty years ago are still roadworthy, but there are two good reasons why the average product of present-day car-makers is unlikely to last to the end of the century. One reason is that cars of such durable quality would cost far more than the typical motorist can afford to pay. Secondly, if long-life cars were to be produced at moderate prices, the market for them would shrink drastically as the stock of reliable vehicles grew. Mass production and low price therefore combine to force us into a cycle of car purchase and replacement that is shorter than we would often like — that is, unless we have been persuaded that having a *new* car is so much better than keeping the old one! The car firm is trading in a market environment in which there is intense competition for a larger and more stable share of a market that is limited by economic, social and technical factors. We are interested in the firm (as economists) both as an organisational unit bringing together the factors of production in an efficient and effective way and also as a decision-making unit within a particular market structure.

WHAT DRIVES THE CAR-MAKERS?

What is the motivation behind a firm? What is it that drives so many employees to perform all their manifold tasks so that cars can be produced? Orthodox economic theory makes another heroic simplification here by referring us to one overriding driving force — to make as much profit as possible. This is in fact quite a useful generalisation that helps us explain much of what we observe in business and industry. Who knows what motivated the great captains of industry of the past — the Fords and the Morrises? Perhaps they beavered away at their motors and cycles because of the sheer challenge of technical development, a kind of 'Everest' complex. The big car firms of today are no longer dominated to the same extent by great 'characters', but are run by boards of directors, teams of professional managers, lawyers and accountants. The motivation for these salaried men might well be different from that of the self-employed businessman. The firm becomes itself a social unit in which the goals of shareholders, directors and senior executives might well be in conflict. If we take this behavioural view of the firm, we see the firm as no longer simply engaged in mechanistic production, but rather as a social structure engaged in managing interactions between its market environment, its social, economic and political background and its own internal needs.

Profits, freedom of consumer choice in a competitive market setting, a concentration on economic activity for mainly self-interested reasons, the presence and accumulation of private property . . . these are all features of an economic system generally referred to as 'capitalism'. In terms of productive efficiency, economic development and the freedom to please oneself, there is a lot to be said for a capitalist economy. But this should not blind us to some of the blemishes on the face of modern capitalism. As we have seen, competitive and technological factors may encourage the development and dominance of very large firms which may then be tempted to use their economic power to control rather than respond to their environment. If one can control one's environment the risks one takes can be reduced; for example, farmers would benefit greatly from an ability to control the weather. But early in 1974, the Japanese Fair Trade Commission warned that the six biggest companies in Japan had become so dominant that they were in danger of destroying the possibility of free competition in that country. When this happens — and Japan may be only a little further along the road than the great Western powers — there will be a need for action by the government to protect the general public interest. It is already a common experience of course that governments in capitalist countries have found it necessary to make 'ground rules' for business behaviour and so we have company legislation, control over monopolies and restrictive practices, and fair trading legislation. Should we expect a private enterprise concern to be 'responsible'? It does seem clear that the capitalist car-maker will not bother about such things as safety, durability, non-polluting exhaust systems, etc., unless there is either a clear commercial advantage in doing so or unless he is compelled by law to do so. Even so, the modern corporation does not wish to create enemies or build up unnecessary hositility that may eventually lead to government intervention. It will try to appear as socially responsible by carrying on research into environmental problems associated with its operations, by making donations to charities or by mounting expensive public relations efforts. Another broad area of problems where government intervention may be necessary is where the market mechanism shows signs of strain or breakdown, or where uncoordinated decision-making by fragmented market elements leads to effects that are unacceptable to the public, as for example when hoarding by individuals in anticipation of a change in market conditions only serves to worsen the situation. We readily accept nowadays the duty of governments to regulate the level of economic activity in an economy, to be concerned with problems of unemployment, inflation and growth. The firm will need to be sensitive not only to its immediate market environment but also to the likelihood of changes in taxation or monetary policy and the effects of these changes on its market.

WORK AND INCOMES — RIGHTS OR REWARDS?

Another significant part of the firm's environment is provided by the other major economic power group in modern capitalism, namely organised labour. So far, we have only mentioned labour as a factor of production, but this is surely not sufficient. The worker trying to keep up with the production line of a car plant is also a human being with drives, needs and desires of his own. We can either see the assembly worker as simply a flexible and adaptable piece of machinery in human form or as a member of society trying to obtain the wherewithal to sustain his family at a satisfactory level of consumption and entitled to some sense of personal fulfilment in his daily work. The UK car industry has been increasingly disrupted by unofficial stoppages and strikes, high labour turnover and absenteesism. The Swedish car firm Volvo is even experimenting with a production layout that does away with the line and reduces the amount of specialisation of tasks in an attempt to enrich the job environment. At present, however, work in a car plant can become almost a way of life, in much the same way as coal miners or nineteenth-century canal bargemen found themselves constrained and conditioned by the particular technology of their work.[2] Of course the car worker does not have to make cars, and we must assume that the rewards are sufficient to overcome any objections he might have. Car workers are often used as examples of overpaid and unskilled employment, but before such simple conclusions are reached we should analyse all the factors that go to determine wage levels and differentials. The profitability of the employers, the nature of the work, whether the industry is growing or in decline, the degree of skill or training required, the freedom or otherwise of entry to the employment, and the power of the trade union organisation are all relevant factors. We can usually find good economic reasons why one man or one occupation should be paid more than another, but there will be many occasions when historical or social factors may be more significant than the market factors. The gradual emergence of the problem of the relative rates of pay of groups of workers as an important factor in the various attempts at operating an incomes policy in the UK in recent years give rise to questions that are as much moral as economic. How does one go about determining the 'proper' relationship between the wages of nurses and car workers? It may be that eventually some countries will attempt to evolve some kind of social agreement or contract which will establish a hierarchy of incomes and social status by general consensus.

In the meantime the hierarchy of income and personal wealth is determined by a complex range of factors. There will be examples of self-made men who by hard work and flair have amassed great (or small) fortunes, others will have had the advantage of a good start in life helped by family wealth and social position. There will be unfor-

[2]An effective insight into the working life of car workers is given in *Working for Ford* by H. Beynon (Allen Lane, 1973).

tunates born into a vicious trap of poverty and inadequacy from which they never break free. Most Western governments are not prepared to accept a situation where the worst miseries of human life are totally ignored. Private charity has never been sufficient to deal adequately with the whole range of problems that need attention and so we have come to expect increasing areas of public intervention and action. Our car worker will be making a compulsory contribution towards an old-age pension and the health service. It is possible that he will not be paying much income tax if he has a large family to support and this is yet another device for altering income distributions. Other taxes will be borne, however, when he buys his cigarettes and pints of beer, his petrol and his hi-fi set. The purchasing power thus taken from the tax-payer is used to finance the social security systems, the defence networks, the education and health facilities, and all the other forms of collective consumption in which governments in both capitalist and socialist economies indulge. There is a tendency for such provisions to absorb larger and larger shares of national output as more needs are recognised and as higher standards of service are demanded. A typical growth area has been in road and motorway construction. Modern cars are expected to achieve a smooth ride with high and sustained speeds, but this is not possible if the road system is poor. The private demand for more cars has therefore generated a demand for bigger and better public roads, and there are many other areas where private and public demands are so interrelated.

Motorway construction leads us on to consider another area of interdependence in modern society. The West affords many examples of the unfortunate environmental effects of motorway development such as noise, pollution by exhaust gases, and congestion. Faster speeds on motorways combine with weakly constructed vehicles and the power-invulnerability syndrome of many drivers to produce more devastating accidents, more serious injuries, bigger repair bills and higher insurance costs. The UK Government has a ten-year rolling programme of road construction that is geared to meeting anticipated demand, while the improvements in the road system encourage more cars on to the road. Another by-product of the road developments is a worsening of the chances of survival of public transport systems. Closed railway lines and suspended rural bus routes give ample evidence of the power of the car to dominate the transport opportunities of the public. Only slowly have governments and pressure groups begun to count the true social costs and benefits of both public and private decision-making. It becomes more and more obvious that we must think of economic man's actions in their social as well as their private setting.

ASPECTS OF COLLECTIVISM

We have so far been discussing the motor-car in the setting of Western capitalist economics, but it might well be worth while considering how different our anlysis might be if we looked at the car in a socialist setting. Socialism, of course, has as many variants as does capitalism, but certain typical characteristics can be found in the socialist economies of which we have experience. These include an emphasis on the public ownership of non-personal property, a preference for economic planning supported by complex systems of bureaucratic control, and a tendency to subordinate the desires of individuals to some expression of collective will. For all of that, Soviet and East German car factories look very much like capitalist car plants — they may even have been designed and built by capitalist firms. The Russian assembly worker is quite likely to find himself struggling to keep up with the line in much the same way as his British counterpart; he may be paid bonuses to encourage him to keep up with production norms. The major difference will be that the Russian is also subject to political persuasion and exhortation as the State will be stressing the industry's and the worker's contribution to national welfare. One may have doubts whether this wider motivation can make the work any less boring in the long run. As far as the enterprise manager is concerned, profit motives have only recently become significant in most East European countries and the reconciliation of selfish profit-orientated drives with the basic ethos of socialism is likely to cause problems for many years to come.

The car, along with many other consumer durables, has not in the past had a high priority in the economic planning of the socialist countries. There are therefore fewer cars per head of the population than in most Western countries, roads are less crowded, and public transport and taxi services play a more important role. Because of the scarcity of private cars, car ownership is probably just as much a symbol of social status in communist states as it is in the West. One gains the use of a car because it is necessary for a socially important job, or because of a position of power in the economic and political hierarchy, or because you have a high income (cars are relatively much more expensive in most socialist states). As incomes rise and consumer goods become more plentiful, the political regimes in Poland and Yugoslavia for example have found it distressing that their people exhibit such capitalistic traits as preferring foreign cars to their own home product. Given long enough, and an absence of world wars, it has been suggested that East and West will grow more and more similar in their life-styles in much the same way that the developed countries of the West seem to be evolving a common 'mid-Atlantic' mass culture. (One has to admit, however, that the Chinese may be embarked on a different route altogether.)

ECONOMIC DEVELOPMENT AND INTERDEPENDENCE AT THE ·
GLOBAL LEVEL

The next question to be asked is, How long can the current trends be expected to continue? Can we really allow everyone eventually to have a car if they want one? Is there not a limit to the amount of land that can be covered in concrete and tarmac? Can we ignore the wants and demands of the developing world where discussions about the advantages and dangers of the growth of private motoring are largely irrelevant? Continuous and rapid economic growth carries with it real problems of energy and resource availability, and also difficult questions of international distribution of income and wealth. The steadily widening gap between the standards of living of the rich industrialised countries of the world and those of the 'Third World' countries helps to set higher and higher aspiration levels with smaller and smaller real opportunity. Wealthy nations have tended to behave as if they were immune from the consequences of a major collapse in the developing world in much the same way that some motorists feel safe and secure while speeding through motorway fog.

The uneven nature of many of the international links and dependences is also illustrated by the pattern of UK trade in cars. Cars and commercial vehicles accounted for some 10 per cent of UK exports in the 1960s and therefore have a special significance for that economy. The markets for the UK exports have not been those in the developing world however, but have mainly been with the USA and the wealthier members of the Commonwealth. We have already referred to the growing demand for more variety in car consumption as demonstrated by the widening interest in foreign cars, and this has been a feature of the increasing sophistication of trade between the industrial powers. Fords, Chrysler and Volkswagen plan their output strategy at the international level with plants spread around the world. The creation of trading blocs like the EEC help to intensify these trends. Huge international companies with no particular national loyalties are already with us and are usually labelled 'the multinationals'. The significance of this 'fourth estate' was clearly demonstrated during the 1973 petroleum crisis when the oil multinationals were seen to be rationing oil supplies in the interests of their international market strategies rather than in the short-term interests of the producing or consuming states. In doing so, of course, these companies may have been displaying a greater awareness of world interdependence than the nation states which were often putting their selfish interests first.

· This survey of the scope of this book is designed to illustrate the obvious fact that 'economic' man does not exist in a set of watertight boxes in the real world. Inevitably, if one pursues the study of economics to more advanced levels, it is necessary to simplify, to attempt to isolate particular effects, to build abstract models based on strict assumptions and using impeccable logic. Sometimes, however, we feel that the more advanced the theory, the more rarefied and useless it is. This book is an attempt to present the complexities of economic relationships with all their uncertainties, and to suggest the areas where the economist may be helped by researchers in other disciplines. Man is a social animal and so we have tried to present his 'economic' aspects in a societal setting, a setting which in turn has historical, political, technological and philosophical roots.

Chapter 2

Wants and Needs

HOUSEHOLD INPUTS AND OUTPUTS

In the previous chapter, some of the benefits, real or imaginary, conferred by the motor-car were briefly considered. The vast majority of cars sold in Western countries are sold to private individuals, and most of these individuals make their decision to buy a car as a member of a household. But what factors would a household take into account when deciding to join the ranks of the car-owner? For most families the expenditures which the motor-car involves will be a significant item in the household budget. There will be the cost of buying the vehicle itself, and this will entail either a period of saving in which other expenditures will have to be cut back, or some sort of hire-purchase commitment. Then there will be the costs associated with the mere possession of a car, the insurance premium, registration tax, and possibly even the renting of garage space. When the vehicle is used there will arise a further set of costs in the fuel and maintenance bills, and looking ahead there is the money to be found if the benefits of car-ownership convince the household that it has all been worth while and the car is eventually to be replaced. The possible benefits to be gained by the expenditure of probably hard-earned money will be a combination of status, convenience, flexibility, and independence from the vagaries of public transport. The household is in effect 'consuming' some of its income in the form of car-owning expenditures and the result of this 'input' of consumption into the household is an 'output' of car-owning benefits (see Figure 2.1).

Households consume goods and services for a variety of reasons. They need food, shelter, and clothing, however minimal, to survive as households. Survival must be regarded as a pretty fundamental goal of the family unit, but most would recognise that there is more to human life than mere survival. The household's life style will be determined by the level of attainment reached in such areas as physical well-being, intellectual and psychological development, and cultural sophistication. We can consider household consumption as a whole, the various goods and services (food, clothing, travel, housing,

Figure 2.1   Car Ownership: Household Inputs and Ouputs

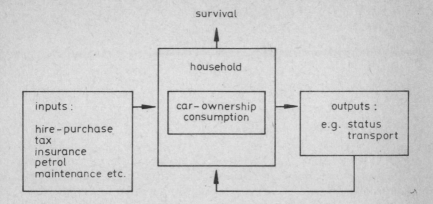

medicine, entertainment, etc.) absorbed by the household, as the inputs necessary to reach the life-style desired by the household. The
life-style achieved will reflect the 'output' of the consumption activity,
just as in the diagram we show that for car ownership the output of
status is achieved as a result of the input of car-owning expenditures.
Now the life-style of a household is clearly limited by the range of inputs available to it. In affluent societies we can conceive of families
setting a particular life-style as a goal and striving to gain control of the
inputs necessary to sustain it. In the diagram, the level of status return-
ed to the household may be deemed insufficient for that family's particular goals, and this can be rectified by increasing the relevant inputs. For perhaps the majority of the world's population, however, the
inputs available are strictly limited. This may seem a rather complicated way of looking at, say, the phenomenon of mass starvation in
India's Bihar State, but for many poor countries the input-output
relationship in consumption has grim significance. Reduction in consumption standards increases malnutrition with its attendant mental
and physical disabilities, making it increasingly difficult to generate the
effort needed to maintain food production, which leads in turn to
further reductions in consumption. If population is increasing at the
same time, the downward cycle will be accentuated, since the
household's needs for inputs will grow just as these inputs are becoming less available.

In Table 2.1 are set out a selection of UK household budgets,
covering a range of incomes over a period of time. For further comparison budgets of village households from Southern India have been
included. The reader should be warned that difficulties arise when

making such varied comparisons. Over long periods of time, changes in the value of money are difficult to allow for. Comparisons between working-class and middle-class families at the beginning of the nineteenth century may for some purposes be more valid than a comparison between a middle-class family in 1825 and one in 1925. Similarly, wide social and cultural divisions make a strict comparison between India and Britain a little tenuous. Nevertheless the data below allows adequate comparison of relative, if not always absolute, differences in consumption patterns.

Table 2.1   Selected family budgets, UK and India, 1810-1970

Social/Income Group	I Lancashire cotton spinner	II Middle class	III Middle class	IV Income range £25-30 p.w.	V Income range £40+ p.w.	VI Madras landless labourer
Family size	6	5+ maid	4	4	4	6
Year	1810	1825	1925	1970	1970	1970
Budget period	Weekly	Annual	Annual	Weekly	Weekly	Monthly
Budget items	%	%	%	%	%	%
Housing	14	10	18	12	12	—
Fuel, light, power	10	5	4	8	5	6
Food	49	46	42	31	24	79
of which:						
meat and fish	5	15				
bread, potatoes						
& cereals	25	7				63
sugar	3	3				
Alcohol, tobacco						
& equivalents	—	8	2	10	7	9
Clothing, footwear	—	15	9	6	11	6
Durables	—	6 (maid)	—	7	9	—
Other goods	—	—	—	8	8	—
Travel, vehicles	—	—	4	13	14	—
Services & misc., including education, medical, savings, leisure	27	10	21	5	10	—
TOTAL	100%	100%	100%	100%	100%	100%

Sources
Group I   Mrs. Rundell, *New System of Domestic Economy* (1825),
              quoted in J. Burnett, *A History of the Cost of Living* (Pen-
              guin, 1969).
Group II   Burnett, op. cit.
Group III   D. Caradog-Jones, *The Cost of Living of a Sample of Middle-
              Class Families* (1928), quoted in P. Wilsher, *The Pound in
              Your Pocket* (Cassell, 1970).
Group IV   Central Statistical Office, *Social Trends* (HMSO, 1971).
Group V   As for Group IV.
Group VI   T. Scarlett Epstein, *South India: Yesterday, Today and
              Tomorrow* (Macmillan, 1973).

Note This Table has been compiled from a variety of sources with the result
that some of the entries are not strictly comparable. The information was
orginally collected for differing purposes. The Group I expenditure pattern
comes from a survey of the early nineteenth-century Lancashire textile industry, while that for Group II is from a book on household management and
is an example of what the young middle-class family *ought* to follow. Groups
III, IV, and V are from samples of large numbers of households, unlike
Groups I, II and VI. Also, where there are blanks in the Table it does not
necessarily mean that there was no spending at all on that item, since (*a*)
spending may be sporadic throughout the year (Groups I and VI), and (*b*) it
may be lumped into the Miscellaneous item. Nevertheless, it is felt that the
general pattern gives the correct impression.

Most of these examples of consumption patterns have little in common with that of the Bihari peasant. Yet a comparison will draw
attention to important differences and similarities. Each of the families
chosen devote a part of their income to groups of items such as food
and clothing. In some cases the proportion spent on food is very large,
and this will be where the income in question is very small. The Table
illustrates a tendency for the proportion of income spent on food to
decrease as income rises and as time passes. Food, for obvious
biological reasons, is a basic need for the household, but we have
noted that once this basic need has been satisfied, once a certain
calorie intake, say, has been reached, our household's attitude
towards food consumption begins to change. Some societies, once
survival needs have been met, apparently develop insatiable consumption wants. The landless labourer in the Madras village has a long
and hungry way to go before this stage is reached, since his income
allows each adult member of his family a calorie intake of only about
1,800 per diem — well below a minimum daily requirement of 2,500.[1]
The relatively well-off peasant farmer indulges in feast-day spending

[1] T. Scarlett Epstein, *South India: Yesterday, Today and Tomorrow* (Macmillan, 1973).

and there is no reason for us to suppose that the landless labourer would not do the same if he had the income. Similarly, if we compare the middle-class UK family of 1825 with their 1925 counterparts, we see that having satisfied their needs, each has turned its attention to wants. The 1825 household has satisfied its wants by buying education and domestic service; for the 1925 family it was holidays and leisure.

NEEDS AND WANTS

It is worth asking whether there are in fact clear distinctions between needs and wants. There are some well-defined physiological needs such as energy intake to replace body cells, and the need to maintain body temperatures, but apart from the very poor this is unlikely to be the way in which a consumer views his expenditure. Certainly a smoker would regard tobacco as being as necessary as food and clothing, although the need for tobacco is less inherent than cultivated. Once the household has passed the point of mere survival, the distinction between needs and wants becomes increasingly less clear, as is demonstrated by the enquiries undertaken late in the nineteenth century into the extent of poverty in Britain. Probably the best known is Charles Booth's *Life and Labour of the People* (1891). In this survey of London, Booth noted that the extent of poverty (and he thought it to be considerable, with 30.7 per cent of about 5 million living below the poverty line) depended upon how you defined it. By shifting this 'poverty line' upwards a little, poverty substantially increased. But how and where was the poverty line to be drawn? A minimum income to maintain a family in 'decent subsistence', taking the size of the family into account, must be based on what the majority of households would accept as normal. For example, if alcohol and tobacco were regarded as regular items of consumption by the community as a whole, allowance for these must be made in any notional subsistence budget, although this argument was anathema to Victorian moralists who regarded alcohol as a principle cause of poverty. The problem is a practical one, however, for if poverty is to be relieved by any kind of social security system, it must be defined and measured, and be continually revised as the community's affluence increases and its consumption horizons widen. Poverty in this sense may not be as grinding nowadays as it was in the nineteenth century, but it might be just as widespread.

Another practical consideration arises from a separation of needs from wants, and which, like the definition of poverty, has its moral undertones. British governments have been accustomed to financing substantial amounts of their expenditures by taxing particular kinds of consumption. In 1973, 22 per cent of the Government's revenue came from excise duties on alcohol, tobacco, and motor spirit. There has been the feeling that it is 'right' to tax such items in view of their 'frivolous' nature, and 'wrong' for foodstuffs to be so treated. Yet items of adult clothing are subject to value-added tax, most of the money spent on tobacco comes from the more numerous lower-income groups, and those who spend money on tobacco clearly regard this spending as essential in view of the failure of tobacco consumption to respond to changes in excise duty. The issue of taxation and morality has generated much heat but less light from past economists, who expended some effort on distinguishing luxuries from necessities. In the twentieth century, however, mass-production techniques have so changed the availability of goods that 'luxuries' such as TV sets and washing-machines, etc., are now standard items of household consumption, and present-day governments are more concerned with the effect that this kind of taxation has on inflation and employment, than with viewing these items as fair game for revenue raising.

CONSUMPTION: GOOD OR SERVICE?

We can, however, see an important difference between, say, food on the one hand and TV sets and cars on the other. For when a household buys food, it will be largely for immediate consumption. Modern packaging and the development of canning and freezing techniques have meant that some kinds of foodstuffs need not, perhaps, be consumed as soon as they are bought, but even so they will be consumed during only a very brief time-span. Once a tin of baked beans is opened the contents must be eaten almost immediately, but when a car is purchased it is not, unless the household is very unlucky, burned up in one frenzied dash down the motorway. Accidents apart, the motor vehicle may have a working life reckoned in years rather than minutes, and consumption of the car will be spread over its lifetime. If status is the main benefit the household sees in the possession of a car it may not even have to be used, merely owned, and thus its durability may be considerable. Most goods which possess this quality of durability, economists refer to as 'consumer durables', and they feature prominently in discussions of consumer behaviour. Not all goods having this durable quality, however, would be considered 'consumer durables' and neither is durability the quality which distinguishes wants from needs. Clothing, for example, is not classed as a consumer durable although items of clothing are consumed over a period of time, and while households in affluent countries, influenced by the dictates of fashion, buy more clothing than they need, a certain level of clothing expenditure is regarded as essential.

Housing too is durable, yet is not regarded as being in the same category as motor vehicles. As with clothing, none would argue that housing is not essential, yet like clothingg many households have a tendency to buy more than they need. Outlays on housing might reflect the desire for a leafy suburb, a second bathroom, a garage, a large garden, etc., as well as the need for a roof over one's head. Unlike most items of consumption, however, housing consumption can take two forms. It can be consumed as a service in exchange for a rent payment, or as a good by purchase, usually in the form of a mortgage. In the former case housing consumption is no different conceptually from taking out an insurance policy, a bus ride, or a continental holiday, where it is an experience we consume rather than a tangible good. Consumption of a service can only take place as long as payment is maintained, although this rather dispassionate way of regarding such an essential commodity as housing has given place to a more humane attitude on the part of many in society, and nowadays eviction does not follow quite so close behind a failure to pay rent as it did in the past. In the latter case, the consumer is buying rather more than simply a roof over his head, for unlike consumer durables, housing can have a very long life, and the mortgagee eventually acquires an asset as well as shelter. In addition, and unlike consumer durables, inflation is likely to increase the market value of a house faster than maintenance costs rise, and faster, if the exerience of the past few years is anything to go by, than the burden of the mortgage, depending on the desirability of the area in which the house is situated. The place where housing consumption occurs may reflect need rather than want, however, since no matter how much, for example, a hospital worker may yearn for the green belt, even if housing there was within his income range, he could not live there if there were no accessible hospitals. Instead he may be forced into buying or renting expensive and poor housing accommodation in inner city areas because of his need for housing near to his work.

If it is not their longevity which distinguishes consumer durables from other items of consumption, it is the fact that expenditure upon hem can be postponed. We have made continual reference to the assumption that income is the main constraint upon the ability of the household to consume. We assumed that if our Madras landless labourer's income were to be increased, he would be bound to consume more, since in absolute terms his level of consumption is very low. A recent contributor to the study of consumer behaviour, George Katona, has suggested that in affluent societies, there may not be such a simple relationship between income and consumption. The ability to consume continues to be important, but behaviour is significantly modified, according to Katona, by the *willingness* to consume.

THE WILLINGNESS TO CONSUME

The willingness to consume becomes important as soon as incomes rise above the level of subsistence. We have seen that such a level is difficult to define, but there is no doubt that in industrial societies today incomes are, in general, well above subsistence level. In the decade following the Second World War, for example, the number of households in the USA receiving income in excess of the bare minimum (however generous this level was in comparison with other countries) increased nearly twofold. The reasons for this growth lie in changes in the productive capacity of the US economy, and we shall be looking at the phenomenon of production in the next chapter. For the moment we are concerned with the consequences of this change.

Savings

Once past the point of survival, choice can be exercised in the disposal of above-subsistence income. The household can choose not to spend this part of its income immediately, but to save it for future consumption. A household possessing such reserves can augment current income, and the greater the accumulated reserves, the greater the discretion which can be exercised in consumption. For example, should current income fall back temporarily to or below subsistence level, consumption can be maintained, even at a level in excess of survival. With the growth in incomes over the past fifty years there has been in most industrial countries a mushrooming of institutions catering for the savings of the lower income groups. Accompanying the growth of savings has been the development of credit purchasing, and this in turn has enabled consumption both above subsistence and, for short periods, current income. The availability of credit (and goods ranging from clothing and household effects to housing itself are financed in this way) has itself allowed more discretion in consumption. In the absence of access to credit a household wishing to make purchases in excess of current income would have no option but to save out of the income in excess of subsistence needs. In this sense 'saving' can be viewed as a form of consumption. A household can spend its income on goods and services, or it can spend it on savings.

Discretionary Consumption — The Importance of Consumer Durables

Consumer credit, however, is associated with the consumption of a particular kind of good — the consumer durable. The proliferation of products such as television sets, washing machines, and the more basic appliances like gas and electric cookers, has added dimension to discretionary consumption. (*NB* There is a value judgement implicit in the word 'basic'. Washing machines, etc., might be regarded as equally essential.) But however essential motor-cars and refrigerators are to the consumer's way of life, they are normally items of postponable consumption. Food, for example, in ordinary circumstances is not of this kind. In the first place it is perishable and in the second it has to be consumed continually. Possibly the essential difference between a luxury and a necessity is that consumption of the former can be postponed, that of the latter cannot. This is certainly true of food, possibly housing, but less obviously so of clothing. There is, however, an important difference between expenditure and consumption in this respect. In affluent societies, while the consumption of food cannot be postponed, expenditure on it can. Canning and refrigeration techniques allow food to be purchased in bulk and in advance of consumption, and within limits stocks can be renewed when the consumer chooses. The postponing or timing of expenditure is particularly possible in the case of consumer durables, from the very characteristics of such goods.

An important influence on the willingness to consume has been the growth of information available to the consumer on factors which might influence the timing of purchase. Discretion will be of value to the consumer only if he sees reason to exercise it. The timing of the purchase of a motor-car, for example, will be influenced by the consumer's expectations of market conditions. The availability of a new model; the trade-in price of the old; the likelihood of a change in the price of motor vehicles in relation to other prices; possible changes in government taxes; seasonal fluctuations; the quality and performance of other makes; projections of sales volumes — information of this kind has become more accessible to consumers through the mass media and through more specialist channels such as consumer protection societies and specialist trade magazines.

Discretionary Consumption is Influenced by Habitual and Contractual Expenditures

The existence of incomes in excess of basic needs does not mean that the whole of this surplus is available for discretionary consumption. Expenditure on basic needs will often be of an habitual nature. A household planning a weekly or monthly budget will allocate so much for general housekeeping, so much for electricity, gas, rates, etc. Other outgoings will have a contractual rather than an habitual claim on the household's income. TV rental payments, hire-purchase payments, rent, mortgage commitments and insurance premiums may have an even stronger claim on income than does customary expenditure, since in extreme circumstances the latter can be reduced, even if not eliminated. The penalty for cutting housekeeping allowances is perhaps to switch to inferior foods or even to hunger for a short period. The penalty for default on a hire-purchase agreement can be to lose much of the outlay already expended. The failure to pay rent may lead to eviction. Some forms of insurance premiums contain a saving element, and cancellation may simply represent a failure to add to an existing reserve of assets. Mortgages are a special case since house purchase is regarded as both a means of shelter and of financial security. Often in excess of the rent payment required for similar accommodation, and therefore theoretically reducible, such payments are placed high on the list of contractual priorities. These outlays, of course, are the result of past decisions to exercise discretionary consumption, as well as the need to cover basic requirements such as shelter. Nevertheless, they affect the amount of consumption choice available from current income.

Factors Affecting Discretionary Consumption

The balance between discretionary consumption and consumption determined by past or customary decisions depends on several factors:
1. The size of the household's income. We have suggested elsewhere that if income is low in relation to basic requirements, the resources for discretionary consumption will be small.
2. The size of the household itself. Two households with similar incomes will have different customary expenditure patterns if one household has more dependants than the other. Large family size in relation to income is regarded as a cause of poverty, although there is a value judgement implicit in this observation. This is because children can themselves be viewed as a form of consumption, and a family can be said to 'consume' children in that they compete for income with expenditure on goods and services. For a variety of social reasons, however, the Madras villager (see Table 2.1) may consider children to be a need.
3. The position that a household sees itself as occupying in the structure of its society. Consumption patterns differ between social groups, and a household aspiring to membership of a specific group must emulate its consumption pattern. Higher education, for example, may be consumed because it is associated with professional occupations. Its real value to the practice of such occupations may not always be obvious, but nevertheless households which seek identification with a

particular social group will regard expenditure of this kind as non-postponable. The need to live in an area associated with, say, middle-class standards will impose on the aspiring household an addition to housing outlays beyond that required for mere shelter.
4. The pressures exerted by producers through advertising. Although nominally informative, advertising is highly persuasive and consumers can be persuaded to exercise their discretionary consumption in favour of a particular life-style.

CONSUMPTION IS CONTAGIOUS

We have referred to outlays which a household might regard as essential to achieve a desired level of status. This level need not be sought consciously. Increasing consumption of durable goods has been due to both the greater availability of such goods and to rising income levels. But rising incomes have to be transformed into consumption, and the observation of the transformation is instructive. In the UK, for example, during the economic uncertainties of the 1920s and 1930s consumption of durables grew, in the main, with surprising steadiness. At the same time, there was a noticeable decrease in the average size of families, not just among the unemployed, but among those groups comprising the main market for consumer durables. Again, since the Second World War the reduction of family size accompanying increasing consumption of this kind has been marked among the affluent sections of even Catholic countries, and in Catholic sections of nominally Protestant societies. Middle-class Catholic families in the UK have tended towards the consumption habits of their Protestant counterparts, with attendant changes in family size (a decreased 'consumption' of children). While family size may still be larger than for Protestant members of the the same socio-economic group, richer Catholic families have smaller families than do poorer. This is not a comment on the economic consequences of a particular reglious belief. It is one illustration of a consumption phenomenon known as the 'demonstration effect'. Socially visible forms of consumption, e.g. foreign holidays, motor-cars, attract the purchasing power of other households. When one household in a street changes the model of its car, other families observe the change and tend to follow suit. When a family moves into a new neighbourhood it will copy the consumption habits it observes around it. Where consumption is less obviously visible, as when consumption takes place inside rather than outside the house, advertising becomes more important in spreading the demonstration effect. One has to be persuaded that others are consuming deep-freezers if one cannot see for oneself.

CONSPICUOUS CONSUMPTION

It is one thing to consume a good which is conspicuous, another to consume it *because* it is conspicuous. In some societies, such 'conspicuous consumption' is blatant and obligatory. Those who possess wealth (even of modest proportions) are obliged to demonstrate it by adopting elaborate and extravagant consumption patterns. Indian Maharajahs paraded their herds of elephants and fleets of limousines because they would be lessened in the eyes of their compatriots if they did not. Conspicuous consumption, moreover, is a demonstration of economic power as well as wealth. Groups who feel free to parade their wealth run the risk of exciting the envy of the less affluent, a risk perhaps acceptable if the power is real. Consumption patterns have a political significance in that they enable the identification of not just different social groups, but those who have power and those who do not. It is perhaps idle to speculate whether the course of French history would have been different if the *ancien régime* had not been so blatantly rich.

OCCUPATIONAL DIFFERENCES IN CONSUMPTION

Market research, in the development of techniques to persuade consumers to revise their consumption patterns in line with the increasing availability of goods, has shown that it is not enough to use income differences to explain variations in consumption behaviour. Occupational differences cutting across income divisions are equally important. Market researchers divide occupations into as many as six categories from A to E, with category C subdivided to distinguish lower-paid white-collar workers from the blue-collar occupations. Groups A, B, and C1 constitute a broad band of occupations which make up the middle-class income groups, while C2, D, and E range from manual workers of varying degrees of skill down to pensioners and others of very low income. This socio-economic grouping was primarily designed to ensure that media advertising was aimed at the relevant prospective purchasers. Products designed for middle-class consumption must be advertised in, say, the newspapers which are most widely read by occupational groups A to C1.

It has been found that there is quite considerable overlap of income between the groups, that ranking occupations from upper middle-class (group A) to lower working-class does not provide the same ranking of incomes. Skilled manual workers (C2) can earn incomes equal to many in the B category of income/occupation which includes some administrative, professional, and managerial workers. Yet the expenditure habits of group C2 occupations are more like the less well-paid D category of semi-skilled and unskilled workers, than those of group B. Again, workers at low levels of pay in nominally white-collar occupations such as retail distribution may aspire to the consumption standards not so much of the better paid C2 category, but of the monetarily inferior C1 groups (clerical, junior managerial). School teachers would be included in the C1 category, yet consumption aspirations tend towards those of the A and B groups.

CHANGES IN CONSUMPTION OVER TIME-
Technology

Consumption of durables has increased partly because they have become more readily available, and this is largely a matter of changing technology. Obviously if a society does not know how to produce a good, or cannot obtain it from another economic system, it cannot consume it. In the absence of technical change society need have no awareness of missing consumption opportunities. A century ago, any conception of a good such as television, which we now take for granted, was beyond the comprehension of all but a tiny imaginative minority. What society did not know about, it did not miss.

We shall say more about technical change in the next chapter, but Table 2.1 illustrates the considerable impact that technology can make over time. The middle-class families are seen to consume broadly similar groups of goods, yet viewed in detail many differences emerge. The middle-class family of 1825 was consuming housing in exchange for rent. By 1925 this had become a mortgage. In 1825 house ownership was far less common than it is now, even among affluent households. By 1925 (and more so today), a mortgage was becoming the rule rather than the exception for households of this kind. Mortgage finance was not available in 1825; the development of the market and institutions of housing finance had not yet taken place. Economists would regard such a development as just as much a technical change as the development of, say, artificial fibres.

All UK households in Table 2.1 consume medical treatment, yet technology has changed that treatment out of recognition. Antibiotics, for instance, have only been available in the past few decades. Remember also that there was no National Health Service available for Groups I to II, and medical services had to be paid for (the same is broadly true of education).

Technology changes not only the absolute but also the relative availability of consumption opportunities. Goods which were once scarce can become plentiful, and thus cheaper. Changes in the production of motor vehicles — in the technology of the industry — have made them one of the most widely consumed durable goods in the industrial countries of the Western world, and this change is reflected in the budget of twentieth-century households.

The increasing labour requirements of industry and the growth and mechanisation of office work, etc., have offered employment opportunities to women who in other times would have had little choice but domestic service. Thus the house-keeping budget of the 1825 middle-class family runs to domestic assistance. That of 1925 does not. Domestic servants were still available in 1925, but had become scarce and thus expensive. Time as a consequence became more expensive for middle-class housewives, and thus strengthened the inducement to undertake the technical change required to cheapen labour-saving domestic appliances. Households of the twentieth century consume the services of domestic appliances rather than those of maids and butlers.

Fashion

Whereas technical change operates on the availability of goods for consumption, fashion changes the willingness to consume. The two are not independent. A change in fashion increases the willingness to consume a particular product, and unless society responds by increasing the availability of the good, its price will rise. The total supply of the good will not have changed, but it will be consumed by different households. Changes in the fashion for food illustrate this point. The low income group household of 1825, and indeed most of the less affluent households into the twentieth century, consumed offal as part of their meat diet. It was suggested in the inter-war period that liver in particular had properties which would benefit sufferers from tuberculosis. Gradually liver became more popular until it is no longer one of the cheaper parts of the beast. This change has occurred as the consumption of meat and meat products *per capita* has increased. Salmon is another case in point. At one time it was a food fit only for servants. As far as we know the taste of salmon has not changed, but people's taste for it has, and as a result it is now a luxury food. Possibly part of its attraction lies in its price — the snobbery of high prices — although its popularity, combined with a reduction in supplies, is also the cause of the increased price.

Occasionally the reaction of technology to changes in fashion has been epoch-making. Reacting against the ostentation of the monarchistic elite, the ruling classes in England of the period in which Parliament gained ascendency over the Crown deliberately chose a style of dress which contrasted which that of their predecessors. Cottons replaced silk because cotton was humble. The reverse, in fact, of the snobbery of high prices. This change took place at a time when supplies of raw cotton were relatively easily available, and when technology was developed sufficiently to permit mechanised production. The new fashions in dress could be copied by lower income groups to provide markets large enough to warrant the risk of capital in machine-based manufacture.

SOCIAL AND RELIGIOUS CONSTRAINTS ON CONSUMPTION

Arbitrary changes in fashion subject to the limitations of technology can restrict particular items of consumption to a certain socio-economic group. If machines of the quality and finish of a Rolls Royce car could be produced cheaply, large numbers of consumers could exercise consumption discretion in their direction. What restricts a Rolls Royce to a particular income group is the price of a good in relation to income. In many societies, past and present, such constraints can be social as well as economic.

Most societies restrict the consumption of firearms by law, for example, and in times of national emergency, governments frequently impose restrictions in consumption ranging from the banning of foreign travel to the physical limitation of even basic consumption goods. From time to time rulers have found it expedient to limit choice by actually forcing the consumption of a particular good. In medieval England, fish had to be consumed on specific days of the week, to provide the impetus for the development of a shipping fleet. In more modern societies, 'public goods' — roads, military equipment, etc. — have to be consumed by society as a whole, and the individual consumer has no choice in the matter. These constraints are upon consumers as a whole and there is usually some purpose, social or economic, behind them.

Restriction of consumption to specific groups has also been the object of government decree, but again with a particular motive. Julius Caesar enacted a series of sumptuary laws restricting the consumption of the more affluent sections of society, and medieval monarchs in times of dearth have restricted consumption of wheaten bread to the gentry. In pre-industrial Japan the Samurai caste had the sole right to bear arms. These again are purposeful constraints with some specific goal, say the preservation of order, in mind. Once the goal has been reached, however, there has been a tendency for consumption taboos to remain as part of socially accepted values. Caste systems, for example, tend to move beyond their social and economic purpose to become even more restrictive. Diet and dress as well as function identify caste membership and as function declines, the other distinctions seem more important. Even in societies less traditional, ossified social barriers and thus differences in consumption remain. Educational advance for women, for instance, has been delayed in many European societies because educational institutions were laid down at a time when women seemed economically unimportant. Only in the past half-century have women been able to consume education on more equal terms with men, and only in the past decade have some Oxbridge colleges become coeducational.

Of a different order are the taboos associated with religious belief. As long as the consumer adheres to the belief, or as long as he regards himself a member of a society that does, he will be bound by its shibboleths. Jews and Moslems, for example, are not allowed to eat pork, nor Hindus meat of any kind. Hinduism in particular is almost an anti-consumption religion, since it places so little emphasis on material existence. Most religious belief is essentially non-material but many religions pay lip-service to some notion of charity, which is extremely material as far as the recipient is concerned. This may seem a peripheral point, but if that religious belief influences attitudes to consumption, important economic consequences can result. The propensity to consume stimulates economic activity, which explains for some the initial stirrings of industry in the Western rather than the Eastern hemisphere. The 'Protestant ethic' may well have been more favourable to capital accumulation than the Roman Catholic ethic.

Chapter 3

Producing the Goods

For most of the history of mankind, and indeed for most of the world's present-day population, the level of *per capita* consumption has been at or near subsistence level. There have been periods of general abundance for some societies, and it has not been unusual for privileged groups within many societies to have more than enough to eat and drink, as witness the banquets of Imperial Rome. An outstanding feature of the twentieth century has been the widespread nature of relative abundance in the industrialised world, but as we shall see in Chapter 11 this does not mean that the basic economic problems of the world have been solved. To use a commonplace expression, in order to eat most men must work. 'Work' in this context usually involves some economically productive activity. We prefer to leave aside for the present the question of whether man has a psychological as well as an economic need to work, because the emphasis in this chapter will be primarily on the harnessing of productive effort to satisfy consumption needs and wants. Production is here seen as the servant of consumption.

THE LONG ROAD TO AFFLUENCE

Man the Scavenger

How has the human race managed to get enough to eat? One thing that even a cursory glance at the development of man as an economic animal will show is that he has rarely been able to do this on an individual basis. For perhaps 90 per cent of the timespan of the existence of the human race the family group has been the economic as well as the biological unit of survival. Indeed, man in prehistory could have survived only in units of at least family size. Man lived then as a gatherer and a scavenger, and the means to support an economic unit from a given terrain could only be found if the unit was small. But even at this level, the way the family was organised illustrates the production relationships within a self-sufficient community. Such a unit would be self sufficient since its entire range of consumption requirements could be provided by its own efforts, and probably the greater part of the unit's activities would be the gathering of food which would be consumed where it was collected (unless it could be found in such abundance that a store could be set aside for the coming winter). The allocation of specific tasks to particular individuals would be confined to the care by the women of children in their infancy.

Pastoral Bliss

The pastoral societies which succeeded the scavengers present a more complex picture. As hunters, men now required tools of greater sophistication than those used to scavenge, and such tools required time and skill to make. Time, then, would have to be allocated between hunting and tool-making. Moreover, in the pursuit of animals, man had to range much further afield than in the gathering of nuts and berries, and children in their infancy could not practicably accompany hunting expeditions. Thus hunting became, as far as we know, a male pursuit; but more importantly, this division of tasks into hunting, tool-making, and child-rearing meant that the family should have some fixed base of operations — even if only for a single hunting season — at which women and children could be left and to which the hunters could return. Hunting trips could be lengthy, and this would allow the women of the family time in which to make clothing from the skins which the hunted animals supplied along with their meat, and to tend the fire which besides giving warmth became essential for the digestion.

The Division of Labour

If the differences between scavenging societies and pastoral societies emerged as we have suggested (and much of our understanding of prehistoric man must be conjectural), we have demonstrated how the range of consumption possibilities was increased by specilisation of tasks. An eigtheenth-century economist, Adam Smith,[1] described this phenomenon as the 'division of labour', which he held to be the basis of factory production. In fact of course it has been practised by mankind for millennia. His various artifacts, stone tools, clothing and primitive pottery developed out of the surplus of time generated by the dichotomy of hunting and child-rearing. Much of our knowledge

---

[1]Adam Smith, *An Enquiry Into the Cause and Extent of the Wealth of Nations*.

of the life-style of early pastoral man comes from observations of extant stone-age cultures, in most of which women do the majority of tasks which do not actually involve hunting. Tool-making seems to have been a male preserve, perhaps for religious reasons, although one suspects that the image of 'man the tool-maker' might be a legacy of male chauvinism! It was the women who had the time on their hands.

Large-Scale Activity

This was another feature of these primitive economic systems which deserves comment. Some kinds of hunting activity involved more than just family units. We tend to think of these societies as being economically self-sufficient, but trapping an elephant in a pit or driving a herd of antelopes over a cliff were hardly one-man jobs. These required the co-operation of groups of families, even of tribes, and this, like the allocation of tasks within a group, required organisation. The more organised a society becomes, the greater the range and volume of consumption and production possibilities, and the less primitive its economy appears.

The Emergence of Urban Society

Sometime between the eighth and fifth millennia BC, man effected changes in the way he organised his existence which added up to one of the major landmarks in the history of mankind — the Neolithic revolution. In this period, man changed from a semi-nomadic hunter into a settled agriculturalist, with epoch-making repercussions. (Not all societies changed, however, and it is common even today for societies at different levels of development to exist at the same time). The pattern which agriculture imposed on human activity meant changes in the way society was organised. The growth of fixed settlements enabled the development of urban communities containing elements which were one or more stages removed from the principal economic activity.

In a pastoral society all able-bodied men are likely to be involved in hunting, with leadership being determined by hunting prowess. Such a community cannot produce much surplus for its leaders. A bed nearer the fire, perhaps, or a choicer part of the animal to eat, but little that the leader of the group can set aside as evidence of his leadership. Agriculture changed this. In its settled forms, agriculture produced grain which, unlike dead meat, could be stored. It became possible for a community in a given year to produce more than its could consume, and the Old Testament abounds with references to granaries. A society, however, which can organise itself to produce surpluses, leaving aside for the moment the question of to whom these surpluses accrue, must be considerably more complicated than a hand-to-mouth collection of hunters. Grain must be stored in suitably constructed buildings, for example, and someone has to take a decision that this should be done. Some will have to undertake the building work, and while they are doing this they cannot be engaged in farming. They will require tools for cutting stone and wood which may have to be provided by other groups of specialist workers. The surplus when stored will normally require some form of documentation, and we find that the development of writing is associated with the growth of settled communities. Settlements, moreover, and particularly those which have accumulated surpluses, are more vulnerable than nomadic groups to the predatory attentions of others, and so they will require protection. This again involves whole groups within a society being divorced from the main production activity. Ultimately all able-bodied males could be involved in the defence of the community, but to be effective, defence had to be organised. If large numbers were involved this organisation would require full-time attention, ranging from the fortifying of cities to the raising and equipping of armies.

An Archetypical Production Pattern

The progress of human civilisation since the Neolithic revolution has been marked by spectacular achievement. We should not lose sight however of the fact that despite the brilliance of the maritime cultures of the Mediterranean or the organisational superlatives of the Roman Empire, life for the majority of the inhabitants of settled societies has been, and still is for a great part of the world's population, largely a matter of subsistent self-sufficiency. The production relationships and the life-style of the Madras villager mentioned in the last chapter would be recognised by a Biblical farmer or the peasants of medieval Europe. The greater part of the output of such production units was, and still is, consumed by the unit itself. Any surplus over consumption may be exchanged for such goods as the unit cannot produce for itself. These would normally be goods related more to production than to consumption activity, e.g. metal products, farm implements, and draught animals. However, before any indulgence in consumption beyond mere subsistence could take place, others would typically take a share, e.g. the feudal lord in the Middle Ages and the landlord in present-day India.

Motivations to Produce

If the continent of Europe was once covered by self-sufficient production units which have their counterpart in modern India, the production activity in modern Europe has clearly changed out of all recognition. A detailed discussion of the pressures which brought about this change lies outside the scope of this book, but some of them originated from the rigid stratification of society. Social movement, and thereby the possibility of lasting material improvement, was only possible, it seemed, by the acquisition of land. Yet to acquire land one had first to accumulate wealth, and wealth in turn came from land-holding. Over the centuries this circularity was broken. From the artisans who supported the warrior elites there emerged a dynamic element which used trade to acquire wealth, and the growing use of money which this process involved enabled the peasant, in Britain at least, to exchange many of their feudal obligations for cash payments.

The fuedal aristocaracy found this process difficult to resist. Farming methods were primitive and the economically self-sufficient manors relied on a plentiful supply of docile labour. When a labour shortage, arising from the catastrophic outbreaks of bubonic plague which swept Europe in the fourteenth century, increased the 'bargaining power' of the village peasant, there became some point in raising production above subsistence level. Farmers could sell their surpluses in the towns, rather than have them arbitrarily expropriated by the landowners, and towns themselves could grow since a larger non-agricultural population could now be supported. This in turn widened the scope for non-agricultural production.

This process was, of course, more complicated than the simplified version given here, and it took place over centuries. The changes described were not arbitrary and although bubonic plague appears as a fortuitous factor it was in fact a symptom of change since it was imported into Europe from the Orient as a result of trading connections. The changes which took place arose from motivations which had their roots in the way in which society was organised, and the pressures to increase the volume of production. The feudal societies which declined in Europe survived for centuries in other parts of the world, yet the means by which change took place were not particularly sophisticated. Indeed, many Oriental countries possessed superior technical knowledge, and until the Renaissance, Europe appears to have been on balance an importer of new ideas from areas she was subsequently to overtake.

THE ROLE OF TECHNOLOGY

The concept of production we want to present here is one where organisational development is as significant as mechanical invention in the process of technical change.

Pre-Industrial Organisation

Feudal societies existed at low levels of mechanical technology. The gradual and sporadic growth of production came largely from changes in the way medieval societies were organised. The leaders of feudal societies saw conquest (or theft) as the key to survival, and conquest calls for the force of arms and a warrior elite. Peasants can be self-supporting while warriors cannot, and so peasants were organised to produce a surplus which would support both the elite in their predatory efforts and the artisans who produced their military accoutrements. The gains, if any, from conquest could be regarded as the final product of society as a whole. But the agriculture which supported this hierarchy had changed little from Biblical times. The two main internationally traded commodities, wine and wool, were the products of low levels of viticulture and animal husbandry. Cloth was occasionally produced in large workshops, but these had their counterparts in the days of Imperial Rome. It was the growth of trade which accelerated the decline of the military basis of medieval society, as trade became an alternative to conquest in the pursuit of wealth, but this change proceeded without any great mechanical invention. Agriculture was merely organised to produce wool rather than food, and the urban growth of monopolistic manufacturing and trading guilds was the product of a division between the organisation of production units on the one hand, and the operational aspects of production on the other, i.e. the emergence of employer-employee relationships.

Factory Production

The economist would view the production increases which arose from these gradual organisational changes as being the result of technical change. Mechanical invention can also result in increased production, but this does not have to be the case. It is the linking of mechanical invention to changes in organisation which has created the impression of technology as simply a mechanical or scientific matter. Mechanical invention is irradically identified with that phase of human history known as the Industrial Revolution, yet the apocalyptical anecdote of Adam Smith[2] emphasises organisation not machinery. He observed, in

[2]*Ibid.*

late eighteenth century England, that methods of pin manufacture varied in different parts of the country. He contrasted the production in some places of pins as a cottage industry, where an individual would carry out in sequence all the many operations necessry to make a pin, with the organisation of pin-making in other locations as factory production. Here each of the stages, the drawing of the wire, its cutting, sharpening, polishing, etc., was carried out by an individual or a group specialising in a particular task. The enormously increased production per worker that resulted Smith attributed to the advantages of 'the division of labour' (see p. 29). What struck him was the way in which this increase had been obtained by changing the way production was organised, for he did not observe great differences in the use of mechanical appliances, although labour specialisation would make their introduction easier. Similarly, that other concomitant to the rise of industry, the railways, would interest the economist partly through the effect they had on the organisation of the economy. Steam locomotion was of course a matter of mechanical invention, but the physical construction of the railroads depended on methods and materials known since the Middle Ages. In Britain at least, the railways were built by men using picks, shovels, and gunpowder, even if the skills of the civil engineer were newly acquired. A mixture, then, of old and new technology. The documentation of the construction of the railways abounds with references to the quantitative aspects of the phenomenon — the numbers of men involved, the tonnages of metal required for the machines and the rails, the volume of household savings utilised, as well as the measureable effects on related industry, etc. But the railways changed the way in which the whole of society was organised. They influenced the growth of towns, the movement of populations, the development of markets for finished goods and for the money to finance these concomitant changes. The development of banking services went hand in hand with railroad construction in the USA, and these services in turn galvanised the rural communities the railroads were built to serve. By itself, the growth of banking would hardly seem to be a technical change. It was neither mechanical nor, in the USA, an invention, yet with the railroads it was to irrevocably alter the basis of the American economy.

The Process of Invention

It was fashionable at one time to regard invention as an 'heroic' act, after the Alexandrian Greek, Hero, who invented a primitive steam turbine nearly two thousand years ago. As the process of industrialisation in the Western world gathered pace, however, it was observed that quite different inventions were made to solve similar problems, and this observation suggested that invention and innovation were the result of systematic or social forces, rather than an arbitrary affair as the term 'heroic' (i.e. out of context) would suggest. The process of invention and its application can be divided into stages. *Stage 1*. It has to be recognised that there is a human want to be fulfilled, and this recognition has to be seen in a social or cultural setting. For example, clothing may be a basic need, but what kind of clothing should come under this category? In nineteenth-century industrial Europe, expensive methods of production in clothing manufacture meant that clothing, other than functional workday garments, often had to be bought secondhand from the more affluent households. This takes us to *Stage 2*. The inventor has to have the knowledge and experience to solve the particular mechanical problems. The inventors of the sewing machine, which revolutionised the production of clothing for sale to the lower income groups, were able to draw their experience from a variety of light engineering pursuits. In *Stage 3*, the human need and the inventor's experience have to be brought together in a particular organisation framework. Material supplies, labour skills, selling outlets, etc., have to exist together at the right time. Just such a setting did exist in North America in the late nineteenth century. There the engineering industry had developed around a large number of small manufacturers who produced component parts for such finished products as Samuel Colt's revolving pistol. Thus the organisation of the engineering industry already suited the manufacture of products like the sewing machine which depended on the supply of small components together with suitably skilled labour, etc. In these conditions, the organisational problems of sewing machine production were of more significance than the admitted complexity of the machines' mechanism. Indeed, the genius of such household figures as Henry Ford lies not in their mechanical inventiveness but in the skill with which they organised production, by controlling the flows of the thousands of components, both human and material, which went into the finished product.

Alternative Methods of Production

Henry Ford's name is associated with the production line 'flow' techniques he developed to such high levels, and seems a long way from the pre-factory pin-maker of Adam Smith's example. The two, however, are linked as examples of alternative production techniques, and the pre-factory pin-maker is by no means obsolete as a production archetype. Processes that involve the making of unique or highly individual products are often known as 'one-off' production, implying that production stages are specially geared to each individual unit of final output. Large parts of the world's ship-building industry are organised on this basis, and 'one-off' production is the rule where an item is made to individual specification. This does not preclude other techniques, however, and even ships, custom-built cars, etc., will contain many sub-assemblies and fittings produced by other methods. 'Batch production', on the other hand, is an arrangement in which work starts simultaneously on a number of identical items — aircraft for example — and proceeds to the final stages before a new batch is begun. In 'flow' production, work begins consecutively on each product, the product being built up in a series of stages so that at any one point in time on a particular production line there will be no two items at an identical stage of manufacture, and the products 'flow' off the assembly line one by one.

The Choice of Technique

In motor vehicle production these three production methods (one off, batch and flow) have followed one another in chronological order, as the number of inventions accumulated. Flow production is nowadays associated with a 'high technology profile' involving the use of large amounts of sophisticated expensive machinery which requires a high degree of design and maintenance skills, even though the machines themselves may not be difficult to operate. But flow methods can and do exist today in the setting of a 'low technology profile', as can be seen in bicycle manufacture which generally uses relatively simple tools and equipment.

At any one time, various production methods can exist concurrently, not just in different societies, or even in different industries within the sme economy, but even in the same industry. The baking industry contains both large-scale firms using assembly-line processes and corner-shop bakeries, while clothes can come from the mass producer or the bespoke tailor. As technology advances it may raise the technology profile, but it does not necessarily erase existing techniques. Thus the more technolgy proceeds, the greater the choice offered by the accumulation of inventions. Road transport preceded canals, which in turn preceded railways, yet today transport economists are preoccupied with the relative merits of all three alternatives.

In the past each of these transport systems presented obvious advantages over the others, and the advantages appeared in the form of differences in cost. Canals became expensive relative to rail since the costs of adapting a canal system, using known techniques, to counter rail's advantage of speed, were prohibitive. Once the development of railways achieved momentum it added to the inducement to advance railway technology, and it brought about organisational changes which reinforced their position. Once a railway line had been built it would then appear advantageous for a business to establish itself near the railway connection, thereby also establishing its dependence on the railway system. Similarly with road transport. Initially a complement to railways — since goods have to be carried to the railway system — it became a competitor by attracting its own technological momentum (the internal combustion engine, the pneumatic tyre, etc.) and by reinforcing organisational change to the railway's disadvantage. When in Britain, during the period 1919-39, population shifted geographically, it moved away from areas in which railways were plentiful and into areas in which roads provided access to the new growing markets and population centres. Additionally, private car ownership was becoming a cultural trait thereby reinforcing the inducement to invest, and the cost advantages of roads over rail continued. The relative costs of the alternative systems, however, also change with the availability and price of the necessary energy sources and hence the present-day re-evaluations of the three systems.

If the decision as to the choice of technique rests on the relative costs of different techniques, it is important that these costs be clearly identified. At whatever level such choices are made, whether by a small productive unit like a market garden with a single owner/proprietor to work it, by a large business corporation, or even by a government, they will be made on the basis of information available on the relative costs of alternative techniques. Information can be inaccurate and it may be wrongly interpreted, but the choice of technique will depend upon the relative costs of the constituent parts of the productive process. The resources of all kinds that are necessary for production are customarily referred to as the factors of production.

THE FACTORS OF PRODUCTION

We will begin this section by examining the constituent parts of the process, parts which are present to some extent in all production activity, and which are conventionally grouped under the headings of land, capital, and labour.

Land as a Factor of Production

Whatever the final produt, every production unit requires space. Even the match-vendor in Oxford Street takes up some pavement space, and the decisions he takes in the siting of his activities are identical in kind if not in degree to those of a much larger organistion. If his fines become too heavy he may move to a less crowded thoroughfare! Some forms of production are clearly more 'land intensive' than others, agriculture in particular, and not all land is equally suitable for all production purposes. Manufacturing and service industries use particular land because of its topographical position in relation to their production activities, its proximity to centres of population, to ports, to other industry, etc., while agriculture and the extractive industries use land because of its physical properties. Certain types of farming can only be carried on in areas of particular climate, soil fertility, etc., and there would be little point in siting a coal mine on land which contained no coal. But land has one property which has interested economists from David Ricardo onwards, and that is that it is extremely difficult to change the amount of land on this planet. Production activity can be transferred from more to less suitable land, but only within the geographical limits of a given economic system. These limits can be increased by altering national frontiers, but only at the expense of neighbouring systems, and they can be overcome by trade between economic systems. In the end, however, land use will be restricted by the area of the earth's land-mass, and it is this fixed supply of land which can give a particular direction to economic activity. In many parts of the world, production is predominantly agricultural, as it was in medieval Europe, and the ownership of the fixed land area of an economic system confers enormous economic power on particular individuals. This economic power has vested itself with specific social attitudes, which have often provided the political justification for the status quo. Indian Maharajahs and the European landed aristocracy have in the past placed barriers in the way of production changes which might reduce the importance of land as a factor of production, just as the planting aristocracy of the southern states of North America once clung to the institution of slavery. Unlike capital and labour, land has this additional quality of being desired for its own sake as well as for its productive possibilities. In parts of the world today, in Cyprus for example, the social attraction of land (or property) ownership, on however modest a scale, can hold back the development of other production activity.

Capital as a Factor of Production

Capital is not fixed in supply and can be increasesd or decreased since it is man-made and exists as the result of human decision. Like land, capital does have some unique characteristics :

1 *Capital creation takes place at the expense of consumption* At a simple level, e.g. for the Madras villager, unable to employ labour, who waters his fields by bucket from the river, the time taken to dig a well or build irrigation ditches means that the growing crops will not be watered while the work is in progress. Thus the crop yield, and hence his family's consumption of food, may be reduced until the benefits of the work appear. Similarly if a manufacturing business buys new machinery, it is at the expense of someone's immediate consumption whether it be worker, manager, shareholder, or creditor.

2 *Capital is almost always an intermediate product* Production units do not acquire plant and machinery for its own sake (if they did they would not stay in business for long) but to increase the flow of goods to the consumer. There may be cases where capital is the final product — the villager may conceivably construct an irrigation work for status purposes, in which case the ditch would be an item of consumption as much as an intermediate good. We would not recognise all intermediate products as capital in the sense that machinery or buildings are capital. These latter items are referred to as fixed capital, while intermediate products such as raw materials for industry, the farmer's seed corn, and the insurance company's stationery, are termed working capital. But both categories are intermediate products since they are necessary inputs to the final product.

3 *Capital creation takes place in anticipation of future benefits* The current sacrifice is gauged against these.The Madras villager would not dig a well if he thought it would make a negligible difference to his crop yields. There is always the chance that he might not find water anyway, and so he faces two areas of risk and uncertainty. First, there is the anticipated effect that the water will have on his crops, and second, the chances that he will find water, or enough of it, when he does dig. The first may be easy to calculate, the second not necessarily so. A firm, for example, may be able to predict what effect a new machine will have on its output, but whether it will be able to sell that output is another matter. So whether or not the firm acquires the machine will depend on how it offsets future gain against present loss. Since there is the risk that future gain may be less than expected, a bird in the hand might not be worth two in the bush. This risk element is present in capital creation at all levels, whether it is the villager with

his well or a government balancing schools and roads forgone against the anticipated benefits of, say, a hydro-electric scheme or a nuclear power station.

4   *Capital tends to deteriorate over time*   Provision must be made to maintain it in working order and perhaps to replace it at the end of its working life. The working life of capital is not only a mechanical matter but also a matter of cost, since the costs of maintenance must be set against the value to the operator of the output. Another reason for scrapping capital before the end of its operational life is when technological change makes it possible to produce the same output by different and cheaper means.

Social capital   Some capital can have a very long life, particularly for the items usully referred to as 'social capital' — such as roads, houses, schools, etc. These are not directly related to a final product, although a house or school will be regarded as one by the building industry, but are complementary to it. 'Social' capital may have no easily measurable output, yet is probably indispensable to the long-term flow of final products. Factory production must be linked to the consumer by roads of some kind, and labour skills often require standards of literacy which can only be provided by formal schooling. The labour force must also be provided with housing, hospitals, etc., and this provision must keep pace with the final product. A society which neglects to provide such social 'overhead' capital will find that its overall ability to produce is impaired, and this is becoming increasingly the case as the production process increases in sophistication. There is, however, an important qualification in that in the short run 'productive' capital formation and 'social overhead' capital are competitive rather than complementary. Just as capital formation as a whole will, in the long term, enable increased consumption to take place, even though in the short term it takes place at the expense of consumption, so in the short term will social overhead capital formation take place at the expense of 'productive' capital or of consumption. Since both factories and schools can only be built by sacrificing current consumption, it is important to get the balance right. Too much as well as too little expenditure on social overhead capital can impare the capacity to produce final goods. Insufficient educational expenditure might reduce the supply of labour skills which in turn can slow down the rate of industrial advance, but then too many schools can mean not enough capital equipment is being created, and this in turn will slow the rate of productive capacity. This reduces to a question of evaluation, since the output of the educational process cannot easily be measured in terms which enable comparison with the output of, say, manufacturing industry, and this difficulty of measurement is a crucial characteristic of social overhead capital. In the end some almost arbitrary judgement may be needed to decide what gain in educational standards is worth what loss in productive capacity, and it will be made in terms of the prevailing social and political attitudes and cultural traits (see Chapter 8).

Labour as a Factor of Production

In a sense, labour shares a characteristic with capital in that they are both man-made, a feature which has relevance to those who concern themselves with the reaction of population change to economic stimuli. We saw, for example (p. 22) that the availability of consumption goods such as motor cars has in more affluent societies at times tended to lead to a reduction in family size. Economic pressure is only one of many influences on demographic change, but it may be the most significant determinant of the 'activity rate', i.e. the proportion of the population engaged in work. Labour, however, does possess one unique characteristic in that it offers itself to the productive process of its own volition. During the productive process, moreover, it retains some control over the rate and manner of its use. This quality remains true even in economic systems in which the degree of individual liberty is small — as in feudal societies, slave-based economies, and sometimes planned economies where labour is directed. It is still possible for labour to work more or less hard, in the face of penalties or rewards, and there is some choice about whether to even work at all.

Like land and capital, however, labour can be infinitely varied in type. It can be more or less skilled, more or less able, and more or less adaptable. But again, labour can to some extent choose to which of these categories it will belong. Skills and training can be actively acquired, subject to certain constraints. These can be in part physical, since particular qualities will be required of brain surgeons on the one hand, and lumber-jacks on the other, and not every individual may be able to acquire the necessary characteristics. Then there may be institutional obstacles in the way. In the past, membership of particular professons — the legal profession in eigthteenth-century Prussia, for example — was restricted by decree to particular social groups, and in Britain now there is still an informal bias towards public schools in some occupations. Custom, even although unenforced, can also present a barrier. In some societies, parental occupation may influence choice, as son follows father in the family trade, and social pressures may also play a part. It may not occur to the children of manual workers that occupational choice exists, since their life-style may condition them into accepting occupational patterns other than those to which their natural abilities are suited (see Chapter 7).

SOME CONCEPTUAL DIFFICULTIES

Another important aspect of labour as a factor of production is that particular types of labour perform an organising function for the whole production process itself. Work done at managerial level may not be regarded as 'labour' in the same sense as the work done by the machine operators. Indeed, a distinction is often drawn between 'labour' and 'enterprise', the latter term being reserved for those individuals who take decisions on the quantity and type of factors used, the way in which they are used, the final product, etc. It may be more appropriate to regard managers as a particular category of labour, since management can be bought in much the same way as labour as a whole can be bought, and the source of management can often be the labour force itself. We can observe, moreover, that organised labour — the trade union — is blurring the distinction between labour and management by developing a managerial role for itself by demanding, and getting, more say over the way in which labour is used.

Apart from the difficulty of separating 'labour' from 'enterprise', it is important to realise that no factor can be used by itself, and even the distinction between labour and capital, or capital and land, may not always be helpful. Even automated machinery requires some labour to operate it, and in operation it is often hard to say what part of the final product accrues to the machine and what part to labour. If it takes a man and shovel to dig a hole, how much of the hole is dug by the man, and how much by the shovel? Again, it is quite valid to regard that period during which a skill is acquired and in which earnings, and therefore consumption, are reduced in just the same way that the process of capital formation is viewed, with the resultant skill being conceptually no different from a capital asset. And what of the employer who, like the apprentice, may have shared in the sacrifice of earnings during the apprenticeship, or the community as a whole which subsidises the medical student? In slave societies, labour clearly was regarded as capital, having maintenance costs and being depreciated over its working life, and being bought, not hired, in the market place. Has the emergence of employer-employee relationships, which replaced slave labour, really been the radical change that it appears? Ultimately free labour can choose between work and privation — unless there is mass unemployment — but social pressures may greatly restrict its freedom of action. We saw in Chapter 2 that much consumption, especially of consumer durables, is of a contractural nature, and depends on the prospect of continuous employment. Thus although technically free not to work, voluntary unemployment would disproportionately reduce consumption. Even freedom to change jobs should not be taken for granted. Debt is a widely used instrument for tying peasants to their land in otherwise apparently free societies, and in Britain it is not unknown for large firms to deliberately pay employees over the market rate so that the contractual consumption based on these levels of income will give the employer the benefit of a stable work force.

Similarly, a farmer may have to maintain the fertility of his land in just the same way as the efficiency of a machine has to be maintained, in which case the distinction for that farmer, between capital and land, is somewhat academic.

Chapter 4

The Market Allocation System

A DECENTRALISED, IMPERSONAL ALLOCATION SYSTEM

Over the last two chapters we have surveyed many of the forces that determine the consumption demands of people and also the stages of development in productive capacity. We must now attempt to bring consumption demand and productive supply together and consider how they interact with one another. At this point in the book, the form of the interaction that will be dealt with is confined to that of market exchange undertaken for the mutual private benefit of buyers and sellers, although a major alternative to this relationship is presented in Chapter 9. The interaction of buyers and sellers within a market environment leads, as we shall see, to goods and services being consumed, to profits being earned, to raw materials, labour, capital and land being directed into particular uses. Market behaviour can determine the What?, Why? and Where? of production as well as the 'to whom?' of consumption.

There are many types and forms of market in a modern economy, from the local street market to the Stock Exchange, from the UK market for colour TV sets to the international oil market. A 'market' is not necessarily a particular place or building where trading takes place, but rather a term describing the presence of trading activity. If there are no buyers or no sellers then there can be no market.

For economists and politicians alike, the fact that economic resources can be allocated as a result of a host of transactions, whether great or small but carried out according to the private interests of all the participants, is of great importance. It implies, for example, that the main economic activities do not have to be organised or directed by a central authority because the markets do this automatically. It has implications for personal freedoms in the sense that people can be left to look after their own interests. On the other hand, as we shall see in Chapters 6 to 10, there are important weaknesses that can emerge if *all* allocation is left to the market process. For the moment, however, our focus will be on the market process as an impersonal and decentralised allocation system.

MODEL BUILDING: THE 'INDIVIDUAL' AND 'THE FIRM'

The determinants of consumption and production patterns have so far been painted with a broad brush so as to provide a general background to our subsequent discussions. But the economist is interested not only in being able to understand economic behaviour in a society, but also in predicting future behaviour. It is in prediction that the economist can potentially be of most use to the world. The great complexities of the real world however are difficult to handle all at once, and so economists attempt to simplify problems by trying to isolate the most important relationships. They set up what they call 'economic models' to represent these behavioural relationships and then use them to make predictions. Models of market behaviour are at the core of much of modern economics, and this chapter presents one version of such a model.

A widely used simplification is to concentrate on the actions of two main participants in a market — the 'individual consumer' who will be regarded as the originator of 'demand' relationships, and the 'firm' which will be the decision unit organising the 'supply' to meet consumer demand.

SOME ASPECTS OF DEMAND

Individual Consumer Demand

'Demand', as far as the economist is concerned, means the market expression of purchasing power. We all have a vast range of desires, needs and wants, but we cannot regard these as 'demands' unless we are ready and able to back them up with real purchasing power. The actual level of demand that an individual consumer will take to, say, the 'shoe market' will be determined by a long list of factors, many of which have already been brought to the reader's attention. A typical list of factors might well include those listed below, but it is not intended to be exhaustive, and the reader can add more based on his own experience if he wishes.

The demand for pairs of shoes per month expressed by Consumer X	depends on→	The income of X, The sex of X, The price of shoes and the prices of other goods available to X, The number of serviceable shoes already owned by X, The degree of status or pleasure derived from wearing shoes in the latest fashion, The season of the year.

It is necessary to express demand as relating to a specified time period for it to have any practical meaning either for the consumer or the supplier. The length of the time period chosen will depend on the nature of the good and the length of the productive process. Foodstuffs are bought on a weekly basis by most households, so demand is perhaps best expressed as so much per week. In the case of consumer durables, however, purchases of such items as vacuum cleaners, cars and refrigerators are spaced out by periods of years for most households. Shoes fall somewhere between those two categories since in the early 1970s people in the UK were buying $4\frac{1}{2}$ pairs of shoes per head per year. Young women between the ages of sixteen and twenty-five years tend to buy rather more at about 6 pairs a year, perhaps because they are more fashion conscious than men and older women, but even so this only amounts to an average for that age and sex group of one shoe per month. Demand relationships at the individual level are important because they determine the total market demand for a good.

Market Demand

The market demand for a good is the sum of all relevant individual consumer demands for that good over a specified time period. For many purposes a sub-section of a total market may be relevant. The total of all sales of shoes per month in a small town could be regarded as 'the market' for shoes in that locality. This may be all the information that a local independent retailer of shoes needs to know, but a manufacturer of shoes sold on a national market or the management of a chain of retail shoe shops will be interested in total UK sales per month. When dealing with market demand, the market reactions of individual consumers get merged into the overall behaviour patterns of thousands and perhaps millions of people. The market researcher trying to forecast shoe sales nationally will not be able to consult all the individual consumers about their purchasing intentions, so they have to rely on sample surveys of consumers and various proxy measures of the factors that influence individuals. One example of a proxy measure might be the use of national wage rate trends instead of individual incomes.

Total market demand for pairs of shoes per month	depends on→	National trends in wages and employment, The age and sex structure of the population, The price of shoes relative to the prices of other consumer goods, The rate at which fashion styles change, Advertising expenditure, The season of the year.

Demand and the Firm

The firm is here assumed to be an organisation manufacturing shoes. There are of course many other types of firm interested in the sales of shoes such as retail and wholesale firms, firms supplying leather or plastics to manufacturers of shoes, and the firms handling advertising and promotional services for the trade. The marketing or sales director of our shoe manufacturing firm may have a diagram something like Figure 4.1 in his office. This will keep him informed about both the state of the total market and about his firm's part in it. We could see the firm's market in two stages as follows:

Demand for the firm's shoes per month	depends on→	The total market for shoes per month, The firm's share of the total market.
The firm's share of the total market	depends on→	The price and quality of its shoes, How fashionable the styles of its shoes are, The firm's advertising expenditure, The extent of the 'goodwill' for the firm's name. } All in relation to rival firms

Figures 4.1   Sales Directors' Chart

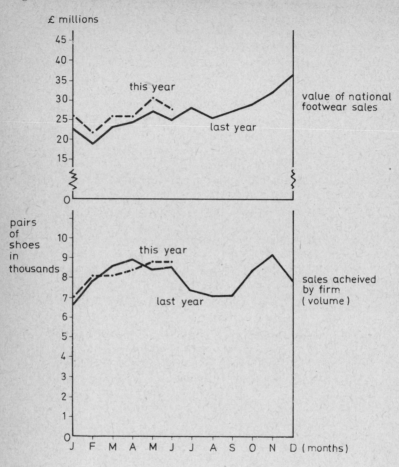

An Analytical Device

Enough has already been mentioned to make it clear that a whole range of inffluences are at work to determine just how many pairs of shoes the firm manages to sell in a particular month. Economists find it difficult to juggle with all these influences simultaneously, and they have evolved a useful (but potentially misleading) device to simplify their problems of analysis. This device is to pretend that all the various market demand influences have been frozen at some given point in time, giving what could be thought of as an instantaneous snapshot where all movement is stopped. Then, assuming that he knows how all the influences work, the economist will attempt to predict what is likely to happen in the market should just one of the influencing factors be allowed to change.

Now the consumer when going to the market place will be engaged in exchanging one good for another. In primitive economies this can take the form of barter, i.e. pigs in exchange for axes, but in developed economies the exchange is between goods on one hand and money on the other. Different goods will be considered as exchangeable for different amounts of money and this money measure of value is of course the 'price' of the good. The consumer contemplating the purchase of goods with widely varying characteristics will at least have a standard measure for comparison in money terms, i.e. relative prices. Given this everyday experience of exchange, it is not surprising that economists have settled on a basic diagram in which only the price of a good is allowed to change and all other influences are held at a constant level.

Assume that we have decided to adopt this procedure by freezing all movement as at the end of February this year. In Figure 4.1 the firm sold about 8,000 pairs of shoes in February this year, and we shall assume that the price to the consumer was £5 per pair. The price of £5 is plotted on the vertical axis of Figure 4.2 while the quantity of 8,000

Figure 4.2   Hypothetical Sales by Firm according to Price

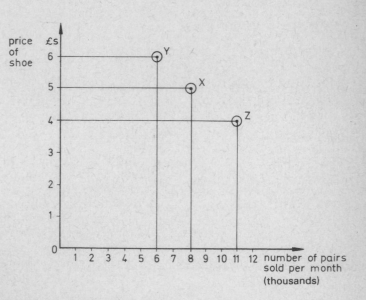

pairs is plotted on the horizontal axis, and these two values yield the point X on the diagram. Now consider the effect on sales if the price, alone out of all relevant influences, is changed; let us say that the price is reduced to £4.

The individual consumer of the firm's shoes is now subject to two main types of influence. First are the 'substitution effects', so called because these shoes are now cheaper in relation to other consumer goods and this firm's shoes are now relatively cheaper than those of its competitors. Consumers will tend to substitute this firm's shoes for other consumer goods and the shoes of rival firms. Secondly, there will be an 'income effect', (a) because the original purchaser will now be able to buy more shoes than before even though their money income is unchanged, and (b) consumers who could not perhaps afford to buy these shoes at £5 are now able to do so at £4. The combined pressures of these substitution and income effects are almost certain to increase the firm's total sales.   As a result of this fall in price, then, sales by the firm rise to about 11,000 pairs.Conversely if the price wereto be raised to £6 per pair (all other factors held constant), then sales would be likely to fall to perhaps only 6,000 pairs per month, since the substitution and income effects now work against the firm. The firm can now consider the position by arranging these results into a table as follows.

Table 4.1   Shoe Sales According to Price

(A) Price in £s per pair	(B) Numbers of pairs sold per month	(AxB) Total sales revenue per month
6	(Est.) 6,000	(Est.) £36,000
(Actual) 5	(Actual) 8,000	(Actual) £40,000
4	(Est.) 11,000	(Est.) £44,000

The information in Table 4.1 is not of uniform quality. The firm has actual experience of how many shoes it can sell at the current price of £5 per pair, but the sales rates at £6 and £4 can only be estimates. Any firm will be interested in the probable effects of price changes on its sales, but few firms are likely to jiggle their prices up and down simply to discover this effect and in any case they are powerless to do so under the special conditions assumed here, namely, all non-price factors constant. On the other hand, the sales director can gain some impression of price effects on those occasions when prices are changed by the firm or when competitors change theirs. In most elementary economic textbooks, you will find a diagram like Figure 4.3 (a) showing a whole range of possible prices and quantities and indicating exactly how much more can be sold should the price fall from say P_3 to P_4. In real life, however, the price-demand relationship is more like that in Figure 4.3 (*b*) where the quantity demanded is fairly certain around the current market price, say P_3, but where increasing doubt surrounds prices further and further away from current experience (the shaded area in Figure 4.3 (*b*) indicates the range of possible quantities at each price). Table 4.1 suggested that the firm could increase its total revenue to £44,000 per month by cutting its price to £4, but the firm must balance the risk of not achieving the potential sales of 11,000 pairs per month against the much more certain information about the cost of producing an extra 3,000 pairs of shoes.

Figure 4.3   The Demand Curve

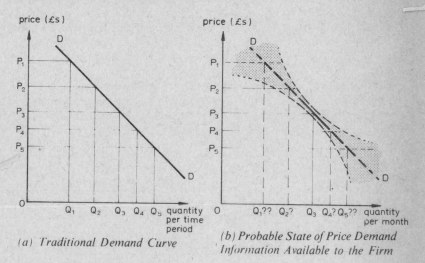

(*a*) *Traditional Demand Curve*

(*b*) *Probable State of Price Demand Information Available to the Firm*

Shifts in the Demand Curve

The demand curve in Figure 4.3 was drawn on the assumption that all the factors influencing demand were held constant with the sole exception of price. The effect on demand of any price change was then seen as a movement up or down the demand curve. The reader should remember that should any other factor than price be allowed to change, then we would have to draw a new demand curve. Let us trace the probable effects of two such changes—

1   *An increase in the firm's advertising expenditure*   In Figure 4.4 (*a*) the original demand curve is shown as D_1, and at a price of P_1 the quantity sold will be Q_1. The increased advertising should mean that

more will be sold than before at a price of P_1, say a quantity of Q_2, and we will then be on a new demand curve D_2.

2   A deterioration in the style and quality of the firm's shoes   We now expect that the firm will sell fewer shoes at each price than before, i.e. in Figure 4.4 (b) the demand curve has shifted from D_1 to D_3, and the quantity sold at P_1 falls from Q_1 to Q_3.

Figure 4.4.   Shifts in the Demand Curve

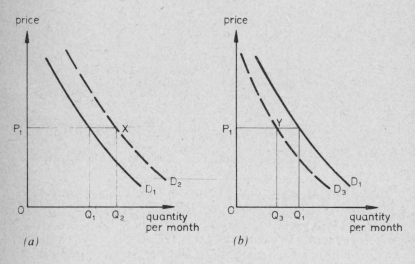

Non-Price Demand Curves

Demand Relationships can of course be illustrated by diagrams that allow any one of the relative determinants of demand to change while holding all the others constant. We might be interested, for example, in how demand for shoes reacts to changes in household income. A diagram like Figure 4.5 might then result showing that higher income households buy shoes much more frequently ·than lower income households of the same size and age/sex composition.

The reader might like to draw for himself a series of diagrams concentrating on one main determinant at a time and speculate on the possible shapes of the curves.

Figure. 4.5 Household Demand for Shoes Related to Household Incomes

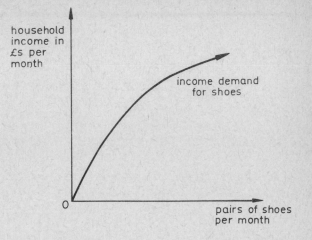

SOME ASPECTS OF SUPPLY

Costs

Whatever the demand circumstances that face a manufacturer, the decision about how far to meet them will hinge on the costs and profits associated with supply. Costs of supply can be broadly divided into two main categories, fixed costs and variable costs. *A fixed cost* is a charge to the firm that must be met whether production takes place or not, and would include such items as rent, interest on borrowed capital, and hire fees for equipment. If a factory is all geared up to begin production there will be in addition the salaries of the managerial and office staff and all the costs associated with their operations. These will tend to be regarded as fixed 'overhead' costs since they do not vary very much with the level of output of the firm. Costs are 'fixed' only in the sense that they cannot be quickly and easily changed, and a distinction is often made between the 'short run' during which it is assumed that fixed costs are largely unchangeable, and the 'long run' when *all* costs can be varied.

Unfortunately, there is a tendency for students to equate 'long run' with a 'long period of time', but a comparison between, say, a motor repair garage and a large automated car factory will quickly indicate that the long run for the garage is shorter *in time* than the short run for the factory.

Variable costs, as the name suggests, are those costs that vary as the level of output of the firm changes. These are the costs directly associated with the inputs to the production process and include raw materials and bought-in components, factory labour, power supplies, and transportation costs.

For the firm to be bothered with all the effort and organisation necessary for production to take place, there has to be some reward or incentive, and in a competitive market economy, the prime motivator or reward offered is profit. The profits that a firm can earn are decided by the way in which sales revenue and production costs interact as output levels change. It is therefore necessary to consider the behaviour of costs per unit of output throughout the output range.

Returning to our shoe manufacturer, we can imagine that the firm has a factory of a certain size in which equipment and machinery has been installed that is capable of a given maximum output. Factories are normally planned by production engineers to have a certain maximum capacity within which there will be a planned normal or design capacity which is expected to be the most economically efficient output level. In practice, these design and maximum capacity levels may not be very precise since firms can often squeeze more production out of the same installed plant by the introduction of overtime working or extra shifts for the work force. To avoid such complications, we shall assume here that the factory has been designed to work with a given number of shifts that cannot be increased for technical reasons.

Table 4.2 is a summary of how costs behave in our hypothetical shoe factory, and the same information is plotted in Figure 4.6 (*a*) and (*b*). In Figure 4.6 (*a*), the total fixed costs are shown by a straight horizontal line indicating that the firm must bear charges of £4,000 per month whatever the output level. The total variable costs rise steeply for the first 1,000 pairs produced as the factory gets 'into gear' and then rise by a constant amount within the output range of 2,000 to 8,000 pairs. When output is pushed beyond the design capacity of 8,000 pairs, variable costs rise more sharply until the theoretical maximum output is reached.

Shoes are sold at so much a pair, so Figure 4.6 (*b*) shows how the cost per pair changes with output levels. Average fixed costs decline continuously as the £4,000 is spread more thinly over the increasing output rate, but average variable costs tend to fall towards a figure of about £1.25 a pair until output exceeds the design capacity when they turn upwards. The firm's average total costs also decline steadily until the firm is producing at its most efficient level of 8,000 pairs, and then they rise.

It is clear from Table 4.2 that the shape and position of the average total cost curve depends directly on the size of the fixed costs and the behaviour of variable costs over the normal output range. Different assumptions about these costs will give different shapes to the average cost curves, and it is not claimed here that all firms face cost curves like those drawn in Figure 4.6. The cost behaviour described in our example which has variable costs per unit constant over a wide range of outputs is, however, believed to be fairly representative of much of modern manufacturing industry.

Table 4.2 Shoe Factory Production Costs

Output per month in thousands	In £ thousands			In £s per pair		
	Total fixed costs	Total variable costs	TOTAL COSTS	Average fixed costs	Average variable costs	AVERAGE TOTAL COSTS
(X)	(A)	(B)	(A+B)	(A÷X)	(B÷X)	(A+B)÷X
0	4	0	4	∞	0	∞
1	4	2.8	6.8	4	2.8	6.8
2	4	4	8	2	2	4
3	4	5	9	1.33	1.66	3
4	4	6	10	1	1.5	2.5
5	4	7	11	0.8	1.4	2.2
6	4	8	12	0.66	1.33	2
7	4	9	13	0.57	1.29	1.86
8 (design capacity)	4	10	14	0.5	1.25	1.75
9	4	12	16	0.44	1.33	1.77
10 (max.)	4	14.8	18.8	0.4	1.48	1.88

Figure 4.6 (a) Total Cost in Relation to Output

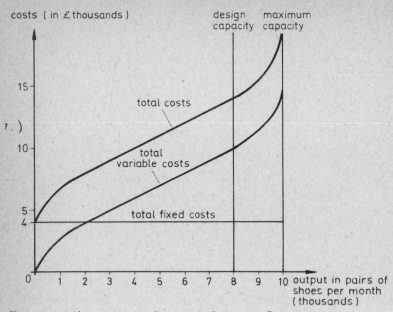

Figure 4.6 (b) Average Cost in Relation to Output

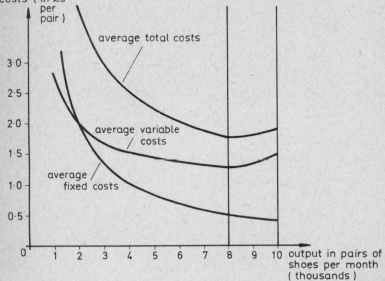

Profits and Capacity Usage

When discussing the demand for the firm's shoes, we began by assuming that there was a rate of sale of 8,000 pairs a month at a price of £5 per pair. A large part of the £5 paid for each pair by the consumer goes to cover the costs and profits of the wholesalers and retailers who distribute the shoes from the manufacturer to the consumer. We shall now assume further that the manufacturer sells his shoes to the wholesalers at a price of £2.50 per pair and that this is regarded as a competitive price when compared with other manufacturers.

In Figure 4.7, the average total cost curve from Figure 4.6 is reproduced and the wholesale price of £2.50 is indicated. With output of 8,000, the average cost per pair of shoes is £1.75, so the profit made is £2.50 less £1.75, or 75p per pair — which represents an approximate profit margin of 43 per cent of costs. With the wholesale price sticking at £2.50 however, this high margin can only be earned when the firm is producing at its design capacity. When the firm was at the point of

Figure 4.7 Mark-Up Margins and Breakeven Capacity

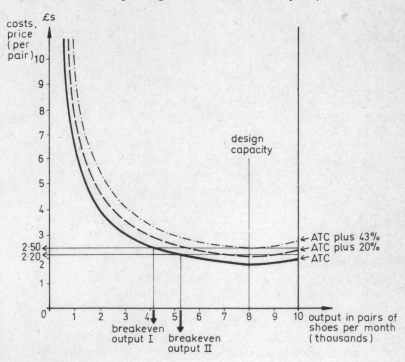

deciding whether to build the factory, it would have had to have estimated its potential or expected price, sales volume and production costs. The owners of the firm would have been looking for some acceptable rate of return or yield on the capital they were investing. From their experience and/or researches in the shoe trade, they may have decided that a minimum margin of 20 per cent on total costs would be necessary to give them the minimum return on their investment that they required given the capacity of the factory.

The implications of this background can be traced in Figure 4.7. The firm is there seen to 'break even' or just cover all its costs at an output rate of 4,200 pairs per month (breakeven output 1) but it does not start to achieve a 20 per cent profit margin until production reaches around 5,600 pairs. At production rates above this level, the profit margin is higher and obviously quite acceptable. Naturally, then the firm would prefer to run its plant continuously at the 8,000 pairs level and would be unhappy if its capacity usage fell below 75 per cent of this level, at which point the firm is just making its minimum acceptable profit of about £2,250 per month. The diagram helps to explain why manufacturers start to lose confidence if their sales and capacity usage falls significantly below their desired levels, because it is obvious that their profit earnings are likely to fall even more rapidly than their output.

Capacity Usage and Stocks

The sales chart in Figure 4.1 suggested that there was a seasonal swing in sales volume in the shoe trade, and this is a not unusual phenomenon in many industries. In these situations, it can readily be seen to be in the firm's interests to try to even out the production flow throughout the year by producing at a higher rate than necessary in low sales periods so as to build up stocks to meet the peak demands. This is a considerable problem for firms that make a highly perishable product or a product that by its nature cannot be stored (as in the case of electricity or transport services). Firms making perishable goods must consider the costs of storage especially carefully, but even our shoe firm has a perishability problem in the sense that shoes are fashion goods and surplus stocks at the end of a season may have very little sales value.

The problem of stabilising production rates is also apparent when sales volumes are unexpectedly high. Stocks may become exhausted as the firm's productive capacity fails to keep up with the current demand. The firm has various courses of action open to it in the face of this situation, for example, the firm could (a) Do nothing and wait for the rush to pass, (b) Institute some kind of rationing of deliveries to wholesalers so as to spread the available output (thinly but evenly), (c) Attempt to increase the capacity of the factory or consider building a new one (a 'long run' solution only), (d) Raise its prices sufficiently to reduce demand to the level of present capacity.

The action taken will be largely dependent on the firm's interpretation of the present and expected future market environment. The firm needs to find out just why its sales have exceeded expectations, and whether the reasons are long or short term. If the situation is believed to be only temporary, then action such as (a) or (b) above is most likely. If high volume sales are expected to continue for the foreseeable future, then both (b) and (d) are possible simultaneous moves. The firm is not likely to choose (d) if the shortage is expected to be only temporary, because it may be afraid of losing the 'goodwill' of customers who may be offended by short-term fluctuations in price in the face of heavy demand. On the other hand, where regular seasonal price variations are normal as with much agricultural produce, action such as (d) may be appropriate. The question of the firm's pricing behaviour is so important, however, that it will be pursued further in the next section.

Pricing Policy and the Firm

Consider a situation where the firm's sales have stuck at around 5,000 pairs for a few months. The firm will be anxious about the excess capacity and its monthly accounts will show that profits are below their desired level. One way to deal with the problem might be to cut its wholesale price to say £2.20, but one immediate consequence of this move would be to raise the firm's breakeven output to around 5,200 pairs (breakeven output II in Figure 4.7). Furthermore, the firm will not earn the same total profit that it was receiving with sales of 5,000 at £2.50 until sales at the new price reach nearly 7,000, so by cutting its price the firm raises the capacity usage requirement for an unchanged profit revenue. Then there is the uncertainty about just how far demand will increase at the new lower price. Price cutting as a way of dealing with poor sales can thus be seen to be a policy fraught with problems and risks. The firm is therefore much more likely to attempt to boost sales at the original price by product improvements and renewed sales and marketing efforts since this leaves more room for manoeuvre. Another danger with a price-cutting strategy is that it will only increase the firm's share of the market if rival firms do not retaliate. Should all firms cut their prices in response to our firm's move, our firm could find itself back with not much more than 5,000 pairs sold but at a price that may not allow it to even break even (unless there is a big increase in total shoe sales of course). Price cutting as a form of competition is therefore unlikely to appeal to firms unless there have been new and genuine reductions in their costs following technological improvements or factor price falls. Price cutting as a market device must otherwise be regarded as a move that is likely to force some firms out of business.

The outline of the firm's behaviour given so far in this chapter is one 'model' or 'theory' of the firm's behaviour. But if the reader pursues economics further he cannot fail to realise that there is more than one 'theory of the firm' in circulation and there is considerable controversy about which one is the 'correct' theory. We have given a common-sense interpretation of some of the price and cost circumstances that a firm can face and of the firm's likely reaction to them. The interpretation is not claimed to be the only possible or the most useful interpretation and our treatment has of necessity been very brief.

THE MOVEMENT OF FACTORS OF PRODUCTION INTO AND OUT OF PRODUCTION

The flow of variable production inputs such as labour and materials depends on production levels which in turn are determined by the volume of sales. The continued application of fixed cost inputs such as buildings, machinery and management services to a particular line of production depends on the profitability of the firm. If we refer back to Figure 4.7, it is quite obvious that the firm's chances of profitability decrease as the wholesale price falls, and should the price fall below £1.75, the firm is bound to make losses. The managers and owners of the firm must then decide whether to continue production or to shut down the factory (incidentally the same dilemma arises if costs increase while the price is held constant). On the other hand, following the example on pp. 58-59, if sales are expected to outstrip capacity by a significant margin for a sufficiently long period, the firm must decide whether an extension of capacity or a new factory are likely to yield enough profit to justify such an investment of time, effort and capital.

Looked at from the point of view of the industry as a whole, these questions can be considered to be about the movement of factors of production into or out of a particular area of production.

Not all firms in an industry are likely to have exactly the same cost and sales conditions. They may indeed use the same basic production methods, but the size of the firm, the age and quality of its plant and machinery, the skill of its workers, the efficiency of its management or any other particular advantages or disadvantages that a firm may have will mean that actual costs and profits will not be entirely uniform.

Let us assume that there are three firms competing in an industry — they are labelled 'A', 'B' and 'C' in Figure 4.8. These three firms are of different size and have different costs although producing a broadly similar product. The diagram suggests that the larger the firm the lower the average costs, but cost differences are not necesarily related to size. The curves shown are the average total costs of each firm, to which has been added a mark-up which will yield the minimum profit acceptable to each firm. With a wholesale price of P_1, all three firms can earn their minimum profit. To achieve this profit, firm 'C' must operate at its most efficient capacity level, but firms 'A' and 'B' have a wide range of capacity utilisation levels consistent with their profit targets. Firm 'C' may decide that it will cease production if capacity usage falls below C_1 at price P_1. Should the price fall steadily to P_2 for some reason, firm 'C' will not be able to reach its profit target at any capacity level and may decide to withdraw from the industry. Firm 'B' is now in the same position that 'C' was in before the price fall, and itself becomes vulnerable to further price falls. Firm 'A' can survive until the price falls below P_3, or capacity utilisation at price P_3 falls below A_1.

The right-hand part of Figure 4.8 indicates the maximum productive capacity that will be available in the industry at each price level. Capacity is withdrawn from the industry as the price falls from P_1 to P_3 (or conversely capacity is added as the price rises). The shading is to suggest that the exact price level at which a firm will decide to pull out is dependent on many circumstances relating to the general financial position of the firm. The general proposition is that higher prices will (a) increase the profits of firms already in production, (b) improve the chances of survival of firms on the edge of failure, and (c) encourage new firms to enter the industry to take advantage of the improved profit possibilities. It should not be assumed that all new firms will have higher costs than the existing producers as seems to be suggested by Figure 4.8, since new entrants may have the advantage of new plant employing the latest technology. Figure 4.8 is best interpreted as a ranking of firms already in the industry, whether new or old, with lowest cost firms to the left. With a larger number of firms in the industry, the discontinuities in Figure 4.8 can be ignored and we approximate to a continuous line perhaps like that in Figure 4.9 labelled *SS*. This curve we shall call the potential supply curve of the industry and it indicates how much production is likely to be forthcoming at each price level. As was suggested earlier, there is likely to be a range of potential outputs at each price level, for example outputs between X_1 and X_2 at a price of P_m as in Figure 4.9, because firstly,

Figure 4.8   Capacity Availabilty and Price

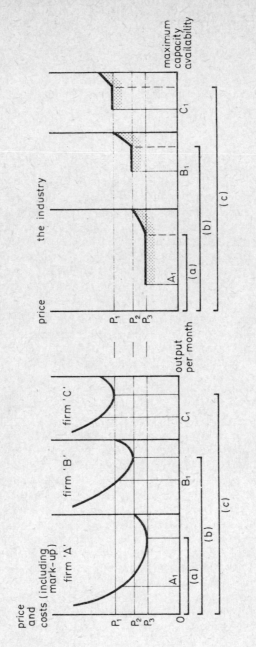

Note: The output rate of A_1 is the minimum capacity utilisation acceptable for firm 'A' at a price of P_3
The output rate of B_1 is the minimum capacity utilisation acceptable for firm 'B' at a price of P_2
The output rate of C_1 is the minimum capacity utilisation acceptable for firm 'C' at a price of P_1

Figure 4.9   The Potential Supply Curve

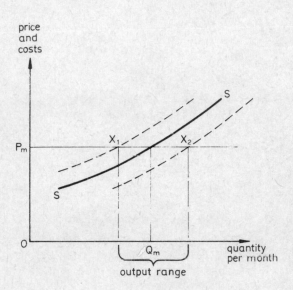

each firm will individually be varying output at each price, and secondly, there is a degree of imprecision about just when firms will enter or leave the industry. Indeed, it could be that the potential supply curve is different depending on whether supply is increasing in response to higher prices, or whether the industry is shrinking in response to falling prices. When the industry's demand is falling during a slump, for instance, firms or factories may temporarily close down but with the intention of re-entering the industry when the economic climate improves. There can then be a fairly rapid response to demand when an upturn in trade comes. If all available capacity is already in use, however, there will be inevitable delays in increasing output until new buildings and plant are installed or new firms enter the industry.

Figure 4.10   Supply and Demand — Price and Quantity Equilibrium

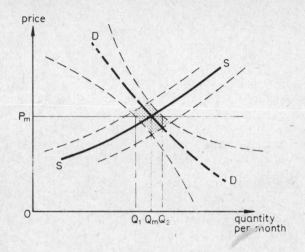

DEMAND AND SUPPLY AND THE EQUILIBRIUM PRICE

We now bring together the demand behaviour in relation to price as indicated in Figure 4.3 (*b*) and the potential supply behaviour of Figure 4.9 in the combined diagram of Figure 4.10. If the supply curve's most likely position is indicated by the line *SS*, and that of the demand curve by *DD*, then the two lines intersect at a price of P_m and a quantity of Q_m. The price of P_m is usually referred to as the 'equilibrium price' because at this price demand equals supply, i.e. the quantity firms are willing to supply equals consumers' willing demands. Our analysis has so far insisted that the realistic view of the market is one in which firms are seen to be operating under conditions of uncertainty and where there is a range of possible supply and demand levels at each price. The shaded area at the centre of Figure 4.10 is consistent with this view and indicates the area in which potential equilibrium is possible. With a given price of P_m however, this shaded area gives a potential output range of Q_1 to Q_2.

CONSUMER SOVERIEGNTY AND THE ADJUSTMENT TO EQUILIBRIUM

Equilibrium price is so called because there is no reason for it to change if the underlying supply and demand conditions are also unchanged, i.e. the market process will be constantly pushing prices and quantities towards their equilibrium values. We are now in a position to summarise this equilibrating process and to bring out the special role of consumer demand in a market economy. Assume that a firm plans to bring a new product on to the market in which the potential industry supply and demand conditions are summarised by Figure 4.11. The firm is not fully informed about these demand conditions, and it introduces its initial supply of Q_{s_1} units to the market at a price of P_1. In fact, the potential demand at this price is Q_{d_1} and stocks are rapidly run down with consumers clamouring for more — there is then an excess of demand over supply equal to 'excess demand (1)'. The original firm quickly realises that it underestimated demand, is able to raise the price without loss of sales, and sets about increasing output by whatever means are available. Other firms may also decide that it is worth getting into the trade since a profit potential seems to be waiting for exploitation. An increase in output is possible only at higher cost however, and the firm(s) now introduce an output of Q_{s_2} to the market at a price of P_2. This quantity is sold at the higher price, but the queues and shortages are now much less with an excess demand down to 'excess demand (2)'. Whether producers press on with increases in both price and quantity depends on their degree of confidence about the exact position of the equilibrium point at Z. Over time, as producers and sellers gain experience of the market, they may well approach the equilibrium price and quantity values more closely.

Figure 4.11 Market Adjustments to Demand

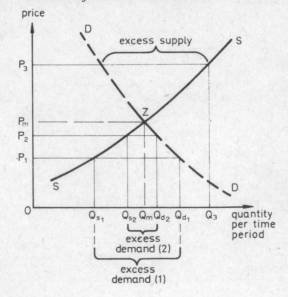

If the producers had pitched their output and price too high initially, say at P_3 with a supply of Q_3, then the excess supply on the market would have forced them to reduce production and prices until the region of Z was reached.

It is because the supply of a good, and by implication all the factor inputs to that good, eventually adjusts to the demand expressed by the consumer via the market, that it has been argued that the market allocation system is dominated by the consumer, that he has 'soveignty' over the use of economic resources. Putting it another way, we might say that as long as the consumer is prepared to pay a price which covers the necessary costs and to provide the producer with sufficient profits to keep him happy, then the market will supply whatever the consumer desires. This conclusion carries a great deal of conviction in most societies based on a competitive market economy where it is not difficult to discover examples of highly individualistic demands being met, at a price, by the market. It is important of course that the price required by the producer is not determined by him unilaterally, but it is usually assumed that the degree of competition present in most markets will keep 'unreasonable' profits down to a minimum as well as costs. The concept of consumer sovereignty with its implications for the expression of personal identity has long been regarded as one of the major strengths of the competitive market economy. But it does also mean that those with the greatest purchasing power will be able to exert the greatest economic choice and influence.

SUPPLY AND DEMAND ANALYSIS AND PREDICTION

The major contribution of supply and demand analysis has been to enable economists to explain movements in prices and quantities and also to make predictions about future movements. Both explanation and prediction as economic exercises are hampered in most real-life circumstances by a lack of full and accurate information about all the relevant circumstances. This means that economists will often feel quite confident about the direction in which a price or quantity will change, but will express many reservations about the precise extent of the change.

To demonstrate these problems, consider the market for, say, petrol-engine-powered lawn mowers (PLMs). Assume that market research has discovered that the demand facing a firm for PLMs is determined by certain main factors and that supply conditions are known.

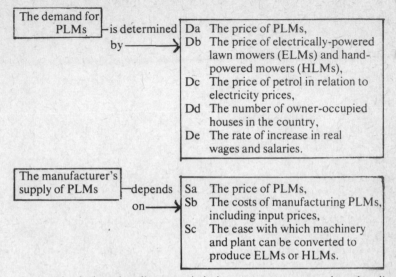

The demand for PLMs	┤is determined by ──→	Da	The price of PLMs,
		Db	The price of electrically-powered lawn mowers (ELMs) and hand-powered mowers (HLMs),
		Dc	The price of petrol in relation to electricity prices,
		Dd	The number of owner-occupied houses in the country,
		De	The rate of increase in real wages and salaries.

The manufacturer's supply of PLMs	┤depends on ──→	Sa	The price of PLMs,
		Sb	The costs of manufacturing PLMs, including input prices,
		Sc	The ease with which machinery and plant can be converted to produce ELMs or HLMs.

In manipulating the diagrams it is important to remember the discussion on pp. 51-52, i.e. changes in 'Da' will mean a movement along an existing demand curve, while a change in 'Sa' leads to a move along an existing supply curve. On the other hand, any change in items 'Db' to 'De' will shift the entire demand curve to a new position, and similarly, changes 'Sb' or 'Sc' will shift the supply curve. The starting position is indicated in Figure 4.12 by the demand curve D_1D_1 and the

Figure 4.12   Supply and Demand—A Shift in Demand Conditions

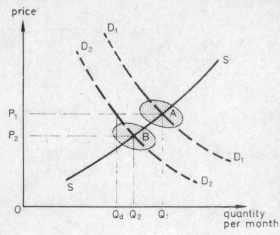

supply curve SS. The initial equilibrium price is P_1 and the quantity is Q_1. Assume that the price of petrol now rises steeply in relation to the cost of electricity; that is a change in item 'Dc'. This change in 'Dc' will shift the entire demand curve to the left to the position shown as D_2D_2. The move to the left is explained by seeing that fewer PLMs will be bought under these new conditions at the old price of P_1, a fall from Q_1 to Q_d.

The new demand curve D_2D_2 intersects the original supply curve at the lower price of P_2. The only item in the list of determinants of supply to have changed significantly is 'Sa', and so the movement is down along the supply curve. The effect of the rise in petrol prices is then predicted to be a fall in the quantity of PLMs sold from Q_1 to Q_2, and a fall in their price from P_1 to P_2. In practice, of course, the exact positions of the supply and demand curves are not known, so the economist will probably be content with a prediction simply that both quantity and price of PLMs will tend to fall, and that the new equilibrium will be somewhere in the shaded area marked 'B' in Figure 4.12. If the rise in petrol prices had been comparatively small, it is possible that the areas 'A' and 'B' could overlap, and it is then possible that no clear prediction of even direction could be given. The alert reader will also have noticed that there is another potential change in our diagram. We said, a few sentences back, that the only significant change in supply conditions was the price of PLMs, but it is quite likely that a rise in petrol costs could change condition 'Sb' significantly so that the supply curve moved bodily to the left. The reader should check that this would lead to a fall in output even below Q_2 but that the equilibrium price will now be either above or below P_1 depending on how far the supply curve has moved.

There are other exercises that should be worked through to ensure familiarity with these diagrams, such as allowing items 'Db' to 'De' and 'Sb' and 'Sc' to change in turn, and then predicting the probable effects on price and quantity. Another useful exercise would be to repeat our example of a petrol price rise but this time trace the effects on electrically-powered lawn mowers.

THE PROBLEMS OF OBSERVING SUPPLY AND DEMAND CURVES IN ACTION

If it is difficult to predict the future position and shape of supply and demand curves, it is nearly as difficult to discover just where they are now or have been in the past. It is possible, over a period of months or years, to collect information on the amounts of a good actually sold at various prices on the market. If this were to be done for some product, say paper used in the packaging industry, we might end up with a series of plots like those shown in Figure 4.13 (*a*). The fact that there are so many different observations must suggest that there had been shifts in the underlying supply and demand conditions during the period September 1971 to November 1973. The observation for June 1972 could be explained by a shift in the demand for this type of paper from D_1 to D_2, perhaps as a result of a fall in demand for the goods to be packaged. The position in June 1972 is assumed to be on the original supply curve $S1$, and if we could be sure that the supply conditions were unchanged then shifts in the demand curves would gradually reveal the position of the supply curve.

In Figure 4.13 (*b*) similarly, if we were certain that demand conditions were unchanged between September 1971 and January 1973, then the shift in the supply curve from S_1 to S_2 would tell us something about the position of the demand curve D_1. Unfortunately, it is not likely that either the demand or the supply curves will be unchanged over time, and typically, one will be faced with an observation like that for November 1973 where both supply and demand conditions have changed since September 1971. Even more caution is necessary once we realise that it has been assumed that such observations are in fact equilibrium values. With the problems of uncertainty and the possibility of non-equilibrium prices as the market adjusts, it seems that an observation like that for December 1971 is consistent with a wide range of possibilities.

Figure 4.13   Hypothetical Prices & Quantities Observed for Paper

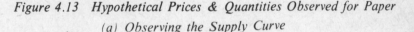

(a) Observing the Supply Curve

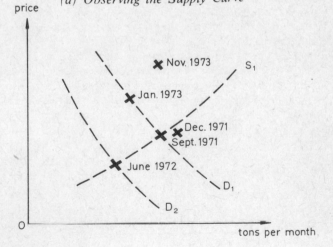

Figure 4.13 (b)   Observing the Demand Curve

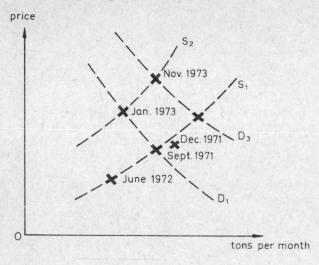

N.B. It is assumed that there have been no inflationary influences on prices over the period, although this alone could account for November 1973.

THE COMPETITIVE ENVIRONMENT

The market allocation process operates by a pattern of response to a variety of informational signals foremost among which is the behaviour of market prices, all under the constant stimulus and motivation of expected profits. The market equilibrium has been described mainly in terms of the tendency for prices and quantities to change in accordance with the underlying conditions of supply and demand. Little has been said so far about the speed and accuracy with which the market adjustments take place, but these can be of vital importance in real-life circumstances.

The Firm and Perfect Competition

One simplified model that economists have often used to make economic questions easier to handle is one which removes all the doubt and uncertainty about the demand facing a firm. The conditions for perfect competition, which is the name given to this particular simplification, can be found in most textbooks of economics and it is not our intention to deal with them at all rigorously. Some of the necessary assumptions are relevant to us here, however, and they are as follows:

(a) all firms are producing an exactly similar product;

(b) there are so many firms in the market that any one firm is too small to exert any influence on the market price;

(c) it is very easy for new firms to enter the market;

(d) full and accurate information about all aspects of the market is available to all buyers and sellers.

The effect of these assumptions on the demand situation faced by a firm is shown by Figure 4.14. With a current market price of £5, the firm could sell any amount it wished and it need only concern itself with its cost of production. If the firm should attempt to raise its price to £6, then consumers would immediately switch all their purchases to the firms still selling identical products at £5 and the firm's sales drop to zero. If the firm cut its price to £4 (a foolhardly exercise since it can already sell all it wishes at £5), then it would be overwhelmed with orders that it could not meet as *all* consumers tried to buy its product in preference to others.

Figure 4.14   The Firm's Demand Curve under conditions of Perfect Competition

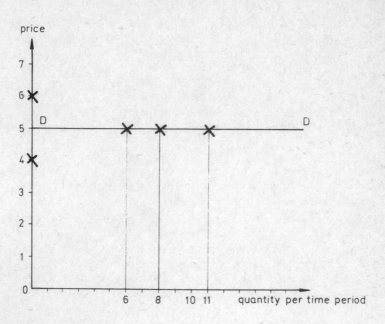

One is not likely to come across competition quite as keen as this in the course of everyday life but rather a range of competitiveness depending for example on how closely the conditions (*a*) to (*d*) above are actually met. As a general rule, we might say that the greater the degree of response of demand to price changes in a market, then the greater the degree of competition in that market. In our analysis of the demand facing our hypothetical shoe firm, we suggested that the firm could not in fact sell as much as it liked at the ruling market price. It was therefore facing a downward sloping demand curve as we have seen, and was operating in a somewhat less than perfectly competitive market.

Error and Disequlibrium

The presence of uncertainty about the nature of supply and demand conditions in areas well away from the current position has already been emphasised. In such circumstances, consumers or producers may form an erroneous view about the market's future position and any decisions based on this view will also be erroneous. The opening price given in Figure 4.11 was a non-equilibrium price, but the signals were then correctly interpreted and a steady adjustment towards the equilibrium price followed. If the suppliers had become over-optimistic as a result of the initial demand, they could have swung the market into excess supply.

Errors can be very expensive to correct if they mean the scrapping or under-utilisation of plant and machinery, so firms will normally engage in extensive market research, test-marketing, and various other information search activities to try to reduce the risk of error when introducing a new product to the market. But even in the relatively stable grocery trade, a majority of the new products introduced each year do not survive more than a few months.

Errors of a different kind are likely when the markets for existing goods are subject to sudden and violent changes as in time of war, social upheaval or natural disaster. Buyers and sellers try to guess where the new demand and supply curves are or will be, and their guesses may be wrong for some time until, by a long process of trial and error, more 'correct' prices are reached.

Time-Lags

One kind of 'time-lag' or delayed response has just been mentioned, i.e. when the market takes time to respond correctly to some shock to it, but there are many other kinds of lag or delay in adjustment that can occur. One is where a firm is unaware of its true financial position until its balance sheet and full accounts are prepared, a procedure that may only take place every few months in some firms, so that the firm adjusts some time after perhaps it should have done.

It is one thing to realise that adjustment or change is necessary, but the adjustment may itself take time to carry out, as when existing plant has to be modified or new equipment installed. The more specialised and capital intensive the production process, the slower will be any adjustment to new circumstances.

Agriculture is a type of production where time-lags are especially significant. The length of the growing cycle can vary from a few months (for pigs) to a few years (for apple trees) depending on the nature of the product, and this poses many problems for the farmer. In addition, agricultural produce is frequently perishable although expensive storage facilities may be available. This means that the average farmer must sell his output as soon as possible, both to maintain his flow of income and to avoid heavy storage charges. The farmer is not able to spread out his production rate in the same way that a manufacturer often can. Farmers are also in a highly competitive relationship with other farmers since their produce is broadly similar, there are very many of them, and none of them are able to manipulate the market in their favour. This intense competition combined with long time-lags can lead to an unstable market for agricultural goods.

A typical example of this situation occurred with UK beef producers in the early 1970s. A 'beef cycle' (see Figure 4.15) develops in the following way. Assume that as a result of a low grass yield the beef supply in year 1 happens to be less than in the previous year when the price was at P_b. The smaller supply of beef, Q_{y1}, can be sold at the higher price of P_{y1}. The producers of beef have a good, profitable year, and become optimistic about the future, increasing their herds in anticipation of being able to sell them at this high price in two or more years' time when they mature. At the same time, others farmers decide to switch from producing sheep to beef animals so as to take advantage of the high price beef has been fetching. All this extra beef, Q_{y1} to Q_{y3}, comes on to the market two years later and farmers seem to be astonished that they can only sell this quantity by dropping their price to P_{y3} (assuming, that is, the demand curve is stable). Instead of large profits, many farmers make losses and some decide to drop out of beef producton altogether. In year 4, the supply could be back around the Q_{y1} level and the cycle starts all over again. The beef industry should perhaps adjust its output to the average of prices over recent years and farm incomes might become more stable. But as long as the majority of farmers are making independent decisions based on the latest price and profit signals, then price and output stability will only occur by accident.

Figure 4.15   Unstable Agricultural Output and Prices—Beef

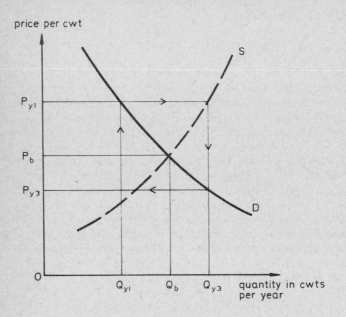

Non-Standardised Products

It was suggested on pp. 59-60 that manufacturers may be resistant to frequent price changes. In fact, they may be more interested in competition based on product variation than on price variation. Unlike agricultural produce, manufactured consumer goods are rarely absolutely uniform and standardised as between different producers. In those industries making machinery and plant, the products will often be 'custom made' for a particular buyer and thus be completely differentiated.

Our everyday experience of 'brand' advertising, new product promotions, and the updating of old products, suggests that manufacturers are anxious to persuade consumers that their branded products are inherently superior to those of their competitors. Much of the expenditure on research and development in industry is concerned to discover an exclusive product for which there are no competitors.

Firms which have successfuly established some kind of product superiority have achieved a degree of stability in and control over their market. Whether this leads to a slower and less satisfactory market adjustment process depends partly on how well the dominating firm can keep control of the market and on how vigorously competing firms try to break that control.

Barriers to Entry

The presence of successful product differentiation, specialised products and processes, significant economies of large-scale production, and control over factor prices and availability can all act as barriers facing a firm trying to break into a new market. The bigger these barriers to entry into an industry, the slower will be market reaction to change. Sometimes such barriers are regarded by governments as 'unfair trading' and will be prohibited by law. On the other hand, it is quite possible for a firm to be simply so superior in both its product and its efficiency that rivals just cannot approach it, and this is not likely to be against the interests of the consumer. Such a firm may have to work hard to maintain its superiority in the face of potential competition and will only become a danger to the consumer if it decides to rest on its laurels for any length of time. Any such 'resting' will of course allow the other firms a better chance of catching up.

Profits

The market process is supposed to encourage the movement of factors of production into areas where above normal profits can be earned. If all markets for all products were to be in equilibrium, then profit rates, after due allowance for risk, should be roughly equal in all markets. By now, it should however be clear that profit levels can vary for very many reasons. Profits can be both above and below the 'equilibrium' or normal level because, (*a*) the market is not actually in equilibrium, (*b*) there are barriers of one kind or another preventing new entrants to an industry from acquiring a share of the above normal profit, and (*c*) firms may not be trying to maximise profits. The typical market that we have depicted does not operate under the theoretical conditions of perfect competition, but there will usually be in most markets a sufficient degree of competition for the market allocation process to function moderately effectively. The efficiency of any particular market can only be assessed by a detailed analysis of all its conditions of supply and demand and their mode of interaction.

Why is Competition Often Regarded as a 'Good Thing'?

Economists in the Western world have come to few generally agreed conclusions, but one which has a very wide measure of support is that 'More competition is nearly always preferable to less'. A full statement of the theoretical backing to this proposition would take us beyond the purposes of this book, but the advantages accruing from a highly competitive market can be summarised as follows:

(a) Production is very responsive to consumer demands,

(b) Costs of production and prices will be kept as low as possible,

(c) Profits will not be greater than necessary to keep firms in production.

In later chapters we shall be dealing with circumstances where even competition cannot guarantee these satisfactory results and where, as discussed on pp. 74-75, competitive activity itself generates fresh barriers to competition.

Chapter 5

Further Aspects of Production: The Firm and its Environment

THE TYPICAL FIRM

The previous chapter was an exercise in model-building which focused on one particular firm engaged in the manufacture of a certain kind of product. This follows a well-established tradition in economic theory of using a medium-sized, single product, single plant manufacturing concern producing a consumer good in wide demand to represent most firms in business. It is as well to remember that the model 'firm' described in Chapter 4 may not be really typical of those operating in modern economies whether advanced or developing, and the aim of this chapter is to suggest some of the complications and deviations experienced by firms in their everyday existence in what are usually very complex economic environments. These environments will, in this chapter, still be market orientated, but many of the problems discussed will be relevant to firms in fully planned economies, as we shall see in Chapter 9.

THE NATURE OF THE FIRM'S ACTIVITIES

The areas of the economic environment of most immediate concern to the firm will depend upon two main considerations, (*a*) the nature of the firm's output, and (*b*) how the firm views the nature of its activities. Consider first the nature of the firm's output. We conventionally classify production activity according to output under three categories: *primary production,* or the supply of foodstuffs and raw materials; *secondary or manufacturing* production in which primary products are processed into a final product; and *tertiary or service industry,* which does not actually produce a physical good but either caters directly for the consumer as in the entertainment industry, say, or eases the flow of goods from secondary industry to the final consumer. It was fashionable at one time to regard production as the creation of usefulness or 'utility'. Thus a manufacturer could clearly be seen to be creating utility when he converted matter from a form in which it was useless to the consumer — as a mineral ore, for example — to a form in which it was useful — as perhaps motor vehicles. But 'form' is not the only condition of usefulness. Whatever the utility of a good in its final form, this will be less if the good is not in the right place, or is not available at a time the consumer finds most convenient. So, in addition to the utility of form, we have the utilities of place and time, and the creation of these utilities is seen to be as much an act of production as manufacture itself. Consumption cannot, in a complex society, take place without ancilliary services which consumers sometimes value more highly than the finished product. Farmers continually complain that farm-gate prices are only a fraction of those eventually paid by the housewife, but the fact is that it often costs more to distribute agricultural produce than it does to grow it!

If the three categories of industry (primary, secondary and teritiary) are equally valid forms of production, then a particular firm need not be confined to a single sector. Indeed, a striking feature of modern industrial societies (as we shall see in Chapter 10) is a tendency for productive enterprise to spread themselves across the spectrum of the three categories referred to above. As this occurs, the points of contact between the firm and its environment change, and we now introduce the second main consideration of this section, namely, how does the firm view itself and its activities? There was a time when firms in the brewing industry saw themselves as simply manufacturers of

Figure 5.1   The Brewing Firm and its environment

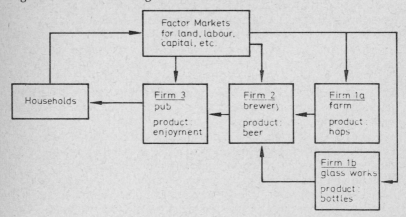

beer. Their place in their general trading environment could be summarised by Figure 5.1

Let us say that the brewing firm we are discussing is represented in Figure 5.1 by Firm 2. It has three main points of contact with its environment. First, there are the factor markets from which it is drawing labour, land and capital services. Then, it acquires raw materials and other inputs such as barley, hops, sugar, bottles, crates, etc. from other firms (represented by Firms 1a and 1b) that would not consider themselves as in the brewing trade. The beer brewed by Firm 2 is then sold to a public house, Firm 3, to be eventually consumed by the households who are the main suppliers of labour and capital. Modern brewing firms, however, have successfully straddled all three sectors indicated by Firms 1 to 3 in the diagram, an this has fundamentally changed their view of their role and environment.

THE FIRM AND ITS NEED FOR INFORMATION

It must be stressed that factor markets are not as formal as the common-sense use of the term 'market' might suggest. Remember that our shoe firm's market was a collection of wholesale and retail organisations spread across the country. Similarly, there is no single point of contact between the firm and either the labour or the capital market. There is no separate 'shop' to which a firm may go in search of information on the availability and prices of factors of production. There are, it is true, labour and stock exchanges, but they represent only the tip of an iceberg of formal and informal arrangements for the purchase and sale of labour and capital. The notice on the factory gate or in the local newspaper is as important as the labour exchange for most firms. Banking firms of various kinds are, for example, also at least as important as the Stock Exchange in the transformation of households' savings into productive investment. Information is sought and provided by buyers and sellers therefore, through a variety of channels, formal and informal, and a 'market' therefore exists. Market activity can be regarded as just as much an exchange of information as an exchange of goods and services. A putative buyer can leave the market without buying, vice versa for a potential seller, and the failure of a transaction to take place is valuable information for both buyers and sellers.

Now Firm 2 in Figure 5.1 could remove the need for information exchanges between itself and Firms 1a and 3 by amalgamating with them or by taking them over, thereby enlarging its area of activity to include what was once part of its environment. To do so, however, would be to exchange one set of contacts for another. Now Firm 2 will have not one but three sets of dealings with the factor markets — it will now be a buyer of factor inputs to agriculture instead of just those specific to brewing. Its final product, moreoever, will now be supplied direct to consuming households. A consequence of such a change may be some reduction in uncertainty, since the firm will now have some control over the supply of its primary inputs and over the sale of its final product (see Chapter 10). But a further consequence will be a great increase in the amount of information the firm will require of its environment. Operating now in the agricultural sector, it will need to respond to the influences on both the costs of farming and the value of agricultural produce. In its tertiary activities the firm will find itself bidding directly against firms in other parts of the leisure field for a share in household budgets. Indeed, brewing firms no longer sell just beer, but a range of services associated with the consumption of alcohol — ambience, live entertainment, etc. A brewery's image of itself, as well as of its markets, has changed, and with this change comes a need for an ever greater range of information. The larger a firm becomes in relation to its environment, the more it will also require information on the activities of competitor and complementary firms, on government policy, and on interrelationships in the markets for final and intermediate products. Depending on the nature of the firm's business, it will also require information on trends in foreign trade and overseas prices.

THE PROCESSING OF INFORMATION

The volume of information a firm receives from its environment is considerable. Some it receives automatically, as it would when the suppliers of raw materials and the labour force ask higher prices for their goods and services. Some it has to collect, as it would have to if a new raw material was required to replace an existing input which was becoming increasingly expensive. This distinction between the information which is presented to the firm in its production activities and that which it has to search out suggests two suppositions. Firstly, that firms are able to sort out the vast amounts of information which could have an effect on production into that which is relevant and that which is not. Secondly, that firms possess some mechanism which enables them to decide that the information they have of production conditions is insufficient, and that they should seek some more.

For the first, we must observe that the order of importance in which input information is ranked will depend upon any bias towards a particular factor in the production relationships. A firm which uses much labour and little capital will watch the labour market more carefully than the capital market. Importance of information will also depend upon the size of the firm in relation to factor and product markets, and to its rivals. If a firm is in the position of being by far the biggest employer of labour in a district or town, then the labour market for the area is bound to be influenced by that firm's activities.

Let us look more closely at what signals a firm receives from and transmits to its environment in its day-to-day production activities. These fall roughly into three categories: information on inputs, on outputs, and on the firm's performance.

Labour Input Costs

Labour costs in production are usually thought of as being a matter of wage payments, whether these are a payment for the time spent at work (time rates) or related to the actual amount of work done (piece rates). The firm will receive its information on these rates from the labour market from two sources. If the firm is considering an increase in its labour force, then information on prevailing rates will have to be sought directly from the market with the organisers of production being aware that any new wage levels set to attract labour must also apply to the existing labour force (see Chapter 7). We have so far presented the production unit as an on-going enterprise, and thus it does not have to *enter* the labour market to be made aware of changing market conditions. Unless the labour force is fragmented or poorly organised there will be a constant exchange of information between employer and employee on such matters as wage rates, working conditions, bonus payments, etc. Industrial labour negotiations (not necessarily ending in strike action) underline the nature of information exchange in the labour market, as buyers and sellers of labour continually assess the mutually acceptable price of labour.

While it is not within the scope of this book to go into the mechanisms of industrial dispute, there are indications that wage rates, etc., give incomplete information on the costs of labour inputs. As consumption levels have risen in industrial societies, conditions of work seem to have gained in importance relative to wage rates as reasons for striking. The environment in which labour is set to work can be made more acceptable by increased expenditures on such fringe benefits as pleasant, cheap canteen facilities, social activities, and perhaps subsidised housing. These will constitute a cost to the employer, but one on which information flows neither automatically nor cheaply. The cost of making work on automated assembly lines less tedious and therefore more acceptable to labour may be at the cost of a slower rate of production in the short term. Yet accurate information on whether an even greater loss of production will arise from industrial stoppages will emerge only with the passing of time.

Capital: Costs and Yield

If there are some areas in which information on labour inputs is not automatically presented to the organisers of production, but has to be sought out, this is even more the case with capital inputs. We have observed that capital in production is used up over a period of time, and that capital formation occurs following the assessment of information on future as well as present market conditions. The decision to invest in capital equipment will be based on the value of some estimated flow of output resulting therefrom. This return on capital is conventionally referred to as its 'yield'. Return on capital is expressed as a percentage which measures the surplus of the value of the output of the capital in a given year over and above the cost of the capital itself. Thus capital which yields 12 per cent is producing a total of £112 of output for each £100 of the capital's original cost. This sum, which is clearly directly related to profit earnings, may or may not be what the organisers of production expected, but before the investment was undertaken, some expectation of future return would have been compared with the cost of financing the project (p. 58). Information on this cost would have been sought from the capital market and this information is relevant even if the firm decides to invest its own ploughed-back profits rather than borrowing the necessary money, in that the market price for capital will allow a comparison betwen potential returns or yields both within and outside the firm's activities. Hence the firm's profits and the return on its capital equipment provide a yardstick for the firm's performance, and is one of the many ways for a firm to assess the success of its input-output relationships. In the long run it is perhaps, in a market economy, the most important. One might be tempted to think that volume of sales or output would indicate success, yet by themselves these indicators take no account of input considerations.

Information Lags and the Performance of Capital

As production proceeds, a periodic comparison of the firm's revenues with the costs imputed to capital will tell the firm whether or not its expectations are justified. But this periodic check is not necessarily straightforward, and may not be flexible enough to allow the firm to bring expectations and performance into line. Information within the firm on capital inputs takes time to collate. If a particular piece of capital equipment has no relationship with a specific output (it may for example generate electricity for the whole factory, or it may consist of a transport fleet which conveys semi-manufactures from one plant to another as well as the finished product to retail outlets), its effectiveness may only emerge when accounts of all input and output flows for the whole firm are assembled on an annual basis. The logistics of collating details of the internal and external transactions of even a small firm are complex. The process of collection and collation of sales invoices, inter-departmental requisitions, wage payments, bank statements, stores purchases, stock inventories and all the other sources of documentation itself requires inputs in the form of office and administrative staff. Thus the measurement of performance against expectation is possible only after a time-lag. Such a time-lag presents the firm with an information problem. If after a period of time — say at the end of the financial year — it emerges that the firm's expectations have been over-optimistic, a search is undertaken to explain the shortfall. The information will already exist within the firm, and much ingenuity has gone into the processing of data by computer and into devising the most informative form of presentation of company accounts to executives in order to keep this search to a minimum. Some time, however, must be spent in this search, and still more in the process of deciding what corrective action should be taken. This may call for still further search. For example, it may emerge that return on capital is poor because the firm's transport system no longer suits the firm's operations; relocation of plant may have changed the balance between road, rail, water, etc., and in order to redress the balance, information on alternative arrangements is necessary. Having decided upon the course of action, work has to be got under way and this takes still more time. Thus working from symptom to diagnosis, prognosis, and through to treatment allows a firm to respond only slowly to changes in environment as far as capital inputs are concerned. The larger the amount of capital investment, the longer is this reaction sequence likely to be.

Each factor input will have its own associated time-lags of course, whether these be, for example, long delivery times for bought-in components or the time taken to train staff to operate machines. The firm needs to understand the nature of all such lags if it is to react quickly and correctly to changes in its environment, as we saw on pp. 73, when a poor understanding of time-lags was the cause of business failures and market instability.

OUTPUT INFORMATION

We have so far confined ourselves to a consideration of information flows which can relate to factor inputs, and yet production is essentially a process for generating output for final consumption.

The output information that we discussed in Chapter 4 was confined to changes in the stocks and sales volumes of finished goods. Stocks will change because the rate of production differs from the rate of sales, and a change in stocks will lead to search into the state of production on the one hand, and sales on the other. There may be a time lag of course, if sales are directed through a network of wholesalers and retailers, but there will be a periodic — weekly, perhaps, or monthly — collection of sales data. As with stock levels, this data tells the firm that sales are changing, but not why they are changing. Nor will they tell the firm what potential for additional sales exists, for, as we saw on pp. 51, this would require knowledge of the demand curve facing the firm.

Stock Fluctuations as an Indicator of Output Change

Stock levels change on a day-to-day basis, and information on any change is quickly available. A change in the rate of production, for example, will alter the rate of through-put and thus the level of stocks of raw materials and finished goods. A given stock level will be associated with a certain flow of production, so as to cushion the firm against any unforeseen disruption in supplies or unseasonal consumer requirements. But holding stocks is expensive, as they represent resources which are not being directly used for production. The money tied up in stocks, whether borrowed or the firm's own cash, is not recoverable until goods are finally sold. The organisers of production must therefore have an ambivalent attitude towards stockholding, setting the benefits of insulation from short-run market change against the costs of tying up cash. The ratio of desired stocks to output will depend on the firm's size and the nature of its business. If a firm's products require a few inputs, and if the cost of inputs is small in relation to the price of the product, stocks can represent supplies for a fairly long production period. The steel industry, for example, carries stocks to last for many weeks. Motor vehicles, on the other hand, using a large range of costly manufactured components, carry stocks for only a few days. When the level of stocks deviates from the required ratio, orders for new stocks change, and the organisers of production are made aware of changed production conditions. Stocks of raw materials will accumulate if through-put is disrupted by operational failures, labour problems, etc. Stocks of finished goods, also affected by change in through-put, can additionally indicate changes in consumer behaviour. The first signals that the firm receives from the market that the demand for its products is changing are likely to be a run-down or a build-up of stocks, signalling that a change in the production rate is in order.

The relationship between stock levels and output has an importance, however, beyond that for a single firm. Conditions which cause stocks to change are unlikely to be confined to a single firm, yet all firms react similarly to a change in stocks. The circumstances in which sales of one consumer durable good increases will be such that increases can be expected for all such goods. The individual firm will experience a run-down in its stocks of finished goods, and if the production process is quick enough, in its stocks of raw materials. Production will have to be increased to replenish stocks as well as to cater for increased demand. Unless the rate of consumption increase is maintained, however, production will increase beyond the level of demand, and stocks at both ends of the production process will accumulate beyond the desired amount. This will signal a reduction in production, and the cycle will go into reverse. The exaggerated reaction of production to a change in stocks affects the whole economy, not just the sector initially involved. This cycle of activity is in fact referred to as the stock cycle, and is a source of information on changes in the level of economic activity across the entire economy.

THE COST OF SEARCH

A firm is an organisation that exists in a time continuum — it is created, grows, may stagnate, and sometimes dies. It is therefore not only concerned with the present and the immediate future, but also with its survival in the longer term. Information on this longer time horizon may not be readily extracted from the current information flows within the firm. The firm must then make a series of assumptions about the future market conditions, and then project expected future sales within this market. Constant adjustments must be made in these projections so as to take into account actual changes in market conditions as they occur. The whole continuing excercise must make demands on the firm's resources, which are limited. The firm must make judgements about how much it can afford to spend on information search, and this will involve in turn an assessment of the potential gains from a better and more complete information flow on the one hand, and the possible losses arising from inadequate preparation for the future on the other. Firms will always be operating under conditions of less than complete information about their environment, and they must be constantly trading the cost (and potential benefits) of search activity against current production costs and benefits.

An area which illustrates this choice well is in the field of research and development. Firms in all kinds of economic systems are well aware of the desirability of spending money on developing new technology and new products. This is not a matter of invention only. The preparation of an invention for commercial production is just as important as the invention itself, and can be very much more expensive. The inventor of the jet engine (in the western hemisphere at least) spent about £300 on the initial invention while the commercial development of the engine has cost untold millions. Historical experience has shown that technological change can create changing market conditions in which firms, and indeed countries, which are not well placed to take advantage of technical change become less successful competitors. Experience also shows that the imitator can ultimately be more successful than the inventor and that in addition, technical change does not proceed in a predictable fashion. If a firm could predict when a technical change will occur, it would be able to decide when to spend money on research and development. Unfortunately this is not possible, and resources must be committed to information search of this kind without full knowledge of either the penalties for failure or the benefits from success.

THE ECONOMIC ENVIRONMENT AS A TOTAL PRODUCTION SYSTEM

The approach in Chapter 4 was to concentrate on small independent decision-making units such as the individual consumer and the manufacturing firm. In this chapter, we have broadened the horizons of the individual firm so as to examine its interconnections and relationships with the economic system in general. Individual consumers, households, firms, factor markets, all live and operate within a particular environment and are to a high degree dependent on one another. Western economists have in the past tended to concentrate on economic behaviour at the individual level and on the process of resource allocation as between producers, consumers, etc. This is usually referred to as micro-economics (from the Greek *mikros,* meaning small). There are much more difficult and complex problems to be dealt with when we try to understand the economy as a whole. Two main approaches seem to have been evolved by economists to help them describe and analyse the entire economy: (*a*) one which sees the entire economic system as made up of a host of micro-economic relationships which all strive to achieve simultaneous balance and equilibrium — the 'general equilibrium' approach; and (*b*) an approach which looks at the behaviour of aggregate measures of economic relationships such as total consumption, the money supply, aggregate investment and unemployment. This is the essence of macro-economics (Greek *makros* meaning long or large).

Now a proper understanding of economic behaviour at the total or macro-economic level requires, in our view, an understanding also of the history and development of the economy and of its political and sociological background. In the next few chapters we shall give

Table 5.1 *Input/Output Flows: Industrialised Economy with Large Foreign Sector (£ million)*

Sources of Inputs → / Where output goes ↓	1	2	3	4	5	6	7	8 Total Inter-industry	Sales to final buyers			12 Total output 8-9-10-11
	(Industries as in rows 1 to 7)								Consumers 9	Investment 10	Exports 11	
1. Agriculture & mining	—	1,180	340	50	60	400	90	2,120	3,600	60	190	5,970
2. Food & drink mfg.	630	—	70	—	—	10	200	910	4,550	110	450	6,020
3. Oil & chemicals industry	260	270	—	210	520	655	425	2,340	925	20	760	4,045
4. Metal manufacture	95	10	50	—	2,285	280	55	2,775	—	80	385	3,240
5. Engineering industry	160	130	170	150	—	615	1,365	2,590	3,550	3,505	4,085	13,730
6. Other mfg. & construction	340	235	235	50	1,115	—	2,070	4,045	5,015	4,365	1,520	14,945
7. Utilities & services	780	965	925	630	1,900	2,050	—	7,250	13,035	780	3,330	24,395
8. Imports	325	1,210	990	615	425	2,110	1,560	7,235	3,700	550	350	11,835
9. Wages & salaries	1,870	1,090	820	1,000	5,520	6,595	12,470	29,365	—	—	—	29,365
10. Profits & return on capital	1,510	930	445	535	1,905	2,230	6,160	13,715	—	—	—	13,715
11. Total input	5,970	6,020	4,045	3,240	13,730	14,945	24,395	72,345	34,375	9,470	11,070	127,260

(Based on the Input/Output Matrix for the UK (1963), Blue Book 1966)

greater attention to these socio-political aspects, but for the rest of this chapter the emphasis will be on certain of the purely economic and technical relationships in a society.

Inter-Industry Relationships

In Figure 5.1 it was suggested that there was a chain of production relationships in which the output of one production activity becomes the input of the next, and so on. Each link in the process, however, in practice requires not one input from the preceding stages, but several; and each link will require inputs such as labour, which are common to the majority of otherwise separate activities.

A summary of all the input and output flows within an economy can be presented in a table like that of Table 5.1. This table or matrix lists seven main industrial sectors, numbered 1 to 7. By following through the row of figures alongside any industry group we can trace what happens to the output of that industry — these are output flows. For example, Industry 1, agriculture and mining, sells output worth £1,180 million to the second industry group, food and drink manufacture, and so on. The total of all these sales to other industries is shown in column 8 as total inter-industry sales, i.e. £2,120 million. These sales by the agriculture and mining sector are therefore inputs into the other industry groups. Most of the sales of Industry 1 are, however, direct to final customers and these are shown in column 9 as £3,600 million. Other sales to final buyers go into investment in stocks or capital goods (column 10) and to foreign sales or exports (column 11). The total sales of Industry 1 are therefore £5,970 million in column 12.

Turning now to the meaning of the columns of figures, these represent the value of the flows of goods and services *into* a particular sector, i.e. input flows. These inputs include not only the raw materials and components bought in from other industrial groups in the country, but also those imported from abroad. In addition there are the payments for direct factor services in the form of wages and salaries paid to the industry's workers and the return on capital invested.

Taking Industry 5 (engineering) as an example, it is clear that the biggest input from another industry is the £2,285 million of goods bought from the metal manufacturing industry, number 4. It will also be noticed that the metal manufacturing industry makes negligible sales to final consumers, which is not surprising since the typical consumer has no use for rolls of tin plate or slabs of pig iron.

Note that the engineering industry itself is not shown as consuming its own products (nor do any of the other sectors), although an input-output table which used finer classifications would indeed show output flows from one section of the industry to another, from heavy to light engineering, etc. This is because each sector is being shown twice, on one axis of the table as a producer, and on the other as a consumer. Reading right across the table to column 12, remember that the total output of each sector is shown, and consequently to include one sector's consumption of its own output would be to count that output twice, and to inflate the total output by that amount.

Households as Sources of Input and Consumers of Output

The industry sectors shown provide basically two kinds of input — fixed and working capital. Labour, as we have observed, is common to all production processess and is provided by households. In exchange for labour services, wages and salaries (horizontal column 9) are paid (as we have seen) which give households access to the final products of the system. What is striking about this last entry is that the total sales to households, as opposed to inter-industry flows, total only £34,375 million, or 27 per cent of a total sales value for the system of £127,260 million. Although the objective of any economic system is consumption, only a proportion of the goods produced in an economy — and Table 5.1 is based on the UK economy — actually take the form of final consumption goods. Besides providing labour, however, households — in market economies — also directly or indirectly provide the money capital to finance the inter-industry flows of output, and they participate in the profits of production either directly by the outright ownership of a productive enterprise — say in the form of a family business, or indirectly as owners of share capital, or as taxpayers (see Chapter 6 and 10). In that their savings finance capital investment and underwrite the concomitant risk, a return accrues to households in the form of interest and profits, which in turn provide access to consumption in the form of sales to consumers.

Changes in Input-Output Flows

Table 5.1 shows the sources and destination of flows of goods and services for a given time period only. The total output for the economy will of course be changing from year to year. As total output changes, so must the outputs of the various sectors, and the input-output table can assist in determining the necessary increases in other sectors. A government may decide it politic, for example, to increase agricultural output by £100 million p.a., in which case the increase in total output would have to be larger than £100 million since no increase in agricultural output can be obtained without increased inputs of tractors, buildings, fuel oils, etc. Of course, there is no question in practice of the equal expansion of sectors, since each industry or group of industries will have its own technological bias. The food and drink industry, for example, obtains most of its inputs from agriculture, so an expansion of food manufacturer will involve a bigger increase in agriculture than it will of metal products, which in turn will be more affected by change in engineering output than would agriculture. It is possible, however, to calculate from Table 5.1 the fractional increases in output required from all sectors by an increase in any one, and these are shown in Table 5.2.

Table 5.2   Input-Output Flows: Direct and Indirect Requirements per £1 of Final Demand

Sector	1	2	3	4	5	6	7
1 Agriculture & mining	1.03	.21	.1	.03	.02	.03	.01
2 Food & drink mfg	.11	1.03	.03	—	—	.01	.01
3 Oil & chemicals	.06	.07	1.02	.08	.06	.05	.03
4 Metal mfg	.03	.02	.03	1.01	.17	.03	.02
5 Engineering industry	.05	.05	.07	.07	1.03	.06	.06
6 Other mfg & construction	.09	.08	.1	.05	.11	1.03	.1
7 Utilities & services	.19	.23	.28	.23	.21	.17	1.03

Each entry in the Table tells us the value of the overall output of the 'row' industry necessary to produce £1 worth of final output by the 'column' industry. Thus, in order to produce £100 million extra of final engineering output, £6 million of output is necessary from the oil and chemical industry, £17 million from metal manufacture, and so on. The output of the engineering industry must itself increase by a total of £103 million because it must in turn produce the £3 million extra to allow the oil and chemical and metal industries, etc., to produce their extra inputs to engineering. Between some sectors the effects can be seen to be minimal. An extra £1 worth of food and drink would require such small amounts of output from the metal and engineering industry that they do not show to two decimal places. The Table is in effect a summary of the technical relationships which exist in an economy at any one time. All of the sectors shown rely heavily on the service industries for example, and the evidence over time is that the service sector is becoming relatively more important in the developed economies. As was pointed out at the start of this section, tables such as Table 5.1 are a record of one year's transactions. Before we can safely proceed to use the coefficients derived therefrom in Table 5.2

to predict future flows, we ought to be sure about two points: (*a*) that there are not likely to be significant changes from year to year in the technical relationships themselves, and (*b*) that a simple linear projection of input requirements such as was done above with the extra £100 million of engineering output is sufficiently accurate for our purpose.

As we shall see in Chapter 9, for a government attempting to plan an entire economy, these considerations of technical change and linear projection are crucial.

Input Combinations and Input Substitution

Input requirements will be influenced in part by the nature of the final product, and in part by existing technology. Motor vehicles must be made to some extent of ferrous metal inputs, and the food processing industry must use inputs that derive from agriculture. Raw material requirements are not fixed for all time, however, and there are constantly increasing opportunities for replacing one raw material for another. The growing use of plastics to replace steel in car production and the development of synthetic foodstuffs are examples. Cars can be produced by more or less capital intensive methods, i.e. the combinations of labour and capital which go into the final product can be varied. The amount of capital used in the US car industry has been higher per unit of output than that in Europe, while European agriculture uses more labour and capital per unit of output than does North American. There must, however, be some land used in any agricultural activity, and therefore some limits to the degree to which factor substitution can go. Fertilisers can be used to increase the fertility of a given hectare of land, and this use is therefore a substitute for land itself. If fertilisers were a perfect substitute for land, however, the whole of the world's food supply could be grown in a flower pot!

'Lumpiness' in Factor Substitutability

The grossly simplified relationships indicated in Tables 5.1 and 5.2 may also conceal the fact that factors cannot be easily substituted for each other or increased smoothly by small amounts. A decision to increase production by using machines rather than men could be thwarted by the fact that each machine may make a large difference to the potential volume of output. However desirable it may be to increase weekly output by, say, 100 units, the effect of installing a new machine may be to increase the productive capacity of the plant by 1,000 units per week, leaving the organisers with the choice of either forgoing any increase in output or of achieving the increase by buying more labour. Labour can be operated in shift or overtime working, and is often available in units as small as a single man-hour.

Technical Optimum

Related to the problem of 'lumpiness' — particularly of capital inputs — is the nature of the technical relationships in a production process. For example, in steel production the raw material, iron ore, passes through a chain of processes to become the finished product (not a final product remember, since most of the output of the steel industry becomes the input of other, steel-using industries such as motor vehicles). These processes can for the purposes of argument be simplified into the blast furnace, the rolling mill, and the strip mill. Each of these processes will be governed by its own set of input-output relationships, and for reasons of technology it is unlikely that production in each process will involve the same combinations of labour and capital. The blast furnace which makes the most efficient use of its factor inputs may be the one which produces 100 tons per week. Similarly the 'optimum' rolling mill produces 200 tons, and the strip mill can handle 400 tons. Thus the technical optimum conditions of production would be satisfied if four furnaces fed two rolling mills, which in turn fed a single strip mill. If the industry were organised into firms which produced steel in multiples of 400 tons, there would be no waste. If a single firm, already producing 400 tons, wished to increase its output to 500 tons, it could increase its blast furnace capacity in line by buying an extra furnace, which would in turn require an extra rolling mill (with 100 tons excess capacity) and an extra strip mill (300 tons excess capacity). These complications cannot be overlooked if one is trying to make serious predictions about the future shape of industrial output by the use of input-output methods, although they are only of major significance if the capacity of the optimum size plant is large in relation to total output.

Factor Costs and Efficiency

We must now admit to having made a vital simplification so far, in that the relative scarcity of factors and therefore of their *price* has been ignored. In the preceding example, the assumption was implicitly made that labour was cheap relative to capital, and that therefore excess capacity would be more expensive than overtime payment, etc. If capital was very cheap, then it would would be quite logical to acquire inputs which are only half utilised. Aside from the technical limitations to factor substitution, factor combinations are determined by the relative costs of factor inputs, and the cost of a given factor is only a reflection of its availability. To say that labour in Hong Kong is cheap is only to say that labour there is abundant relative to other factors of production. But can we say that production in labour-intensive Hong Kong is as efficient as capital-intensive USA?

Efficiency can be defined by either an economist or an engineer. The engineer would indicate 'technical efficiency' by comparing the physical volume of input with the physical volume of output. To the engineer the airships of the 1920s and 1930s appeared more efficient than aeroplanes because larger loads could be moved per unit of energy input. The economist, however, measures efficiency by comparing the costs of input against the value of the output. In these terms airships compared poorly with aircraft. Fuel was cheap, the costs of developing the airship were high in comparison, and society placed a greater monetary value on the superior speed and safety of the aircraft. In recent years, however, rising fuel costs and advances in technology have brought the economist's appraisal of the airship more into line with that of the engineer. The present very sharp rise in oil prices, if sustained, is bound to have a significant effect on the technical relationships in Western economies, and this would not be allowed for in a simple projection of the relationships in Table 5.2.

Chapter 6

The Capitalist Economy

We have made many references to a 'capitalist' economy. The two previous chapters have been set in the framework of a capitalist system. The reader may have accepted the setting because of his or her familiarity with the capitalist world, which consists in the main of Western Europe, North America, parts of South America, Australasia, Southern Africa, and Japan. These areas on the whole enjoy high living standards in comparison with much of the rest of the world, and it might be tempting to associate capitalism with affluence. They also contain highly developed industry, which again is sometimes taken for a hall mark of capitalism. Both associations are misleading. There are poor capitalist economies — Nicaragua, the Philippines — as well as rich. There are industrial societies in Eastern Europe which are held to be the antithesis of capitalism. Certainly the economic problems of the USA are in many ways more like those facing the USSR than those facing Zaire. The importance different between the USA and USSR is the way in which they solve their problems. In this chapter we will discuss the relationships and institutions which characterise economies such as the USA, and which the reader through familiarity might take for granted.

THE CHARACTERISTICS OF CAPITALISM

We can give no universally accepted definition of capitalism, so we must instead indicate its main characteristics.
1. In a capitalist system there will be the right of the individuals to private property.
2. Private property allows the existence of 'market' relationships, not just for goods and services but for factors of production, labour and capital.
3. Markets for labour and capital are particularly important because they indicate the existence of conflicting interests in the production process.
4. There will be a tendency for the ownership of capital to be concentrated into a relatively small section of the population.

5. This tendency is reinforced by the process of capital accumulation.

6. Associated with private property is a degree of economic liberty which allows individuls to seek income and wealth.

7. Thus the 'Pursuit of profit' is generally regarded as the catalyst which activates the whole system, and the profit motive is the key determinant of the allocation of resources in production, and of the choice of production techniques.

8. The process of capital accumulation and the existence of market forces leads to some inequality of incomes.

The order in which the main characteristics have been given is not intended to suggest an order of importance, although it could be argued that private property is the primary characteristic since all the others depend on it. Certainly various observers have stressed one or other characteristic. Max Weber thought that it was the rational pursuit of profit which was the most important, while for Karl Marx it was the reduction of labour to the status of a commodity. What we will stress as we consider these characteristics in more detail is that they are *all* present in a capitalist system to some degree.

Private Property

Consumer demand for a pair of shoes has been expressed in terms of the factors upon which that demand depends. An omission from the list of determinant variables was the right, legal or customary, to own a pair of shoes. We tend to take this right for granted. In Chapter 2 we saw that in the past the right of particular groups to own particular goods has been proscribed. In customary societies the consumption of more than is required for survival can appear senseless. Only one pair of shoes, after all, can be worn at a time. In such circumstances, a market as outlined in Chapter 4 could never develop. A prospective buyer could not be certain that he would be able to keep goods once he had parted with his money if it were customary to regard goods in excess of need as being common property. The development of the legal right to private property, and the enforcing of this right, has removed an important area of uncertainty from economic activity. Handicraft production, for example, might flourish within a village or town offering a secure market, but if piracy and brigandage were the rule outside only the most foolhardy would risk expanding production beyond the requirements of the most immediate customers. Peasants the world over have reacted to random expropriation (e.g. taxation) by reducing their output to the barest subsistence. No one is going to produce goods which they may not be able to keep. It is no coincidence that organised production occurred first in societies which devised and enforced rules of economic behaviour.

Besides reducing uncertainly, the right to private property has emerged as the result of a social need. It has been a convenient way of enabling society to adapt to changing technology. For example, the invention of mounted warfare involved heavily armed men riding large, expensively reared horses. The existence of each unit of horse and rider depended upon the efforts of numerous individuals. Yet the effective use of the unit required a flexibility of action which was only possible if the rider could act without reference to those upon whom he depended economically. Flexibility could be secured if the rider 'owned' the horse and weapons, although he may have contributed little or nothing to their existence. We are not saying that high levels of organisation have been impossible in customary societies with communal ownership of property. The impressive civilisation of the Aztecs of Mexico incorporated communal property ownership. Aztec society, however, was inhibited technologically. It would be unwise to draw too sweeping a conclusion from this, since other factors besides communal property, such as the nature of religious belief, had a bearing. Western European attitudes towards private property, by contrast, have been a major influence on the pattern of economic advance during the present millennium.

This is not to say that the only way to resolve uncertainty and to maintain flexibility is to confer the right to private property. The organisation of production and trade based on communal property would have been unsatisfactory in the absence of effective communications, which themselves depend upon technology. Alternative approaches to property ownerships did not become practicable until after the industrialisation of Europe. By that time private property had become a deep-rooted institution of those societies now regarded as 'capitalist'.

The Development of Trading and Market Relationships

The right to private property is inextricably linked with the development of exchange and trade, and the existence of trading relationships is a further characteristic of a capitalistic society. Trade of sorts has been a feature of most societies, even the most primitive. As the means for survival became more numerous and more complicated, self-sufficiency became more impracticable. It is one thing, however, to exchange surplus goods of one kind for others in short supply, but another matter for the trade in goods to be a means of survival itself. We have elsewhere drawn a distinction between different kinds of production activity and noted that in the contemporary world the difference between production and trade is academic. Yet this distinction has relevance for the nature of capitalism. Some historians think in terms of the 'natural' economy of the Middle Ages, in which the functions of the producer and the trader are merged. A trader would be a manufacturer, buying raw materials, processing them, and selling the finished product in local markets. With the growth of intranational and then international trade, the problems of supplying distant markets changed relationships. Given legal title to the goods he bought, the merchant engaged in trade for a return beyond mere subsistence. Conditions of the times were risky. Piracy and vagaries of sail-driven ships meant that not only would trade take place for gain, but that this gain would have to be considerable. Firstly, it must compensate for the risks involved, and secondly it must go to secure economic power in order to control the trading environment. The merchants of the Hanseatic League and the Italian city states, for example, were ruthlessly exclusive, and their behaviour has many parallels in the industrial societies of the twentieth century. Not for them were the conditions of a perfect market (p. 72). Having restricted entry into their ranks, they sought state patronage for their activities. They obtained exclusive rights for the sale of particular commodities in their home market, territorial monopolies abroad, and in both charged prices based on what their customers were able to pay, not upon the cost of the operations. In this they defended their departure from the medieval notions of a 'just price' by pointing to the great risks they undertook. Great as these risks may have been, they did not prevent the amassing of princely fortunes. This was, however, capitalistic behaviour rather than capitalism itself. Trading monopolies had existed in the ancient world, as had 'markets' for particular commodities. The right to private property is equally time-honoured, and, as far as consumer goods are concerned, is permitted in contemporary socialist states. Private property and developed markets may be characteristics of capitalism, but their presence alone does not constitute capitalism.

The Accumulation of Capital. 1—Capital and Wealth

Property consists of more than just trade goods. It consists also of land, buildings, and all the other paraphernalia we term 'wealth'. Wealth, however, can take many forms. It can consist of property which is largely a repository of value, such as works of art, jewellery, etc. It can consist of property which has social value as well as intrinsic value. Land, for example, is both a store of value and in some societies a mark of social status. Land has a further important quality. It can be combined with other factors of production to produce an output. Capital goods are similarly both objects of property and productive assets. They are a form of wealth which can create more wealth. The concentration of property of this kind into the hands of a particular social group is a precondition for the emergence of a full-blooded capitalist system. It comes about in two stages. First must come the accumulation of wealth *per se*, and second must be the existence of means whereby unproductive wealth can be converted into productive capital.

1   *The Accumulation of Wealth*   For wealth to be accumulated, it is necessary that some means exist whereby property can change hands. This means is provided in part by the institution of private property, but it also requires that property should exist in a transferable form. Perishable goods and services are obviously unsuitable. Land is not wholly suitable either. It is certainly durable, but ownership may be restricted to particular social groups. It certainly can be accumulated if ownership can be transferred, but may not be divisible into sufficiently small parcels. A peasant farmer, for example, may at the end of a consumption period have a few chickens in excess of his consumption needs. It would prove practicably impossible to convert such perishable goods into a sufficiently small piece of land. Money in various forms serves as a store of value if it is durable, and it can be added to in small amounts. (Some forms of money have been eminently unsuitable. The Masai use cows, and while this form of money can reproduce itself, it can also run away or be eaten.) In the past two or three centuries the growth of banking and credit institutions has provided a repository for wealth in a highly transferable form. A feature of pre-capitalist societies in Europe which distinguished them from similar societies in Asia was this growth of forms of holding and transferring wealth other than land or bullion. Where the form of wealth takes on social significance, it lacks the transferability which is so important in the accumulation process. However, trade and the other means of acquiring an accumulating wealth, such as conquest and theft, can be slow and uncertain, and the accumulation process has been greatly assisted by historical events, both fortuitous and contrived. Wars and economic crises have caused fluctuations in the prices of property, making it occasionally very easy to acquire. In the wake of disturbances such as the currency upheavals of sixteenth-century England, land passed from old feudal owners to a new landed gentry. After the First World War, industrialists of the Weimar Republic reorganised their plant at zero cost by borrowing money which, because of inflation, they never had to repay.

2   *Owners of Wealth Become Owners of Capital*   Until the industrial revolutions of the eighteenth and nineteenth centuries, the conversion of wealth into capital was a lengthy process, largely conditioned by opportunity. We say largely, because there can be social constraints to the search for wealth which might inhibit the conversion of wealth into productive capital. The Catholicism of sixteenth-century Spain prevented bullion wealth from Spain's American empire from being put to productive use, and it was used on church ornaments instead. In parts of eigthteenth-century Europe opportunities for conversion were growing. The cheapening of labour from population growth, and a geographical expansion of markets for raw materials and finished products, coinciding with technological development, allowed profits to be won on favourable terms. Many of the early industrialists, particularly in Britain, were landowners with exploitable mineral resources. Much of the new technology was applicable to small-scale undertakings, and was cheap enough to be financed by the savings of a single household. The step from blacksmith to ironmaster was not impossibly steep. Capital produces an output, unlike wealth, and once wealth had been transferred into capital, an upward spiral began. Income from capital could be reinvested as more capital to produce yet more income, and so on. The process was intensified by the pace of technical change, which has so far tended towards an ever larger scale of production. As production became increasingly capital intensive, it required larger and larger amounts of previously accumulated capital, amounts greater than could be financed by reinvested income.

Joint Stock Enterprise

The process by which wealth is transformed into capital does not always require that the owners of wealth engage directly in production. Indeed, as capitalism has developed it has become exceptional for those who organise production on a significant scale to finance the process from their personal assets. As the capital requirements of large-scale industry exceeded, from time to time, the capacity of a business to generate new capital, or as the capital cost of a production venture exceeded the assets of those who wished to carry it out, ways had to be found to draw upon the reserves of households outside the production process. To this end an institution has been developed which has become an associative, if not a causative, characteristic of capitalism. This is the joint stock enterprise.

There are two ways in which a business can obtain money capital with which to finance production. It can borrow from those who have assets in excess of their consumption needs, or those who can be persuaded by the offer of an interest payment to postpone consumption. The physical ability to borrow, however, depends upon the development of suitable credit institutions. Alternatively, the firm can offer a share in its business in exchange for a cash payment. The money is used to acquire productive assets, and the 'share-holder' becomes part-owner of those assets. As a proprietor, the shareholder becomes entitled to a share in the company's profits in proportion to the size of the shareholding. The company's assets, or 'stock', are held jointly by the shareholders, each of whom has a say in the running of the enterprise, again in proportion to the size of the shareholding.

Shareholding became an attractive way to hold wealth. Certainly there are risks that the investment might prove unsound, and unless the shareholder's stake in the company is limited by law to the size of his shareholding, those risks can be very great. But shareholding in a profitable company is to possess an accumulating asset, as well as a source of income. In the experience of the UK, once the advantages of holding wealth in this way had become accepted, the transference of wealth into productive capital gathered pace. Even land-holding, with its attendant social cachet, seemed less attractive by comparison. Oscar Wilde has Lady Bracknell observe, when she approves of Ernest's income from investments, that land had ceased to be a profit or a pleasure.[1]

Consequences of the Joint Stock Principle

The introduction of the joint stock principle has had two important consequences for the development of capitalism.

1. It enabled the emergence of a managerial class by allowing for a separation of the ownership from the control of a business. It became possible for those with managerial ability to exercise their talents without having first acquired wealth of some kind. It is arguable that this is true save only in the larger firms. Production in most capitalist societies is carried out by both large and small businesses, and in the latter the strength of family shareholdings, if indeed the business consists of more than a one-man enterprise or a partnership, often means that control can be exercised by the owners. In large businesses, with numerous and diverse shareholdings, hiring of management skills is the practicable way to run the organisation.

2. It enabled the process of capital accumulation to become pervasive. While the distribution of wealth has remained uneven in capitalist societies, shareholding has become possible for relatively humble

[1]*The Importance of Being Earnest* (1895).

households. In earlier stages of industrial development, the production process has been dominated by a narrow group of wealthy households, easily identified as 'capitalists'. As institutions for channelling money capital into real, productive capital have become more sophisticated, however, the savings of relatively low income groups can be utilised. Such savings take the form of trade union subscriptions, pension fund contributions, and insurance premiums.

We shall refer to this development again (Chapter 10, part 1), but its importance in the present context is that a large number of households have a stake in the process of capital accumulation, even if they are predominantly suppliers of labour.

The Capital Market

The purchase and sale of productive capital is a unique feature of a capitalist system. While aspects of a labour market can exist in other systems, a capital market can only exist where capital is privately owned. In planned economies, for instance, different wage levels can be offered by the State to induce a flow of labour in a desired direction. But controlling labour is not the same thing as owning it. In a capitalist system, capital, like labour, is owned by households and used by firms. Labour, however, provides a service and does not change its nature as the houschold offers it to the firm, or as it flows between firms and industries. This is not true of capital. We have seen that the form it takes while in the household's possession differs from that in which it is used by firms, as bank deposits, etc. in the former, and machinery in the latter.

The capital market is the institution in which the conversion takes place. The conversion can take two forms. Money deposited in the banking system can be re-lent to producers, or a company's paper securities can be bought for cash. It is important then that a company's shares and loan stocks should be freely transferable. In each case the market will be performing an allocative function. Loans from the banking system will flow towards firms and industries prepared to pay the highest rates of interest, and the public will subscribe to shares which offer the highest rates of return. It is important to remember that at any one time the supply of money capital is limited, and that for funds to flow towards one firm or industry, there has to be a corresponding reduction elsewhere. Capital will thus flow from the less to the more profitable production possibilities. It is important to remember, too, that there is a distinction between new paper capital and existing paper capital. Shares which have already been issued are held by individuals as a form of wealth and they change hands as investors seek to maximise the value of their assets. There is an indirect allocative effective here, since the company whose shares are highly priced will find it easier to raise new capital than the company whose existing shares are held in disfavour by the market.

The Money Market

A capitalist system will have a money market as well as a capital market. Money is, in fact, the commodity dealt with in both markets, but what separates the two is the purpose of the transactions. The capital market is a channel through which money is converted into productive capital. The money market is a market for loans for all purposes. Producers can use it to raise money to finance production, but they will be competing with hire-purchase companies, seeking to finance consumer spending, and the Government, borrowing to finance its day-to-day expenditures. The separation of the two markets is in a sense artificial, since they are so closely interrelated. Household savings are attracted directly or indirectly into one or the other by the rates of return offered, and a paradox may arise as producers, for example of motor vehicles, in order to finance production, must attract savings away from those consumers who would finance their purchases of motor vehicles by hire-purchase.

The Separation of Labour from the Means of Production

The existence of a labour market is also a feature, but not a unique one, of capitalism. For Karl Marx, however, the existence of a labour market was especially significant. It was a sure sign that feudalism had given way to capitalism. What in his eyes distinguished capitalism was its particular 'mode of production'. This was not reference to a production technique, but to a situation in which the owners of labour services sold not the products of that labour but the labour itself. The merchant capitalism of the sixteenth and seventeenth centuries, which he referred to as a system based on trade rather than industry, was not full capitalism, according to Marx, because in it labour had not become fully divorced from the ownership of the production process. Industry, with some exceptions, was dominated by handicraft methods, in which the operator owned his own tools, bought by his own raw material inputs, and sold a finished product. Of course, there was a substantial labour element in the final product. Production was not yet 'capitalistic' in that it was not capital intensive. Nor did it matter that the product might be sold, not to the consumer, but to a powerful middle-man who used his market position exclusively to his own advantage. We have observed that such acquisitiveness might be capitalistic behaviour, but not necessarily capitalism. Capitalism, as Marx saw it, did not emerge until the rise of modern industry in the nineteenth century. It is worth noting in passing that Marx's understanding of the phenomenon has been in retrospect more relevant than that of those who, like Max Weber, emphasised aspects of capitalism which did not confine it to a particular epoch. The development of markets, the pursuit of profit, are present in societies which we would not nowadays recognise as being capitalist. The 'mode of production' which exemplified capitalism for Marx has been in existence only since the turn of the nineteenth century, although its emergence rested on foundations laid down in earlier periods.

The Accumulation of Capital. II — Capital, Labour and Technology

Broadly speaking there are three variables at work in the process of capital accumulation: the availability of labour, the productivity of capital, and the state of technology upon which the productivity of capital depends. The three are not independent of each other, and a change in any one is likely to affect the remaining two. In the accumulation process the owners of capital combine it with labour and raw materials to produce an output, and the amount of output so produced depends upon the technical conditions of production, upon technology. But what is the output for? It is to enable consumption by both labour and capital owners. The more labour consumes, the less will be available for the owners of capital to consume or reinvest as they choose. The less labour consumes, the lower will be the level output required by society, and the less point in adding to society's productive capacity. At the same time, technical change seems to input-saving, particularly of labour, and so the more capital per unit of labour will be required. Relationships of this kind have led to a series of predictions that the process of capital accumulation cannot be self-sustaining. They fall into three groups, and in each one emphasis is placed in turn on the limitation of natural resources, the consequences of an increase in the use of capital, and the possibility of a failure of technology to change.

1. Natural resources are not unlimited, and thus the greater the volume of production, the more scarce and expensive raw materials will become. The output from each successive addition to capital will decline, and the owners of capital will find greater satisfaction from using their incomes for consumption than from reinvesting them.

2. This declining rate of return can alternatively arise from a growing preponderance of capital over labour. The development of capital in-

tensive, mass production techniques increases on the one hand the amount of capital used per unit of labour. On the other hand, by reducing the demand for labour per unit of output, the owners of capital reduce employment and with it the consumption of their mass-produced goods. The return on capital will thus fall relative to the amount of (employed) labour to capital.

3. In the absence of such technical change, the decline in the rate of return on capital and thereby the rate of capital accumulation will come about by a decline in the productivity of capital. So-called 'diminishing returns' set in if output can be increased only by adding equipment of the existing type to the existing capital stock.

The three possibilities are not mutually exclusive. They could all combine to bring the process of capital accumulation to an end, or they could operate in pairs. Natural resource limitation and slow technical change are currently discussed in the context of the outlook for the UK economy. To date, however, capital accumulation has continued. Technology has so far prevented the pace of resource exploitation from holding back the growth of output. It has been fast enough to prevent diminishing returns. In specific industries it has been biased towards capital intensity, but the creation of capital has required labour inputs on a scale to prevent the reduction of labour content in the final product, and the growth of capital intensive industry itself has promoted the growth of ancillary service industries which, as we have seen, have been labour intensive. Continual technical change may underwrite the process of capital accumulation, but in itself does not explain it. Why should there be a propensity to harness technology to the production process and why should capital owners and household savers behave in an accumulatory manner? For this we must turn to a consideration of the motive force of a capitalist system.

The Pursuit of Profit

There are three aspects of the search for profit to be emphasised. Firstly, it is not confined to capitalist systems. Secondly, it has a role in the allocation of resources so important as to set capitalist societies apart from other economic systems. In this it must be linked with private property and the accumulation of capital. Thirdly, much of the justification for profit-seeking must be seen in historical context. Capitalism is continually changing, and, as we shall see in Chapter 10, so perhaps is the place of the profit motive.

In common with private property and the development of markets, the pursuit of profit is a necessary but not sufficient characteristic of a capitalist system. Other societies, past and present, may tolerate profit-seeking to some degree, and it is present even in socialist systems. Within a capitalist system, however, the pursuit of profit is regarded as a catalyst and a very justification for the system itself. Briefly, the protagonists of capitalism argue that if there are no restrictions place upon the determination of market prices, a competitive system will result in the 'right' amounts of each good being produced at the lowest price. This will involve the most efficient use of an economy's resources. We have seen in the previous chapter how this allocation takes place through a host of market transactions, and the point is the manner in which resource flows follow changes in profitability. In the archetype of a pure capitalist system, this profit must be sought rationally. Individuals in the market, consumers as well as producers, are seen making continual adjustments to their activities so as to maximise their personal advantges. Consumers make purchases of goods to the point at which the pleasure of consumption is balanced by the pain of parting with money. What a consumer is parting with when he exchanges money for a particular good is, of course, the chance of consuming alternative goods. Producers change their outputs and inputs so as to maximise the difference between cost and revenue, i.e. profit. Changes in consumer satisfaction are reflected in changing prices, and output is adjusted accordingly. Similarly, changes in the availability of factors will be reflected in their prices, and producers will make adjustments to their factor combinations so that costs are minimised. As long as the pursuit of profit is allowed to flourish untrammelled, the result will be to the greater good, it is argued, since, (a) all goods produced will be consumed — if the price is lowered sufficiently, (b) all wants will be satisfied — at a price, and, (c) all factors of production fully utilised — at some level of remuneration.

Profits will accrue to some individuals and not to others, but this is justified principally by showing that profits as a source of income are a reward for taking risks. If the pursuit of profit is successful, this is because correct decisions have been taken on changes in market circumstances. In any case, the market mechanism contains checks and balances which prevent rewards becoming disproportionate to risks, since persistent success will attract imitators who will collectively ensure that excess profit is only a transitory phenomenon. This schema should have the chance to take the risks which could result in profit. Samuel Smiles in his *Self-Help* showed that entry into the property-owning, profit-making groups was open to all who practised industry and thrift. Smiles's work (1859) remained popular into the twentieth century, but few of the multitudes of people who had worked very hard actually made the transition from rags to riches. It may be enough that one or two did.

Laissez-faire

In the last chapter we saw that in practice the market does not always work smoothly, and we will turn to some important consequences of this later. Nevertheless, the ethos of the pursuit of profit has its attractions, if only because profits, by involving the self-interest of the organiser of production, provide both a sensitive indicator of changing economic circumstances, and a stimulus for reaction to such changes. To the nineteenth century proponents of 'market' capitalism, the market system would only result in an optimum allocation of resources if governments did not interfere with the economic decisions of individuals. Adam Smith wrote of the 'unseen hand' of the market mechanism which, although activated by the self-interest of individuals through the pursuit of profit and the maximisation of consumer satisfaction, would act for the common good. This notion suited an age whose intelligentsia were influenced by the works of Charles Darwin. 'Social Darwinism' presented a natural progression towards material advance which governmental intervention, to prevent the least fit from going to the wall, would only hinder. The politico-economic doctrine which was the repository of such ideas is known as *laissez-faire* (to leave alone). While social acceptance of *laissez-faire* is not itself a characteristic of capitalism, there will nevertheless be present in a capitalist economy a degree of economic liberty not found in alternative systems. As well as the right of the individual to own property, there will be less of the social restriction on economic activity found in customary or traditional societies, and fewer of the state monopolies associated with command economies. This does not mean that similarities cannot exist. In a traditional society the consumption of particular goods may be restricted by custom or edict to a particular social group, such as the priesthood. In a capitalist system, Rolls Royces may in practice be restricted to a particular social group by virtue of purchasing power. Similarly job opportunity will in practice be constrained by economic rather than social considerations, although in principle there should be greater mobility. Perhaps the freedom of a capitalist system can be summed up as a 'freedom to' as opposed to the 'freedom from' of customary and command economies. Where economic freedom is reduced, the individual can be said to be free from the consequences of his economic activities. If he is not allowed to make profits, he cannot make losses either.

CAPITALISM MUST BE A NATIONAL SYSTEM

We have listed and described the characteristics of a capitalist economy, and we have seen that very few of the characteristics are unique to capitalism. The existence of markets for factors of production is perhaps the hallmark of a full capitalist system, since they must incorporate both the ownership of private property and the separation of labour from the means of production. But even here there is a qualification. The markets must be national markets, and they must permeate every aspect of economic life. A good example is the relationship between the capital market, the money market, and the economy as a whole. In a capitalist system these markets have so developed that the vast majority of consumers are involved with each other through their bank deposits, building societies, pension funds, as well as the markets for goods and services.

The factors operating in the housing market of the UK in the 1960s and early 1970s illustrates this point. Savers found that building societies offered an attractive outlet for their savings, and funds began to flow out of bank deposits, unit trusts, etc., and into the building societies. These funds were used by the building societies to provide loans for house purchase. With the rise in purchasing power and relatively fixed supply, the price of property began to rise. This had two effects. Firstly, resources began to flow into the building industry. Builders expanded their activities and bought land and labour with borrowed money, which was becoming more expensive as the flow towards the building societies continued. Secondly, the rising property prices increased the attraction to large savers of investment in land and buildings relative to industrial investment. For the economy as a whole, labour was already scarce, and the increase in building activity made it more so. Thus producers in general, not just building firms, were faced with two alternatives. They could either raise wages, or replace labour with capital. But we have already observed that the costs of borrowing were increasing with the attraction of the property market. Indeed, this was becoming so attractive that even the main sources of external capital (as opposed to ploughed-back profits), the insurance companies and the pension funds, were investing directly in property. At the same time, the increasing number of houses being bought and sold meant an increasing demand for furnishings, furniture, and consumer durables associated with setting up house. To meet such demands resources must be attracted from other uses. The interrelationships could be traced indefinitely.

DEFICIENCIES OF THE CAPITALIST SYSTEM

We have presented capitalism as having evolved over a period of time into an economic system in which resources are allocated by the free interaction of market forces. Market forces direct the economy towards a combination of resources which produces the highest possible output. That this goal may never be achieved does not invalidate the use of market forces to this end. In a world of constant change, the availability of resources is constantly changing and thus the notion of what constitutes the most efficient allocation must be elusive. Nevertheless, however elusive this goal may be, capitalist systems in the main have been able to accommodate rapidly changing technology, and viewed over the long term have generated high levels of income per head in comparison with the rest of the world. It may be, as we shall see later, that some of this success has been at the expense of other countries, but we could accept that at least as far as the populations of the developed capitalist world are concerned, the market system has worked well.

There are, however, some important reservations to be made.

1. Capitalist systems do not always work in the way they are supposed to. Competitive forces which should direct the economy towards its optimum allocation of resources are sometimes dulled. Markets, whether for goods or factors, are rarely, if ever, completely competitive. This can be due to inherent imperfection — labour, for example, is seldom mobile in the short run — or to imperfections deliberately introduced.

2. Competition can sometimes be wasteful, leading to needless duplication of products.

3. Wasted resources, particularly unemployment of labour, are a periodic feature of capitalism.

We shall examine these deficiencies in more detail in a moment. There are additional shortcomings which, while within the scope of this chapter, are more appropriately dealt with elsewhere.

4. Social costs considerations do not enter into production decisions, and consequently the allocation of resources can be distorted. In Chapter 8 we shall discuss ways in which the State can reconcile private with social costs and benefits. We can note in passing that state involvement in this respect has been a feature of the 'Welfare State' capitalism of the twentieth century, in contrast to the 'market' capitalism of the nineteenth century. This latter was characterised, in contemporary terms, by little state intervention.

5. 'Alienation', the low level of job satisfaction found in capitalistic industry, was a feature of capitalism emphasised by Karl Marx, and this is dealt with in our discussion of the socialist system.

6. Income inequalities are a particular consequence of the ac-

cumulation of capital, but we will consider this under the broader
heading of income determination (Chapter 7).

Monopoly

Monopoly or monopolistic practices are terms used to suggest the
deliberate restriction of competition. Strictly speaking the word
'monopoly' means 'single seller', and in this sense it need have
no pejorative connotation. A monopoly can exist 'naturally' when the
economies of large-scale production indicate a plant size large enough
to supply the whole market, or where the supply of a particular output, theatre talent for example, can come only from one source. The
creation of these conditions can be a policy objective in order to increase the firm's revenues beyond the level obtainable under competitive conditions.

1   *Establishing Monopoly*   Firms already in an industry use a variety
of devices collectively referred to as 'barriers to entry'. In motor
vehicle, nylon and computer production the amount of capital a new
entrant would require at current technology constitutes a 'natural'
barrier. Where technical conditions allow a larger number of firms,
collusive action is possible. Production costs of new entrants can be
artificially increased by the use of patent law. Heavy advertising outlays and brand differentiation make it unduly expensive for a prospective producer to acquire a market share large enough to bring unit
costs of production down to the level of existing producers. Trading
agreements by existing firms can make raw supplies unavailable to
prospective competitors, or make it difficult for them to find retail
outlets for their goods.

2   *The Use of Monopoly Power*   Monopoly practices distort market
relationships at many levels. Prices paid for monopoly output can be
those most advantageous to the producer, and may bear little
relationship to the cost of production. Output may be, as a result, less
than would be produced in competitive conditions. Possibly higher
prices could be justified socially, since the wants of all consumers for
the monopolist's products can be theoretically satisfied. Television
broadcasting is a favourite example. A large number of competiting
channels will each attempt to cater for the largest section of viewers;
the minority with either very highbrow of very lowbrow tastes will
either be ignored, or will be accommodated at inconvenient times. A
broadcasting monopoly will cater for all tastes, having no viewers to

lose to competitors. One group of consumers will, in effect, be sub-sidising the consumption of others. The consumers of minority programmes, if no one else, would regard this aspect of monopoly behaviour as beneficial. If the monopolist's revenues, however — whether this is a single firm or a group acting in concert — are greater than would accrue to the industry in competitive conditions, then the purchasing power of consumers will have been distorted. Expenditure on goods other than those of the monopolist will be less by the difference between what the firm received as a monopolist, and what it would have received in competitive conditions. Fewer goods will be produced in the non-monopoly sector, and if the monopolist has max-imised his revenue by decreasing his output, total production across the economy will be smaller than it would have been under com-petition. Hence both total output and product mix will be different un-der conditions of monopoly against competition.

Competitive Waste

The virtues of competition are part of the ethos of capitalism, yet un-restrained competition is by no means wholly beneficial. While monopoly can offer wide consumer choice, it will not necessarily do so. Quantity and quality of output will be decided by the producer, with less need to cater for consumer preference. Henry Ford had a monopoly of cheap cars, but they were all painted black. On the other hand, a proliferation of small producers each offering a virtually iden-tical product cannot represent wide choice. Before the advent of high turnover retailing techniques, a product such as tea would be bought from a wholesaler and packed by small retailers in an individually marked bag. Each retailers suggested to the consumer that his tea was a different product. The concentration of retail sales into chain stores has meant a great reduction in the number of brands available, but a cheaper product in real terms. Waste can result from competition when the resources used in production are durable, and cannot be easily transferred to other uses. The vast amounts of railway in-vestment in the UK in the 1840s resulted in surplus capacity which took years of traffic growth to eradicate. The investment itself was the result of strong, even frantic, competition to cater for growing traffic, but the volume of traffic had been overestimated, and the result was considerable duplication of services. But once a railway had been built, its owners had debts to service which could only be done by offering rates that would attract a share of what traffic was available. The return on railway investment fell below market rates, but firms were unable to leave the industry because they could not convert their physical capital into cash, and railway lines have few alternative uses. The result was that the travelling public received a service at a price less than they would have been prepared to pay. More recently in many countries competition between road and rail has lead to duplication of services and distortion of resource allocation.

The Waste of Unemployment

Perhaps the most dramatic result of market imperfection, and the greatest waste of a capitalist system, is the periodic fluctuation which takes place in the level of economic activity. The nature of these fluctuations is complicated and beyond the scope of this book. We have seen that factor movement and output change do not immediately follow changes in price. Time has shown to be false the notion of *laissez-faire* theorists that goods which are produced are automatically consumed. Production in excess of demand will cause prices to fall, it is true, but with them will fall producers' revenues. As firms adjust to the lower prices by cutting back on employment and investment. they reduce overall purchasing power causing further reduction in demand and increasing unemployment. Economic activity will only increase again when firms can be persuaded that the outlook justifies reviving investment plans. Such fluctuations have persisted in capitalistic societies since industrialisation began, with periods of high economic activity — 'booms' — followed by periods of low activity — 'slumps'. The unemployment of resources during depression can be considerable. For the UK in the period 1919-39 the average annual level of unemployment scarcely fell below 10 per cent of the labour force, and in one year, 1932, it reached 24 per cent. This was actually lower than in many other leading capitalist countries. In Australia, Germany, and the USA it reached 28 per cent, 44 per cent, and 23 per cent respectively. Since that time, when observers predicted that capitalism would collapse under the weight of the mass of unemployed, greater understanding of the nature of the cycle in economic activity has been a factor enabling governments to greatly reduce the severity of unemployment. From 1945 the annual level in the UK has never so far reached 5 per cent. Nevertheless, fluctuations still occur and unemployment still persists. The fact that it tends to be concentrated on particular grades of labour—particularly the unskilled, on particular age groups in particular industries in particular locations and especially on the older employee—makes it a serious social problem.

REPAIRING THE DEFECTS OF CAPITALISM

The deficiencies of capitalism have been the object of government policies to some extent in all capitalist societies since capitalism began, but there have been considerable developments in the twentieth century. The reasons are part political, part economic, and the balance between the two varies according to the particular case. The cynic might argue that the growth of social security in the UK was in response to increasing competitive pressures abroad, since the Victorian economy had been highly wasteful of labour; this waste became costly once the UK lost her monopoly position in world trade. Certainly universal suffrage has made for greater governmental sensitivity to problems of unemployment, poverty, and social costs, while policies on monopoly and competition seem to be influenced more by economic considerations. In the circumstances of the interwar period there seemed little virtue in unrestrained competition, while the growth in industrial concentration in the UK since 1945 has swung the balance of government thinking the other way.

In Chapter 10 we shall consider the forces for economic change in both capitalist and socialist societies, and elsewhere in the book we shall discuss attitudes towards aspects of market imperfection such as income inequality, social cost, etc. For the moment, we will briefly consider just one area in which it has been found necessary for the Government to act, that of control of monopoly.

The Control of Monopoly

Public policy on monopoly has to strike a balance between the needs of technology on the one hand, and the loss of factor mobility on the other. There are two approaches to the problem. The dogmatic approach outlines features of monopolistic practice which are regarded as undesirable, and declares them illegal. The pragmatic approach is to examine each case of monopolistic practice on its merits, and to act accordingly. Under a dogmatic policy a firm may be statutorily forbidden to sell more than a certain proportion of the market for a particular commodity. Firms may be confined to a prescribed geographical area. Specific practices such as resale price maintenance, where a firm or group of firms control the retail price of their products, can be outlawed. The virtue of such dogmatism is that it establishes rules to which producers can adjust. On the other hand, it tends to protect society against some of the abuses of monopoly power at the expense of flexibility to adjust to pressures for larger scale production. If technical conditions make for larger size, dogmatic monopoly control may either cause the total output of the system to be less than the maximum, or producers may find ways round the regulations so that control becomes more difficult. Restrictions on market size in the USA, for example, have been a factor in the growth of multinational companies.

The pragmatic approach, on the other hand, possesses flexibility since each case is examined on its merits. In order to do this, however, some clear understanding of the nature of monopoly is required. Otherwise monopoly will go undetected, let alone controlled. Excess profits are associated with monopoly, but how excessive is excess? To examine suspected instances of monopoly, in advance of pronouncing on the possible merits of each case, can require substantial administrative machinery which, by its bureaucratic nature, is likely to lessen the flexibility that pragmatism offers. The most usual measure of monopoly is the size of a firm's share of the market. Yet an economist is likely to define monopoly in terms of 'monopoly profit' — that level of profit earned in excess of that required to keep the firm in the industry. Some firms with a small share of the market may earn 'monopoly profits' by product differentiation, while a dominant firm may be doing little more than break even. Another indication of monopoly is the existence of restrictive practices. Some collusive agreements, such as price fixing, 'loyalty' rebates designed to place competitors at disadvantage with retailers, tender rigging, etc., are clearly designed to restrain competition, and where they exist, firms are acting as monopolists. But by what criteria can it be decided whether an agreement to pool research expenditures is of the same order? Questions of this sort lead to some consideration of what is or is not 'in the public interest', and into the subject matter of Chapter 10.

Chapter 7

Income Distribution and the Power to Consume

SHARE-OUT, LOTTERY, OR LOGICAL OUTCOME OF MARKET FORCES?

In this chapter we concentrate on trying to explain why it is that individuals and households have different levels of access to an economy's available supply of consumer goods and services. In doing so, the distributions of income and wealth in a society will be fundamentally important. In the context of a purely market economy, the words 'distribution' and 'share-out' are inappropriate since incomes are primarily determined, as we shall see later, by the impersonal interaction of the forces of supply and demand and not by a conscious decision on the basis of agreed principles. The man in the street may think it sheer chance that he missed being born a son of the landed aristocracy, and modern Western man may thank the stars for not being born a poor Latin-American peon. Any observed pattern of distribution of income and wealth across a community will be the result of a multitude of factors and the problem will be to isolate those elements that are most important in any particular case.

Equality by Necessity

A brief examination of a 'share-out' approach to distribution will reveal some of the preconditions necessary for this concept to work in practice, and a start is made here by looking at the behaviour of a small closely-knit community living at a fairly primitive level. Anthropologists tend to concentrate on the cultural, social and religious aspects of their subjects, but sometimes the economics of the life-style emerges.[1] The Nambikuara of Brazil are a dwindling tribe of Indians forced to spend the seven months of the dry season searching

[1] Claude Levi Strauss, 'The Social and Psychological Aspects of Chieftainship in a Primitive Tribe' in *Comparative Political Systems* ed. Cohen and Middleton (National History Press, 1967).

through the northwestern Mato Grosso for the roots, wild fruits, small animals and insects that form their diet. Hence they are still at the scavenging level. One square mile of bush provides very little food and this forces the tribe to operate in small bands travelling over great distances. The bands are linked to each other by kinship and this facilitates the regrouping of the bands should this prove desirable. The chieftains of these two-to-ten-family bands 'evolve' as they demonstrate their natural and acquired skills in leadership, hunting, dancing and warfare. If a leader makes the wrong decisions there is an immediate impact on the wellbeing of the band which will then tend to disintegrate and join more successful bands. Here then, we have the factors which will tend towards an equal share-out of available resources: (a) whatever wealth there is in the band in the form of knives, ornaments, shells, etc., must be small enough to be carried by the women of the families and this precludes great concentrations of wealth, (b) the chieftain is constantly forced to share his food and wealth with his band in order to maintain its cohesiveness and his position as leader. The chief's main reward for what seems to be an onerous and difficult job is that he is allowed to have more than one wife! (c) if the members of the band are not satisfied with their leader's performance they can opt out of his leadership.

Equality by Choice: The Commune

Another way that some communities have sought a generally acceptable share-out has been to form a commune. There have been many types of commune formed throughout history and their distinguishing feature is that they are voluntary groupings of people into smallish economic and social units united by a common belief or philosophy. Most communes have had their roots in religious or socialist ideology and hence such concepts as equality before God and man, brotherhood, the holding of property in common, democratic decision-making and the weakening of family ties tend to appear. Communes seem to work best when they are small scale, have great unity of purpose, and are not subject to too many external pressures. The Israeli *kibbutzim* have been successful modern communes, but the compulsorily formed communes to be found in some communist countries have often violated the 'free choice' condition, especially when they have been imposed on an ancient and stubborn peasantry.

THE EXERCISE OF ECONOMIC POWER BY COMMAND AND BY CUSTOM

Once we move much beyond the 'family' scale of economic activity, we find that mutual belief and support are rarely sufficient to organise a complex society. Sir John Hicks[2] suggests that pre-market-dominated societies tend to fall into two main groups, 'customary economies' and 'command economies', but recognises that elements of both types are usually present.

Command Economy

This suggests the use or threat of physical power, an economy where the ruling elite determines the political, social and economic structure of society in accordance with its own wishes. Wealth, social status and public office become rewards for loyal service to the rulers. Sometimes the central direction of the economy is so powerful and detailed that it permeates down to the lowest levels of economic decision-making, as in the case of the Soviet-type war economy, but historically one more often finds that absolute rulers are content to accept heavy tribute from their peoples while leaving those so oppressed to raise their payments in any way they can.

Customary Economy

According to Hicks, this requires stability in the structure of society and in political and economic organisation. Privileges and duties, by long usage, become rights, and in a situation where little is changing, the way of passing on rights that is most likely to develop is by inheritance. Pure examples of either command or custom economies are rare and it is more common to find mixtures of the two. One typical line of development can be seen when societies become command economies in times of invasion or revolution. If stability follows these upheavals, the elements of command can evolve into custom and inheritance. The development of the feudal system in Britain following the Norman conquest is an obvious example. Western readers may be less familiar with an example that illustrates the command/custom mixture very well indeed, and this is the economic framework of Moghul India in the eighteenth century.[3]

Moghul India had a ruling aristocracy descended from nomadic invaders and conquerors. Unlike the European feudal system, this aristocracy did not have the stability of the manorial land system

[2]John Hicks, *A Theory of Economic History* (Oxford University Press, 1969).

[3]A. Maddison, *Class Structure and Economic Growth* (Allen and Unwin, 1972).

behind it, but was instead allocated a share of the Emperor's revenues arising from the villages and farms. This upper class depended on the power and might of the Emperor but could be shuffled around or dispossessed according to his whim. There was a clear incentive for the nobility to squeeze as much out of their revenue sources as possible. Against this background of a shifting band of noble predators, the economy was held together by the stability of village society. This social stability had its roots in ancient Hindu texts which divided people into groups or castes. There were (*a*) the Brahmins, priests banned from manual labour and subject to food and drink taboos, (*b*) Kshatriyas (warriors), Vaishyas (traders), and Sudras (farmers and servants), each of these often being divided into grades of various standing, and (*c*) the Melechas (untouchables) destined to a life of servile and 'unclean' drudgery. These castes provided impenetrable barriers to social mobility in that sons always followed their fathers' occupations, castes could not think of eating together, and inter-marriage between them was impossible.

The distribution of goods and services under such a system is not difficult to predict. The relatively small class of aristocrats enjoyed palatial living quarters complete with the pleasures of exquisite landscaping, servants in abundance, and well-stocked harems. Their clothing was of the finest silks and cottons and was adorned by the costliest products of jewellers and sword-makers. As far as the vast mass of the population was concerned, they lived in abject poverty, but at least they were reconciled to their lot by a general recognition and acceptance of their place in a strict social hierarchy. Only the unfortunate untouchables had no one to look down on and it is significant that Mahatma Ghandi called them 'Harijans' or 'The Offspring of God' as part of his attempt to lift them from centuries of servitude. Later in this chapter we shall have to assess how significant tradition and custom are in determining the distribution of income and wealth in modern Western economies.

Charity or Natural Right?

A brief word is relevant here about two other forces that can affect the allocation of the power of consumption, although they will receive fuller treatment in the next chapter. Many societies have considered it a public and private virtue for their better-off citizens to assist those less fortunate than themselves. Often, religion provides the strong moral impetus towards charity as in the case of Christianity and Islam, but Tawney's telling comments on the various and often mercenary motives behind charitable actions should always be kept in mind.[4] It is

[4] R. H. Tawny, *Religion and the Rise of Capitalism* (Pelican Books, 1938).

unlikely that charity has ever led to a significant redistribution of income and wealth, while the recipients of such assistance have often had to give up some of their personal freedoms in order to qualify for it. These days we usually expect people in need of help to be entitled to it 'as of right' and that there should be no loss of human dignity in the acceptance of such help. The 'rights' that people may feel entitled to will change over time in much the same way that acceptable living standards adjust to past and present circumstances. Occasionally, some definition of human rights at the religious, political and economic level is enshrined in a widely accepted code such as the Constitution of the USA or the Charter of the United Nations, but these pronouncements tend to be less effective than the practical legislation and action of governments in their day-to-day wielding of political and economic power.

THE ALLOCATION OF CONSUMPTION POWER BY THE MARKET

In the previous chapter it was suggested that a basic characteristic of Western capitalist economies is a general belief in, and reliance on, the market mechanism as the method for the allocation of economic resources. We need now to examine how far market forces determine the extent of the individual's and the family's command over goods and services as well as the way that power is used. Table 7.1 shows the sources and distribution of factor incomes in the UK in 1972 and the average percentage distribution over the decade 1962-72.

Table 7.1   UK Factor Incomes Before Tax

		1972 £ millions	% 1972	Av. % 1962-72
Wages and salaries—including pay of HM forces and employers' NI contributions		37,138	68.2	67.9
Professional persons	866			
Farmers	986			
Other sole traders & partners	2,912			
Self-employed total	4,764	4,764	8.8	8.3
Gross trading profits of companies		6,584	12.1	13.4
„ „ „ „ public enterprises		1,790	3.3	3.5
Rent		4.182	7.6	6.9
Total domestic income		54,458	100.0	100.0

Source National Income and Expenditure Blue Book 1973, Tables 1 and 19.

One important point to remember is that the Table shows the original sources of income for the population as a whole. Any individual household will often be receiving income from more than one of the sources mentioned, but note that this table excludes incomes received in the form of social security payments, etc. The combined effects of taxation and social security benefits can be very important in the case of individual incomes, as we shall see in the next chapter. Table 7.1 is intended to focus on payments for the use of the various factors of production. The self-employment category, for example, represents the payments to those who run their own business, although a casual observer may be unable to detect any difference in the behaviour of a window-cleaner or a managing director according to whether he is a paid employee or running his own business. The essential difference between employed and self-employed is that the latter supplies his own capital and resources to his business and has a much deeper commitment to the success or failure of its operations. The rewards to the self-employed, then, are a mixture of a number of elements such as payment for labour services, interest on capital invested, and profits on risks undertaken. The determination of the rate of payment to each of the services provided will now be considered.

Profits

The previous chapter dealt with the usual justifications for the existence of profits as a motive or reward for the taking of risks and for the organisation of business activity. It is difficult however to explain or justify particular levels of profit. It is a long-standing presumption that the taking of high risks requires the potential of high profits to offset potentially high losses. But in addition, as we suggested in Chapter 4, the competitive process would tend to set the rate of return or profit regarded as acceptable or normal in a particular trade.

In practice of course one can usually find sound reasons why profits are higher in some businesses than others, and these might include the following: (a) Some businesses are more efficient than others and therefore have lower costs, (b) the extent to which the business has monopoly power over the consumer either because of deliberate strategy or just good fortune, (c) the extent to which the business can control the prices it pays for the services and goods it buys into the business.

The question of the profitability of business and the return to entrepreneurship has become more complex in modern economies with the growing division between the ownership and control and increasing government regulation of profit rates (see Chapters 6 and 10).

Interest

Classical economists explained the determination of the market rate of interest in terms of the supply of savings and demand for investment funds. There are many different interest rates ruling in the money market at any one time because there are in practice many separate markets for particular kinds of money linked together in a very complex way. Here are some of the reasons why rates will vary from market to market: (*a*) The use to which the money will be put and the degree of risk associated with it, (*b*) the security or collateral that can be provided by the borrowerer, (*c*) the length of the loan and the ease with which it can be recalled, (*d*) the general supply and demand conditions for money, (*e*) the degree of ignorance and/or desperation of the borrowerer, and, (*f*) the avarice of the lender. The last two factors are not normally referred to the textbooks since they are not believed to be very important in Western economies, but a brief examination of the plight of those impoverished rural peasants in Asia and Latin America who have fallen into the hands of the village money-lenders will convince one that these points are worth making. The medieval Christian Church held that usury or the taking of interest rates was a sin, and there is still a widespread sense of moral revulsion against 'excessive' interest rates, especially when the borrower is in desperate need of funds. It is significant that UK governments have often subsidised the interest paid on house mortgages but not the hire-purchase charges on washing machines, because a roof over one's head has been given a special social significance.

Rent

This is the price paid for the use of land and property. Rent levels will be mainly determined by the forces of supply and demand. The rent that anyone is prepared to pay will depend on his assessment of the potential satisfaction or profit that he expects to get from the use of the land or property. The owner of the property will have to decide on the relative merits of using the property himself and of charging somebody else for letting them have the use of it. Governmental intervention in the market for rented property has most often been in the form of fixing or regulating house or flat rentals in situations where the demand and supply conditions were pushing rents beyond the means a large number of people. The rents of commercial or industrial properties are not normally regulated.

Further Consideration of Table 7.1

The proportions of total income in Table 7.1 are not constant over time, and important developments in the nature of an economy will show up in such a table. In a predominantly agricultural country characterised by large numbers of absentee landlords, we would expect the rent share to be larger; but if there were a large landowning peasantry then the self-employed sector would be larger.

In the Uk, as well as in many other Western countries, there has been a tendency for the share of total factor incomes which takes the form of salaries to increase over the last fifty years, while the self-employed share has declined, and this is mainly a reflection of the decline in the number of small independent businesses and the steady expansion in the importance of the large joint-stock companies managed by paid employees (see Chapter 10).

On the other hand, another feature of most Western economies has been the remarkable long-run stability in the share of total income going to labour as a factor of production. There have been short-run changes in relative shares of course, especially during periods of recession or rapid economic growth, but the shares have always come back to their original level. An attempt to explain this phenomenon is beyond the scope of this book and the explanations (and their implications for the long-run effectiveness of trade union activity) are in any case highly controversial.

WHAT IS LABOUR WORTH?

If we can answer the above question, we shall have explained nearly three-quarters of UK sources of income. As with interest, rent and profits, the forces of the market process will be seen to be of great significance but by no means the whole story.

Payment According to Output or Contribution

The theory most often used by Western economists to explain how wage rates are determined is the 'mariginal productivity theory'. Put very simply, the argument goes like this: Assume that there is an inexhaustible supply of labour of uniform quality available to the labour market and that it is willing to move freely between jobs. An employer will need labour in order to keep his business in operation. This employer is only one of very many all competing for labour so we have a highly competitive situation on both the supply and demand sides of the labour market. The employer hires men one at a time until he reaches the 'ideal' number of workers. As each man is hired, the employer will assess the extra revenue that will be earned by the firm as a result of this man's labour: this last man added to the work-force we could think of as the 'marginal' employee, and the value of the increase in total output that results is the 'marginal revenue product'. The employer now compares this marginal revenue product with the extra wage costs that arise from hiring the marginal man — this is called the 'marginal cost' of labour. As long as the marginal revenue product is greater than the marginal cost of labour, the man will be employed. The 'ideal' size labour force will be hired at that point where marginal revenue product equals marginal cost i.e. the wage rate. The labour force is 'ideal' because it will be maximising the employer's profits, and the wage rate for the last man will equal his marginal product. Figure 7.1 illustrates some aspects of this theory.

Figure 7.1   The Demand for Labour and the Wage Rate

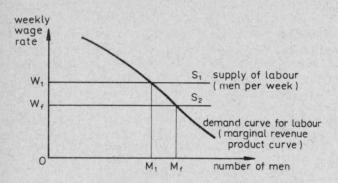

The supply curve for labour is horizontal in Figure 7.1 because it is assumed that there is an unlimited supply of labour available at a wage rate of W_1. The marginal revenue product of labour falls because it is assumed that labour output falls as more and more workers are crammed into a given capacity factory or office (i.e. diminishing returns to labour input). Now assume that the diagram is a summary of the position for the entire economy and that there are altogether M_f workers willing an anxious to work. At the wage rate of W_1 only M_1 workers would be employed, and it would seem that the only way for the employers to take up the surplus labour would be a reduction in the general wage rate to W_f. Hence the general conclusion that the wages paid to any given available labour supply will depend on its marginal product.

One reason why the marginal revenue product theory has proved popular for a century or so is that it seems to be not only an explanation of wage rate determination, but also a 'fair' solution to the allocation problem, since workers can be seen to be paid what they deserve in relationship to their contribution to the productive process.

This simple approach becomes unsuitable, however, once we introduce the complications associated with the willingness of labour to be hired. The classical economists of the early nineteenth century used the concept of 'subsistence wages' to indicate the minimum payment necessary to keep the existing labour force alive and just reproducing itself. The implications of this idea were extended to suggest that any payments to labour over and above subsistence would either reduce the labour supply by encouraging idleness, drunkenness or worse, or would lead to a rise in the birth rate which would ultimately increase the labour supply to the point where wages would be competed back to the subsistence level again. It should be obvious by now from the earlier chapters of this book that the accumulation of capital and technological progress in developed countries not only allowed wages to be paid well above subsistence levels, but also led to worker/consumers so adjusting their life-styles that their willingness to work at certain wage levels has become more important than mere survival. In much of the developing world of course, as we shall see in Chapter 11, the so-called 'iron law of subsistence wages' is unfortunately still very relevant.

Now consider Figure 7.2 which illustrates the case where the employer is large and the labour supply is limited. A minimum wage rate exists but is now determined not by subsistence, but by, say, nationally organised trade union bargaining. The employer needs M_1

Figure 7.2   Wage Rate Determination and Bargaining Strength

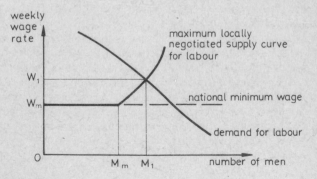

men in order to run his business effectively, but can only attract M_m workers at the minimum wage. To recruit his required work force and to hold on to it, he must offer all his workers the rates necessary to attract the last few employees he needs. The supply curve of labour therefore rises as more men are hired. Wage bargaining could be seen as taking place between the limits set on the one hand by the national minimum wage and the marginal revenue product of labour on the other. If workers are in a weak bargaining position locally, the employer may get his employees at only a little above W_m, but a strongly unionised work-force could insist on W_1.

To Assess Productivity we Need a Measurable Product

As we have just suggested, an industrial process carried out by a complex of installed machinery and plant may require a certain number of workers to enable it to work efficiency — indeed, it may not be able to operate at all with below a critical number of workers. The employer will not then be engaging men one at a time, but rather hiring a team of workers. Trade unions and workers have not been slow to realise that in many modern integrated process-industries the absence or strike of a handful of men can bring the plant to a halt. As business and industry become organised into larger and more closely integrated units, so the joint responsibility of every worker for the final product becomes more pronounced. In these situations, however, what meaning can be placed on the concept of the 'marginal product' or the 'marginal worker'? It is clearly ridiculous to claim that the last man employed to complete the team was responsible for the entire output of the plant, while all the others produced nothing.

A further difficulty in the practical application of the marginal productivity theory arises in the area of the public services. The concept of marginal revenue product that has so far been discussed clearly implies that there is a product or service to be sold. Some 25 per cent of those employed in the UK are paid by public authorities, and they range from civil servants, teachers, local authority road workers to doctors and scientists. The public does not normally pay directly for the services of these people and hence there is rarely a market price for their output. Public employees have sometime sought to establish the principle that they should be paid the wages and salaries that equivalent employees can earn in private employment. This makes some sense for some groups such as the professions and some manual workers where a large part of that kind of labour is employed in the private sector. But the vast majority of nurses, teachers and, of course, *all* civil servants are employed by public authorities, and the small

private markets that may exist are not likely to be a satisfactory guide.. Public bodies, in such circumstances, are instrumental in determining the stanard of living of their employees.

Figure 7.3   Distribution of Gross Weekly Earnings of Manual and Non-Manual Male Workers over 21 years (Great Britain) as at April 1972

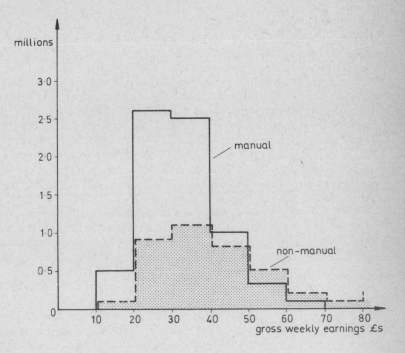

Source   Table 45, 'Social Trends No. 4', (HMSO, 1973).

Figure 7.4   Cumulative Distribution of Gross Earnings of Manual and Non-manual Workers as at April 1972 Great Britain.

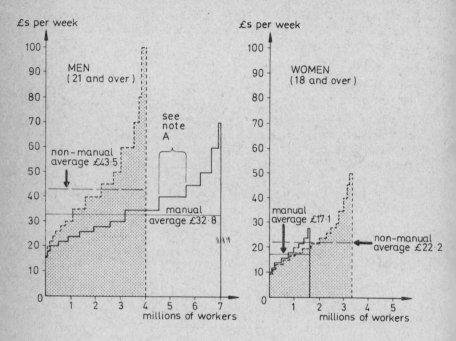

Note A   The diagram indicates at this point that 1.1 million workers were earning between £35 and £40 per week.

Source   Table 45, 'Social Trends No. 4', (HMSO, 1973).

The Non-Monetary Rewards and Dis-Benefits of Work

It should be recognised that the payment for labour services is not always in a money form, and that therefore money wages do not give a complete picture. Sometimes there are payments in kind, such as free coal for miners, cheap housing for policemen, or company cars and flats for company executives, but these can be fairly easily evaluated in money terms. Much more difficult to evaluate are the more intangible benefits or dis-benefits of a particular job, such as social status, danger or inconvenience. In theory, workers should be prepared to work for a lower wage if the job they do is in itself pleasant and satisfying but should demand more payment for dirty and unpleasant jobs. Before Figure 7.2 could be used to illustrate such occupations, the supply curve for labour would have to be adjusted, if possible, for these non-tangible rewards and disadvantages. (The reader might like to pursue for himself the question of whether the presence of considerable intangible benefits will affect the bargaining power of workers such as nurses and teachers!)

Wages and Salaries in Practice

There are various ways that the pattern of incomes received can be displayed. One common method is shown in Figure 7.3 which is essentially a bar-chart indicating how many workers there are in each earnings band, e.g. there were about $2\frac{1}{2}$ million manual workers earning between £30 and £40 per week in the UK in 1972, while there were only about 1.1 million non-manual workers earning the same amounts. The pattern or 'distribution' in Figure 7.3 demonstrates a typical feature of both wage rates and earnings levels, and that is the lack of symmetry in the distribution. There tend to be more 'steps' to the right of the highest bars than to the left, i.e. at higher income ranges. This phenomenon seems to be linked to the nature of wage differentials and will be consider on pp. 128-9.

What the diagram does not clearly show are the earnings relativities, and this is why we have presented basically the same information in the alternative format of Figure 7.4. This time we show the gross weekly earnings of both men and women manual and non-manual workers. The reader can check that, as in Figure 7.3, some $2\frac{1}{2}$ million manual male workers were earning between £30 and £40 per week (Note A in Figure 7.4 should help in understanding the chart). The diagram shows gross earnings which include overtime payments and bonuses rather than bare wage rates, but this need cause us little difficulty since the cost still has to be borne by the employers and there is some evidence that workers tend to regard regular overtime and bonuses as part of their normal payment for the job. A number of points can be derived immediately from Figure 7.4:

1. The range of earnings is large. At the top of the manual workers range a few men are earning twice the average of this group and four times the lowest rate. In the non-manual group, the range is wider still with the top-paid men getting eight times that of the lowest paid but still twice the average level.
2. Women are generally paid substantially less than men, with the average man earning nearly twice that of the average woman.

3. Only about 1½ million manual workers out of a total of 7 million are in the range £30-£35 p.w., which includes the average for manual workers, and thus emphasises how misleading averages can be.

4. Non-manual workers earn, on average (remember 3 above!) about one-third more than manual workers.

5. The better paid manual workers earn more than the lowest paid white-collar workers.

6. There are twice as many female non-manual workers as female manual workers — the reverse is roughly true for men.

At the top end of the non-manual workers scale you will find company directors and senior executives, managers, engineers, scientists, academics and the professions — law, medicine, accountancy. Among those at the bottom end of the manual scale are catering, domestic and hotel staff, farm workers, and employees in the textile and clothing industries. This pattern applies to both male and female workers.

If we are to accept the argument on p. 121ff, we need to be able to demonstrate that the differences in payment that we have been observing can be explained in terms of the differing contributions workers make to the well-being of the employer. Unlike the assumption made in Figure 7.1, we know that people vary considerably in their natural abilities, their education and training, their determination, temper and general physical attributes. It would not be surprising, then, if individuals made very differing contributions, but are they paid according to their contributions?

SOME COMPLICATIONS IN THE LABOUR MARKET

Group Differentials

Whether the reasons be economic or social, over time, workers find themselves established in certain group relationships. A hierarchy is evolved such that skilled workers always get paid more than the unskilled in a particular industry, and groups of approximately the same level of skill but in different industries will tend to compare their relative status and pay. This could be explained simply in terms of supply and demand and relative productivity, but once established, the human propensity to consolidate positions in society together with the other rigidities in the labour market that will be noted below, all tend to harden and perpetuate relativities. Occasionally, this question of comparability becomes a major issue in wage negotiations, as it did in the Guillebaud Committee report[5] on railway wages in 1960, when it was claimed that railwaymen should be paid a similar amount to those doing roughly comparable jobs in other industries. A very com-

[5]Report of the Railway Pay Committee of Inquiry, March 1960.

mon cause of industrial dispute in some industries is the discovery that some employers are paying more for the same kind of work than others. There are also frequent labour problems arising from awards of pay that close the gap between skilled and unskilled workers, even though the market forces favour the unskilled. There is no doubt that existing differentials tend to be very durable even when under strong market pressure for change, and in these circumstances current wage rates may for some time represent past market valuations rather than up-to-date values. The lack of symmetry in the distribution of earnings indicated in Figure 7.3 may well be the result of determining differentials in percentage terms rather than absolute terms, as the reader can quickly test for himself by adding 50 per cent to a given range of income levels. Sometimes observed differentials seem quite illogical, and it has been suggested that once high relative pay levels have been established for whatever reasons, this high relative status will also grant high social status to the job, which will then be used in turn to justify the continuation of high rewards.

Are Women Underpaid? Consider again the generally lower payments to women indicated in Figure 7.4. It is widely accepted that various types of intelligence and ability are distributed among any human population in a particular way, that is the so-called 'normal' distribution. In the normal distribution, most people are clustered around the measured average or mean level, while a few people are distributed symmetrically around the mean or average at the upper and lower ends of the scale. The general shape of the normal distribution is shown by the dotted line in Figure 7.5. Let us assume that intelligence (however measured) is a major determinant of an employee's contribution to an organisation, and insert the actual distribution of non-manual earnings in the UK for 1972. The result is something like Figure 7.5. The distribution of male earnings is flatter and less regular than the assumed normal distribution, but the distribution for women is wildly skewed towards the lower levels. Who will dare deny that women are just as intelligent as men? The reason for the divergence is not, we will assume, a matter of intelligence but rather the status and role of women in society. Women are frequently paid less than men even whey are doing the same work, but equally important is the fact that there are fewer women than men in the better-paid jobs.

This pattern of lower female earnings is common in most countries of the Western world, and arises from centuries of social, political and even religious attitudes that have restricted the opportunities available to women for personal and economic development within male dominated societies. Does this mean that employers have deliberately exploited women by paying them less than their productivity deserved or have deliberately not been prepared to hire potentially highly profitable labour? One way to answer this controversial question might be to observe the results of legislation introduced to enforce equal pay for equal work and to ensure equal opportunities for women. If employers have been exploiting female labour, then equal pay legislation should merely cut the employer's profit margin. If employers could only stay in business because they were able to employ cheap female labour, then equal pay could lead to female unemployment. Should the employer be convinced that women *are* inferior to his male employees, then we should expect the prospects of the lower-paid male labour force to improve at the expense of female labour. The legislation at present in force in the UK has not yet had sufficient effect for these propositions to be tested, but by the late 1970s some of these questions should be answered.

Figure 7.5   The Distribution of Men and Women's Earnings in Full-time Non-Manual employment as at April 1972 UK.

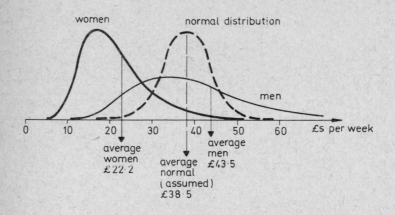

Source   (Diagram based on chart on page 104 of 'Social Trends No. 4', HMSO, 1973).

Training and Education One major reason for there being many fewer women than men in the better-paid jobs is that there are fewer women with the necessary higher education and training to qualify for those jobs. Society in general may have restricted the educational opportunities for women, but quite often employees have themselves limited entrance to training programmes. The apprenticeship system has for centuries been both a way to provide trained and skilled manpower and a way to keep down the number of qualified entrants into the trade. By restricting the supply, the price of the skill can be kept up and the future employment prospects secured, a situation that has appealed to the professions and skilled manual trades alike.

It has often been argued that money and time spent on education and training is a form of investment in human resources (see Chapter 8), and that the higher rewards subsequently obtained should be seen as both interest and profit on this investment. Unfortunately, although this interpretation may seem reasonable where the market mechanism is working freely and competitively, the rewards may in practice be partly in the form of monopoly profits if access to this investment is restricted. Nevertheless, it is often accepted that the contribution of the better educated and more highly skilled is greater than those less well qualified, and that in any case inducements will be necessary to persuade people to undertake the effort of acquiring skills. Inevitably however, those born with the highest natural ability tend to be those that go highest up the qualification ladder and hence the arbitrariness of birth may dominate what may appear to be a 'fair' system of allocating income.

Trade Union Activity Trade unions are set up to look after the interests of their members but they only become really effective in forcing employers to take notice of their representations when they can control all or a large percentage of the labour available to the employer. Taken to its extreme, this idea leads to the 'closed shop' situation where the union is able to insist that only union labour is employed. A widespread feature of trade union activity in the Western world is nationally organised wage bargaining on behalf of all the workers in a particular industry or with a particular skill. As we saw in Figure 7.2, the employer faced with this form of collective bargaining in fact faces a fixed minimum price for labour. Quite often the employer will be involved in further negotiations at the factory level that may raise the actual payments to his employees above the nationally agreed level. Imagine that the horizontal minimum wage line in Figure 7.2 is steadily raised. The diagram would then suggest that union action was gradually reducing employment possibilities and unemployment would rise. This is certainly a possibility, but unions are aware of the danger and try to prevent redundancy occuring in various ways:

1. The unions may argue that the employer should take a lower profit margin so that workers can be paid more than their presumed marginal product without an increase in the price of the product. More often, of course, the employer will try to maintain his profit levels by passing on the increased wage costs in higher prices. This is easier to do if the demand for his products is not likely to be greatly affected by price increases, for example in times of consumer boom.

2. The union may be able to force the employer to keep more men on his payroll than he needs. This most often occurs when there have been technological improvements which cut manpower needs or when the employer's demand for labour fluctuates frequently.

3. The union may co-operate with the employer to raise general productivity in return for increased pay.

Under highly competitive conditions with an unrestricted and uniform work force it was predicted that wages would tend to equality in all occupations. As has been pointed out in earlier sections of this chapter, labour is not uniform in quality, neither is it in unlimited supply to any occupation, nor does it move freely from occupation to occupation. Individuals place additional restrictions on their freedom of movement in the form perhaps of special preferences for particular types of work or in the form of family and social ties to certain localities. It should now be clear that there is not one labour market but a whole series of markets, some of which are closely linked together while others exist in almost watertight compartments.

WEALTH AND INCOME

Income can be measured in terms of a flow of payments over given time periods such as weeks, months or years. Capital and wealth, on the other hand, is measurable only as a stock which has a value fixed at some particular point in time. The ownership of wealth is important to us in this chapter because it is a source of actual and potential income and is therefore a determinant of an individual's command over future flows of resources as well as command over current resources.

The Wealth Cycle

Wealth can be accumulated in very many ways, some of which were outlined in the previous chapter. We have, for example, the stereotype self-made man who scrimps and saves to build up his capital and who steadily ploughs back his profits into his business. The very simple process of accumulation over a lifetime will itself ensure that older people will tend to have more wealth than the young. In this section, however, we wish to concentrate on a particular process by which wealth is distributed and accumulated — inheritance.

Research[6] in the UK has shown that a man is much more likely to leave a high value estate to his heirs if he has already inherited a substantial amount himself. This may not be surprising, but it is worth having the point made that paterns of inheritance are important in determining the distribution of wealth. Furthermore, it helps to explain why the distribution of wealth in a capitalist economy will always tend towards inequality unless very strong measures are taken to counteract the reinforcement cycle. Figure 7.6 illustrates a hypothetical life-cycle for the son of a wealthy father in Britain.

Figure 7.6   Hypothetical Reinforcement Cycle for Wealthy

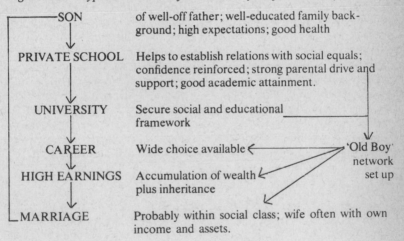

SON	of well-off father; well-educated family background; high expectations; good health
PRIVATE SCHOOL	Helps to establish relations with social equals; confidence reinforced; strong parental drive and support; good academic attainment.
UNIVERSITY	Secure social and educational framework
CAREER	Wide choice available
HIGH EARNINGS	Accumulation of wealth plus inheritance
	'Old Boy' network set up
MARRIAGE	Probably within social class; wife often with own income and assets.

The reinforcement process will be strengthen by such factors as:
(a) The right of primogeniture preventing the break-up of estates.
(b) Low or ineffective taxes on the inheritance and holding of wealth.
(c) A low level of social mobility.
(d) Restrictions on the opportunities for low wealth holders to acquire wealth.
(e) An economic and social system that grants high rewards to the successful but which discriminates against the failures.

[6] C. D. Harbury and P. C. McMahon, 'Inheritance and the Characteristics of Top Wealth Leavers in Britain' in *Economic Journal*, September, 1973).

A Cycle of Poverty

Poverty also produces a reinforcement process that has been called the poverty 'trap'. Such a cycle of poverty may run as follows:[7] a man with poor educational qualifications is likely to be restricted to an un-skilled job which carries low pay; low pay can lead to the man's family living in bad housing conditions on an inadequate diet and with a poor cultural environment; the children of the family (and there are likely to be many) are hindered in their educational development by their home background while the health of the head of the household and the mother suffers; this can lead to the mother neglecting her children and an erratic working life for the father. In many cases the result of this accumulation of handicaps is unemployment, homelessness, psy-chological disorder and family break-up. The unfortunate children have a tendency to go through the same cycle as their parents.

On another level, this concept of economic flows and forces tending to perpetuate and reinforce themselves has been used to explain the growing divergencies between the rich and the poor nations of the world (see Chapter 11). It has not been the intention of the last two sections to suggest that movement up and down the social and economic hierarchy is impossible, but rather to suggest that there is some stability at the top and bottom. There is normally constant movement, but a measure of the extent to which groups change their social and economic rankings (the former tends to lag behind the latter) could be a good indicator of how 'open' the society is. It is often argued that even if everyone was born socially and economically equal in a market economy, general inequality would develop within one generation. If this were so, the existence and the nature of barriers to movement would be of more interest than the actual degree of ine-quality observed. In our view, however, most of the world's societies are far from being 'open'.

How Unequal is the Distribution of Income and Wealth?

This is clearly a question of great interest, but not one that is easily answered. In the first place there is no single entirely satisfactory index of inequality in a society. Secondly, even if such an index were to be widely accepted, comparisons made over time or with other societies are not in themselves necessarily very illuminating. The scale of ine-quality is well illustrated by Figure 7.7 which is based on a suggestion by Jan Pen.[8] Annual income before and after tax is shown on the ver-

---

[7]D. Jackson, *Poverty,* (Macmillan, 1972).   [8]J. Pen, *Income Distribution,* (Allen Lane, The Penguin Press, 1971).

tical axis and the number of income holders on the horizontal. In this respect, the diagram is constructed in the same way as Figure 7.4, but this time total income is illustrated whether earned or 'unearned', i.e. derived from land or capital. The diagram is based on figures for individual incomes (compare number of incomes with the UK population of 55.7 million in 1970) and will not therefore give an adequate picture of the income of particular households which may contain more than one income receiver.

Figure 7.7   UK Distribution of Personal Incomes before and after Tax, 1970-71

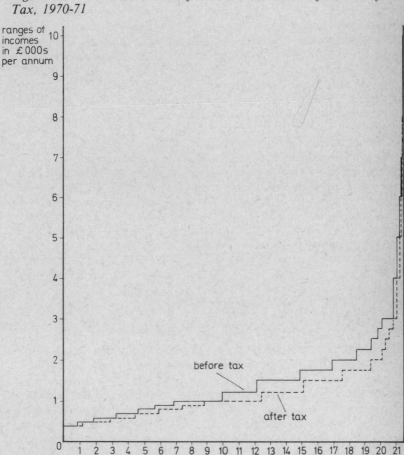

Source   Survey of Personal Incomes 1970-71, Inland Revenue, HMSO.

Figure 7.8   Estimated Distribution of Wealth 1971 (UK).

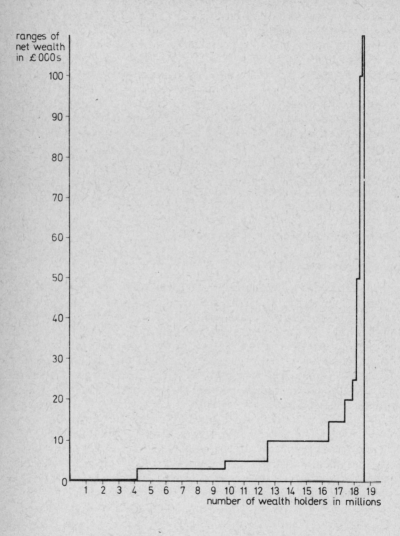

Source Annual Digest of Statistics

The diagram does bring out well the relativities of income receivers with half the number of pre-tax incomes in 1970-71 at or below £1,000 p.a. and about a quarter of about £2,000 p.a. and above. The extremes of income are dramatic on the diagram and would be even more so if the very few highest income holders were correctly shown, but this would require us to have a vertical scale that extended three times the height of that in Figure 7.7.

The distribution of wealth is also difficult to illustrate. The statistics on wealth holdings are subject to considerable errors since they are usually based in Britain on returns arising from the payment of estates duties. Most people in Britain do not have enough wealth to be liable to estate duty, while the wealthy find various ways to avoid paying it. There are also very great problems in placing valuations on many types of asset. In spite of these difficulties, there is enough evidence to suggest that wealth is even more unequally distributed than is income in the UK. Figure 7.8 is drawn on the same lines as Figure 7.7, and simple visual inspection will suggest that wealth is concentrated in fewer hands than is income. The same dramatic difference in relative wealth holdings remains and is probably compounded when one realises that those with the greatest wealth tend to be also those with the highest incomes.

A 'FAIR' DISTRIBUTION?

Having looked at various aspects of the way people are rewarded for effort and the way they accumulate wealth, can one conclude that the results are 'fair' and 'reasonable'? There are undoubtedly strong market forces of supply and demand that can be observed at work in the labour market, but there are also many examples of market manipulation and social constraint. We might expect that the more developed a market economy is, the stronger will be the effects of supply and demand and the weaker the influence of command and custom. Expectations may not be fulfilled however, and a detailed study of particular economies is necessary to determine the balance of forces. Even if the markets are working relatively smoothly, the working of cycles of reinforcement will tend to reproduce past patterns in a way that could be called 'fortune' rather than 'fair'. We must conclude that 'fairness' is not a concept that can be handled by market forces alone, and much of the next chapter will be concerned with collective action towards socially acceptable solutions.

Chapter 8

Aspects of Collective Consumption

ON SHARING AND SELFISHNESS

In spite of the many examples already produced in this book showing man's behaviour in a social setting, it is worth remembering that economic man is depicted in traditional economic theory as a solitary creature motivated by self-interest. The discussion of economic relationshps often begins by simplifying to the individual, perhaps a Robinson Crusoe figure on a deserted island where self-interest is obviously paramount. As more complex relationships are built up, however, there is still a tendency to see these relationships as being between individualised bodies, i.e. the household, the firm, the Government. What can be and often is overlooked when this approach is taken is that these 'individual' decision units are usually collective or social units. The behaviour observed in a given unit will normally be the result of complex decisions within a group context as when household spending depends on a balance between the competing needs of parents and children. It is this group dynamic that has so often been neglected in the past.

The areas of social and collective decision-making that we shall explore in this chapter are those associated with acts of charity or altruism, the pooling and sharing of facilities on a voluntary basis in the form of clubs and societies, and at the public level, the provision by State and local authority of goods, services and cash for the benefit of the community at large as well as for individuals. The cynic will no doubt argue that most acts of charity and altruism are motivated deep down in man's unconscious by what are in fact selfish motives, as when gifts are made to curry favour or avoid attack. It may be believed that charity will help to store up 'riches in heaven', and that 'good works' are a way to establish one in a position of high public and social esteem. When contributions to charity are allowable for tax deductions — as they are in many countries — motives are bound to be somewhat mixed. At the national level it may indeed be difficult to detect much 'charity' in the mind of a heavy payer of taxes who sees the situation as one in which his hard-earned income is confiscated and handed over to the 'undeserving' poor in the name of public assistance. The reader must reach his own conclusions about the true nature of man's morality, and this chapter will simply be concerned to indicate some of the areas where group and collective activities and interests are more important than private interests.

VOLUNTARY ASSOCIATIONS

The Role of Charities

It is estimated that there are some quarter of a million charities of all shapes and sizes in the UK. Some of these have histories going back hundreds of years to the bequests of wealthy men grateful for having avoided the poverty of the majority of their fellow citizens. These early charities were mainly for educational purposes or for the relief of the poor and aged and were usually very small, but an outburst of growth of new charities with wider aims appeared in late Victorian England. Hundreds of new religious, missionary and educational charities sprang up alongside newer types such as friendly socities, working men's clubs, and youth organisations. Since World War II, the most typical new charities are concerned with medical research and the welfare of the young, the old, and the physically and mentally handicapped, and help for the developing world.

The motives for setting up and running a charity under modern conditions must include a strong element of idealism and altruism. Such organisations have advantages in that they can spring up quickly to meet social needs as they are recognised. Often the charity will be instrumental in discovering and then meeting areas of social distress that are at the moment not adequately covered by official public provision. Charities can pioneer and develop new methods and can operate experimentally in a way that state services would find difficult. It is perhaps significant that more charities concerned with poverty and welfare have appeared since the UK became a so-called 'welfare state' than was the case formerly. Often, having demonstrated that its activities were of real value, a charity has had its functions taken over by the State and this may be the best indicator of its success.

It is not easy to assess the importance of charities in the overall scale of things. A recent study[1] analysed some thirty-six of Britain's largest charities with incomes varying from £200,000 to £7.5 million, and es-

---

[1] Consumers Association, *Money Which?* (December 1972).

timated that in total they were spending over £71 million in 1972. Most of this money was spent on welfare services and was about 1 per cent of the central government's expenditure on similar areas. Such a calculation must understate the true value of their contribution to society since much of the work done by charities is performed by un- paid volunteers and helpers. In addition, these figures only refer to charities that depend on public contributions, and to ascertain the full impact of charitable activity we should include the vast sums paid out annually by the great foundations and trusts set up by the Nuffields and Gulbenkians of this world.

At this point an interesting juxtaposition of altruism and selfishness can be suggested. One considerable incentive for wealthy men to set up charitable trusts is that big tax liabilities can be avoided. Such ad- vantages have not escaped the corporate sector of the economy. One estimate suggests that in 1972 about £38 million was given by limited liability companies in the UK for charitable purposes. Apart from tax advantages, it would seem that companies see benefits for their public image and the future strength of their business in a judicious support for worthy causes. The ambivalence in such forms of giving are clear when tobacco companies finance cancer research and distilleries assist in the welfare of alcoholics.

Clubs and Societies

If information on the economic significance of charities is limited, there is even less data available on the economic and social significance of clubs and societies. The concept of a non-profit- making club or society implies the voluntary association of people for an agreed or common purpose. Commitment to the club is usually ob- tained by restricting membership in some way, perhaps by making an undertaking to support the ends of the society and by paying a membership fee, thereby gaining access to the activities and facilities of the club. Generalisations are difficult in view of the vast range and variety of such organisations. There are social clubs for instance which exist mainly to provide opportunities and facilities for conviviality. Then there is the proliferation of sporting clubs and associations. These exist to provide the facilities for training and practice and to assist in the organisation of the competitive activity that is of such vital importance to sportsmen. Some sports such as golf, yachting and rac- ing require facilities that are normally beyond the means of individuals and hence co-operative and collective provision is essential.

Some sports can be performed by individuals but most are group activities. Many cultural pursuits are essentially group activities — if you wish to sing in a choir or play in an orchestra or act in a play there is no alternative to combining with others of like mind. The economic significance of clubs and socieites can only be guessed at, and estimates of revenue and expenditure would again tend to undervalue the unpaid service rendered by members. If developed countries do manage to sustain their past improvements in living standards with increased leisure time, then clubs and voluntary societies will be of growing significance in the output of enjoyment, health and cultural enrichment available to those economies.

SOCIAL AND COLLECTIVE PROVISION

Is State Action Inevitable?

The mere existence of a 'state' in the sense of a geographical area ruled by an acknowledged authority must imply some kind of regulation or control of the inhabitants of that area. From the earliest times, effective governments have had to perform two basic functions, (a) the protection of the State from outside interference and attack, and (b) the provision and enforcement of a set of laws and rules dealing with social and business relationships. No matter whether the government is based on dictatorial power or democratic processes, these two functions are essential.

If one examines a typical nineteenth-century government, one finds that its major roles were in national defence and the waging of war, the preservation of law and order, and the regulation of trade both internal and external to the State. It may appear that these functions are so obviously the proper duties of government that no further analysis is necessary, but the economist has attempted to rationalise the situation by applying the concepts of 'externality' and 'joint supply'. As was pointed out on p. 138, the market economy assumes that individuals make economic decisions by comparing the potential benefits of an action with the costs associated with that action. By implication, both costs and benefits are relevant exclusively to the individual. In practice, some costs and benefits can spill over to others not directly involved. Consider a modern housing estate where a fairly uniform pattern of colour schemes is used on the houses. An individualistic plumber moves into a house in a prominent position and proceeds to have the entire premises painted in lurid colours to his own immense satisfaction. Our plumber made a private decision, but there are important public implications. Most of the other householders in the estate may be outraged by the colour scheme and may feel that the satisfaction they derived from living in the area has been considerably diminished (a few may be highly delighted, of course). The results of this particular piece of decoration are both internal and external to the plumber. The effects beyond those calculated and intended by the new owner are called 'externalities'. Closely linked to externality is the question of joint supply, since in providing the owner with pleasure, the coats of paint so vigorously applied give pleasure or pain to anyone who enters the street — the direct painting costs are unchanged no matter how many people come to wonder or to curse. Similarly, passers-by cannot be excluded from the effects of the masterpiece but are subjected to it willy-nilly. It is precisely because of problems of this nature that various authorities lay down rules and regulations or consider special taxes to avoid the worst excesses of individualism where they are likely to impinge on others. An important point made by this example is that private costs and benefits cannot always be assumed to be equivalent to social costs and benefits.

The concepts of externality, joint supply, and non-exclusivity are clearly relevant to national defence systems and to law and order provision. All inhabitants of a State are jointly supplied by a general defence system and it is difficult to imagine how they could be excluded from the benefits. A good or service which has these characteristics present at a high level is known as a 'public good'.

Very many goods and services provided by present-day governments have some of the characteristics of the public good, but as we shall see later, the degree of externality or exclusivity involved varies greatly. The major point to be understood at this stage is that goods or services with these qualities are unlikely to be supplied at the 'correct' level by the market mechanism. A citizen cannot choose just how much defence or law and order he personally will consume, because he is presented with a predetermined package. In order to calculate the value to the citzen of the defence provided we might present him with the package and ask him how much he is prepared to pay towards it. If the sum of payments from all citizens was just enough to cover the cost, then the package could be bought by the State. If the contributions were inadequate or greater than the cost, a new package could be devised and once again submitted for assessment. Apart from the sheer difficulty of mounting such a complex auction, there is another reason why valuation would be a problem. It is likely that many citizens would be convinced that the Government was going to provide a system of defence whatever private evaluations they set, and that since the cost was bound to be recovered in one way or another they might as well try to reduce their own burden by declaring an artificially low value for defence. This dependence on others paying the bill has been called the 'free rider' problem and is applicable to many areas of public life where a section of the citizenry is prepared to let others do their duty for them.

Collective Insurance

One way to ensure that one's social status can be preserved even though income suffers a sharp decline is by putting something aside out of current earnings to provide a stock of wealth that can be drawn on during lean times. One manifestation of this desire for greater security was the proliferation in nineteenth-century Britain of mutual friendly and provident societies. These would provide some assistance during sickness and a decent burial in the event of death in return for a small weekly contribution — in effect, an insurance against the workhouse and the pauper's grave. Even so, the vast majority of working people had no adequate source of income to fall back on should they be injured, ill, unemployed or just old, other than the minimal aid of public and private charity. Unfortunately, such charity as was available was not only hopelessly inadequate, but also frequently administered in ways that offended the dignity of the recipient.

As long as poverty and social distress were regarded as the result of idleness and shiftlessness, those in need could expect little help, but the investigations into urban poverty by reformers such as Booth (see Chapter 2) and Rowntree at the end of the nineteenth century shocked a generally complacent middle class into recognising the sheer scale and depth of suffering. In addition, two of the most important causes of distress could hardly be blamed on those afflicted. Booth emphasised that loss of earnings and worsening health comes with old age, while Beveridge drew attention to the increased tendency of Britain's free enterprise economy to lurch into periods of economic depression and high involuntary unemployment. The pressure for change in public and private attitudes was building up from other quarters, some internal to Britain such as the growing political awareness of the working class, and some external to the country as in the developing Anglo-German rivalry.[2] Old age pensions were introduced by Act of Parliament from 1908 and unemployment insurance and health insurance followed from 1911. Initially, only a small proportion of workers was covered, but gradually the scope and coverage of social security provision has been extended until Britain has a claim to be called a 'welfare' state.

[2]Bismark created wide-ranging schemes of social insurance in Germany between 1883 and 1888.

It should be noted that William Beveridge, the architect of most of this country's social legislation in this field from 1908 to the 1940s, always conceived of state provision in terms of publicly assisted self-help. In his view, pensions and other benefits should not be free handouts but should be paid for by the recipient out of contributions made in periods of employment and affluence. Beneficiaries would then be able to claim help as a right that they had earned and could avoid many of the stigmas attaching to the charity concept. In practice of course, as social security benefits have been extended and deepened, many people are now entitled to assistance even though they never have contributed and perhaps never will. In addition, most of the finance for the schemes comes from employers and taxpayers in general. Nevertheless, the basic principle is still officially adhered to that such benefits should be regarded as being based on compulsory contributions from those able to pay and are essentially a form of collectivised insurance. Voluntary or compulsory insurance schemes are the basis of most of the unemployment, sickness, old age and health benefits provided in developed countries and inevitably those schemes which are compulsory have the most comprehensive coverage.

Public Redistribution

Redistribution by Benefits in Cash and Kind   In Chapter 7 various aspects of the distribution of income and wealth were discussed, but the role of the State in altering that distribution was passed over. In fact social security payments in Britain have accounted for nearly 9 per cent of total post-tax income in recent years. Most of this is accounted for by the payments such as retirement pensions and unemployment benefits that were discussed in the previous section. To the extent that these benefits are provided out of contributions they are hardly redistributive (except over time), but as already noted, contributions do not cover the full cost, and in so far as the additional costs are paid for out of taxes paid by the better off members of society, there is a redistributive effect. In addition to the elements of social insurance, there are welfare payments specificially designed to help those with the lowest incomes. These range from supplementary pension payments to income supplements for the poorest families and special allowances for the disabled and handicapped. Not all benefits are paid in cash and further help is provided in such forms as cheaper food, rent and rates, or in some cases, especially where there are children at risk, various goods and services may be provided free of charge.

Redistribution by Taxation   To assess the overall impact on income distribution of social security provision, it is necessary to consider further the revenue sources that finance the schemes. Modern governments do not normally use particular taxes to pay for particular services, but rather they raise their desired revenue by pooling the proceeds of a complex system of taxation. Most taxes fall into one of two broad categories, (*a*) taxes on the income and profits of individuals and companies — direct taxes, or (*b*) taxes on the purchase or use of particular goods or services — indirect taxes. Much detailed analysis is necessary before it can be decided whether a given tax redistributes income or wealth, and there is space here to discuss only a few of the complications involved.

If everybody had one-third of their income deducted in taxation, it is true that a rich man would pay more in total money terms than a poor man, but such a tax system does not in itself alter the relative positions of each income group. It is more usual therefore for governments to operate some kind of 'progressive' income tax system that has the essential characteristic of increased percentage deductions as income levels rise. In this context, it is worth making the distinction between 'average' and 'marginal' tax rates. The average rate of income tax is the proportion of total income taken for tax. There are very many low income earners in the UK who pay no income taxes at all. Most people fall into the middle range of incomes and they pay roughly 25 per cent of their income in taxes while the very rich may pay 50 per cent or even more of their income in income taxes. These are average tax rates, but the marginal tax rates people face may be much higher. The marginal tax rate is the percentage of any additional income received that goes in taxes. For the middle income group, the marginal tax rate is around 30 per cent in the UK, but for the highest income groups 70 per cent or 80 per cent of an extra £100 earned can be deducted for tax. There are in addition even higher rates on 'unearned' income. Surprisingly perhaps, many low income earners also face a high marginal tax rate. This is because a number of benefits in cash or kind are paid only after an assessment of 'need' and 'means', of which current income is a major determinant. For those in receipt of such benefits, an increase in earnings can mean the loss of the earnings-related benefits and the net increase in income may be very small. Old age pensioners can also find themselves facing quite high marginal tax levels if they go out to work while in receipt of a pension. It is often argued that very high marginal tax rates will act as a deterrent to effort and initiative, but the evidence is not conclusive and is in any case almost entirely confined to studies of the work behaviour of the better off. Our concern at this point is to emphasise that an assessment of the redistributive effects of state policy must include both taxes and benefits.

Before indirect taxes can be classified as being redistributive in effect, we must first consider the consumption patterns of the income group in question. Taxes on food, clothing and tobacco are generally regarded as having an adverse effect on the poor since these items form a large part of their budget (Chapter 2). For this reason it is quite common to find that so-called 'luxury' goods carry higher than average taxes, while 'essentials' have low or zero rates.

Figure 8.1　The Combined Impact of Benefits less Taxes: UK 1971

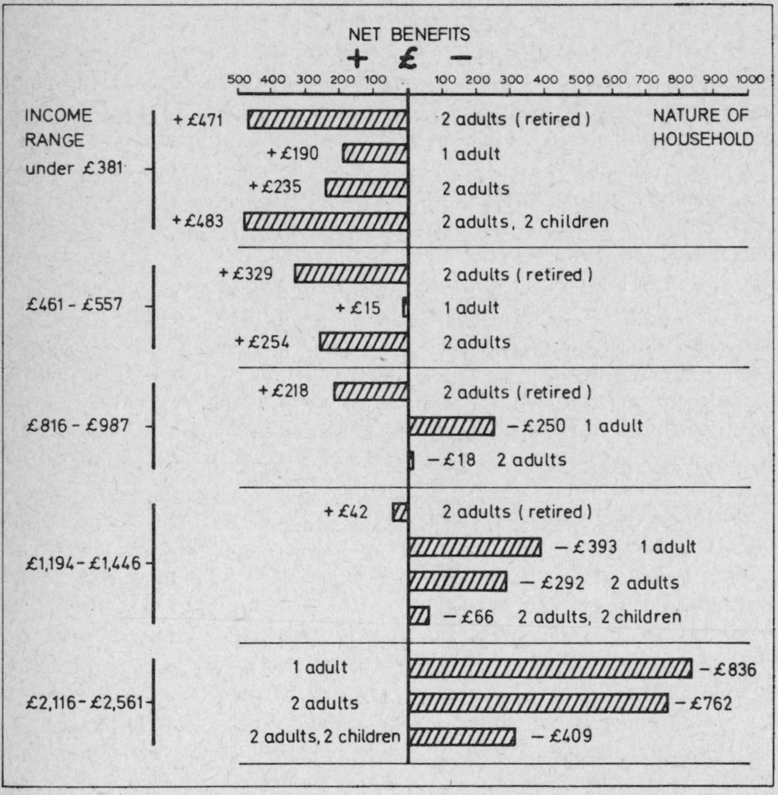

Source　Social Trends No. 4, 1973, HMSO

The Distributive Effects of Taxes and Benefits Combined The combined effects of social benefits and taxes in the UK for 1971 is indicated in Figure 8.1. The length of the bars to the left of the centre line show the extent to which the value of estimated benefits received outweighs the value of taxes paid for different income and family groups. Benefits are here defined to include all cash benefits plus the estimated value of educational and health services and welfare foods received. It is clear that at incomes below about £800 p.a., net benefits generally exceed taxes paid. As the income level rises so the taxes increasingly outweigh benefits. Note that families with children are more favourably treated than two adult families in the same income group. This is partly because allowances against income tax rise with the number or children in a family and partly because there are larger totals of benefits in cash and kind accruing to the larger family.

The chart is intended only to indicate the general tenor of the redistributive effects of taxes and benefits and caution should be exercised in its interpretation. The estimated value of the educational, health and welfare foods supplied to a family may not seem relevant to that household if it feels that what it really needs is extra cash. The estimates are in any case based on a voluntary sample survey of family expenditure budgets and may therefore reflect the position in the better regulated households. It is also known that many households that are entitled to various social benefits do not in fact claim them — a problem especially severe with those in the poverty trap or in old age. The actual income bounds are also continually disturbed by inflation. Since income taxes and many benefits are directly linked to money income, the liability and entitlement levels need to be constantly revised in times of rapid inflation. Hence, Figure 8.1 gives only an impressionistic indication of the actual impact of benefits and taxes.

We have been concerned so far with current flows of benefit and tax, but Figure 8.1 does not adequately reflect all the aspects of redistribution by the Government. The Table shows the balance of tax and benefit on individuals and households, but a major source of state revenues are the taxes on companies. A large part of company profits are used to pay dividends to shareholders and this is then covered as income in the Table, but a significant part of company profit is used for the purchase of new plant and machinery and all manner of assets that enhance the value of the company and it shares, and thus the wealth of the shareholders. The ownership of wealth has important effects on purchasing power as was pointed out in Chapter 7, but the taxation of wealth is far from being as comprehensive as the taxation of income in this world. Where countries have introduced wealth taxes they tend to be of three main types, (*a*) an annual levy on current wealth holdings, (*b*) a tax on gifts during the life of the donor, and (*c*) taxes on the estates of the deceased. In the UK, the wealth tax that has been levied for the last seventy years is essentially of type (*c*). Its main effect seems to have been to redistribute wealth from the extremely wealthy to the very wealthy. The main reasons for this lack of wider impact are firstly that it has proved too easy to arrange one's affairs so as to avoid the full burden of the tax, and secondly, the tax has been charged against the value of the wealth of the deceased and not against the wealth of the inheritor. From 1974, the estate duty is replaced by a gifts tax levied on the transfer of wealth where the tax rate is related to the value of gifts that the donor has made over his lifetime. A further tax of type (*a*) is planned for introduction in 1976.

Collective Consumption and Investment

On pp. 141-142 we considered some of the theoretical and practical reasons why public authorities have found it necessary to perform certain functions and to supply certain goods and services. The characteristics of a public good were linked to a discussion of defence

Table 8.1   The Pattern of Public Expenditure in the UK (1972 and 1961)

Function	£ millions 1972	%	1961 %
Social security	5,119	18.9	15.8
Health and personal social services	3,191	11.8	10.5
Education	3,508	12.9	9.8
Housing	1,449	5.3	5.4
Environmental services	1,321	4.9	3.8
Libraries, museums and the Arts	130	0.5	0.3
Justice and law	731	2.7	3.0
Roads and public lighting	934	3.4	2.7
Transport and communication	1,016	3.7	5.1
Commerce and industry	2,998	11.0	11.7
Defence and external relations	3,465	12.8	18.0
Other expenditure	862	3.2	2.8
Debt interest	2,420	8.9	12.2
	27,144	100.0	100.0

Source   Table 168, 'Social Trends' No. 4, 1973, and Blue Book HMSO.

and law and order, but when the range of goods and services currently provided by the governments of the world, especially in western Europe, is examined, the 'public good' approach is seen to be inadequate. Table 8.1 shows the main areas of central and local government expenditure for 1972 in the UK.

It will be noted that in 1972 under 16 per cent (down from 21 per cent in 1961) of the total expenditure is for the purposes of defence and law and order, while the collective insurance of social security provision comes to nearly 19 per cent (under 16 per cent in 1961). How far can public good criteria be applied to the major expenditures remaining? Roads and public lighting and many of the environmental services such as sewage disposal do often display joint supply characteristics as is easily demonstrated if one tries to imagine street pavements provided for the sole use of ticket holders! When the State or local authority spends money on education, personal health services, housing, and the Arts, however, the justification cannot properly depend on public good theory alone. It is clear that the market system can and does provide the services of teachers, doctors and actors in this and most Western countries. Many philosophical, political, social and economic reasons have been put forward over the years to justify the public provision of such services and only a few of those that seem to be most relevant at the present time can be mentioned here. Most of the arguments put forward seem to derive from a belief that the private market standard of provision will be inadequate. 'Inadequacy' can be variously defined, but in this context will usually involve the following areas:

(*a*) Distribution: only those who can afford the charges will be able to make use of the services.

(*b*) Social efficiency: bad health and poor education hinder social mobility and efficiency — remember poverty cycle, Chapter 7.

(*c*) Consumer ignorance: many people will tend to undervalue or not be aware of the long-run benefits of education and preventative medicine, especially when faced with substantial short-run costs such as forgone potential earnings during training or treatment.

It should be obvious that any assumed inadequacy of provision is based on judgements about how much of a social good (or bad) people should be exposed to. This area of discussion is at the heart of much of modern political debate and cannot be resolved solely by economic argument or logic since the attitude an individual assumes will mainly depend on his view of the 'proper' relationships between the individual, society and State. For example, someone who believes that both the market system and individual choice are efficient, just, and democratic ways of allocating resources is likely to argue that points (*a*) to (*c*) above are paternalistic, dictatorial and wasteful. An alternative view might suggest that a democratically-run State is quite entitled to determine the use of society's resources providing it has the support of a majority of electors. This approach would allow us to describe all public expenditure as collective consumption and investment, and we return to this theme on pp. 157-158.

THE GROWTH OF PUBLIC EXPENDITURE

One of the most significant developments to take place in most Western developed economies in this century is the long-run growth of public spending both in absolute volume and in relation to the size of the economy. This growth as regards the UK is clearly shown in Figure 8.2. Over the period 1890 to 1970, public spending grew from about 10% of Gross National Product to around 50 per cent. (Note, however, that only three-fifths of spending in 1970 was directly on goods and services for the provision of public services. The remaining two-fifths took the form of 'transfer' payments such as social security, debt interest, students' grants, etc., and most of this money will have been spent on the products and services sold by the private sector.)

Various attempts have been made to explain this shift in the balance of economic influence from the private to the public sector, but no one theory can be said to tell the whole story. One of the earliest approaches goes back to the 1890s with Adolph Wagner's analysis of the forces leading to greater governmental participation in and control of the market economy. He argued that as economies become more sophisticated and complex they inevitably throw up inter-firm and inter-industry relationships that could be harmful if not regulated in the public interest, for example, a need for monopoly control and consumer protection. Also, the weaknesses and inadequacies of the market system would gradually be more clearly recognised and understood and a steady expansion of social services provision would result. Wagner's Law, as it is called, does provide a useful frame of reference to investigate this question but can only be an explanation of long-run trends.

A shorter-run explanation is provided by Peacock and Wiseman's 'displacement effect'. [3] This approach focuses attention on the process by which a population adjusts, (*a*) its willingness to pay taxes, and (*b*) its demands for public provision. In this context, the very high levels of governmental expenditure during the world wars is seen as leading to the acceptance of higher tax rates as well as to the raising of public ex-

[3] A. T. Peacock and J. Wiseman, *The Growth of Public Expenditure in the UK* (OUP, 1961).

pectations about future living standards. Wars are also likely to reveal weaknesses in an economy and its social structure in much the same way that the Booth and Rowntree reports exposed previously concealed problems — a so-called 'inspection effect'. These shifts in public attitudes (which are ratchet-like in that they have so far always been upwards) constitute the 'displacement effect'. Although the timing of these shifts in public spending may well be explained by this displacement effect, it does not fully explain the long-run upward trend.

Apart from these theories relating the growth of the public sector to the dynamic development of society, there are others that treat the Government as a collective entity representing to a greater or lesser extent the wishes and desires of the population. The problem then is to balance these publicly expressed private demands against the costs of provision so as to achieve the greatest possible welfare of the people.

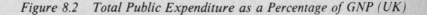

Figure 8.2   Total Public Expenditure as a Percentage of GNP (UK)

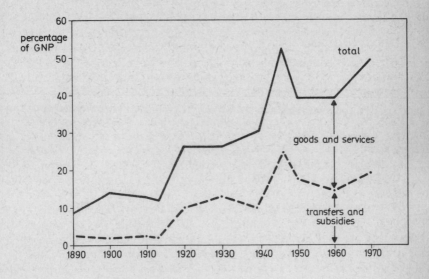

Sources   A. T. Peacock and J. Wiseman, *The Growth of Public Expenditure in the UK,* (OUP, 1961), and Blue Book, HMSO

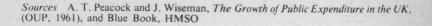

It may be that there are important elements of truth in all of these explanations, but the difficulty is in applying any one of them to predict the future development of spending. If the trend established so far this century is simply projected into the future, it would mean that the UK will have become virtually a socialist state by AD 2050. It may be that the growth of the public sector will slow down once it becomes responsible for rather over half a country's Gross National Product, but there appears to be no *a priori* level which can be said to be 'correct' other than in the context of the overall needs and aims of a particular society and economy.

ASPECTS OF DECISION-MAKING IN THE PUBLIC SECTOR

Needs, Aims and Means

Much of the foregoing discussion is linked to the problem of recognising a society's 'needs' and then deciding how far and in what ways the needs can be met. To use the term 'need' can be misleading in much the same way that 'necessity' can be variously interpreted. For example, how does a government assess the need for nursery school places? It can receive advice from educationalists and commissions, sociologists and trade unions, and any others with an interest in the issue, about the value that pre-school education might have, but the difficulty is in deciding just how many nursery places can be provided within current financial constraints and in relation to all the other pressing 'needs' the Government is expected to meet. In a 1972 White Paper,[4] the UK Government accepted a recommendation that nursery school provision should be sufficient to meet 'demand', which was estimated to be about 90 per cent of all four-year-olds and 50 per cent of three-year-olds. It was noted that most countries in Europe with a similar standard of living had provision at this level already and this was taken as confirmation of the level of need. The Department of Education and Science admitted that it had no way of knowing whether the extra millions of pounds to be spent on nurseries would yield a higher welfare than if it were spent on, say, part-time further education, but did feel that this was an area where the UK was falling behind in relation to other services and other similar countries (this latter view being perhaps an international version of 'keeping up with the Joneses').

As the size of the public sector increases and as the pressure on resources grows, public authorities are being forced to be more aware of the importance of clarifying their aims and objectives before mak-

4'Education — A Framework for Expansion', Cmnd 5174 (1972).

ing decisions on spending programmes.

One area where a greater clarification of aims might be helpful in the UK is how far the Government should use the provision of goods and services as a way of redistributing income. The traditions derived from the charitable and voluntary societies in the supply of cheap or free food, clothing and shelter, together with those political interests favouring much greater social mobility, have tended to encourage governments to build up a complex of income-related benefits in both cash and non-cash form. If the aim of these policies is simply to raise the income of the worst-off members of society, it would perhaps be cheaper and more efficient to fix some minimum acceptable income and then remove the plethora of income-related benefits. In practice, of course, the objective of these benefits is not simply a matter of income but rather a paternalistic concern to ensure that any help given is used in a 'proper' way by the recipients and to retain casework-type links with those in need. Much of the heat that has been engendered by political debate on this general topic could perhaps be removed with advantage to all concerned if only aims and objectives were more clearly specified.

Efficiency

The desire for economic efficiency was discussed in Chapters 2, 3 and 4, and as we saw then, the level of profitability of an enterprise is one important measure of efficiency in a market context. In the public sector of modern economies, the question of profitability arises with particular force in connection with the problems of running various publicly owned enterprises. Most publicly financed activities have no obvious output however, and they are not carried out for profit, so it is consequently difficult to measure their efficiency.

In the sphere of education, the Government will determine the percentage of any age group that shall have access to or be compelled to partake of the various levels of educational provision. There is a tendency to measure the amount of educational output in terms of the size and cost of the inputs to education by calculating the number of places provided in the various institutions, the number and quality of teachers, the amount spent per pupil on buildings, books and equipment. There is much less discussion of the actual output of the education system other than the use of crude measures such as numbers of examination successes and their grades. At the very least, this approach will tend to neglect the value of education to those who do not manage to pass examinations and may go some way to explain the continued presence in the UK of illiteracy on a surprising scale.

The problem is not helped by the very divergent views to be found among educationalists, and the absence of any clear way for the population in general to express its attitudes to aims and objectives means that we are usually confined to an aim simply of 'more and better'.

When we turn to public health provision, a similar lack of good output measures emerges. There are plenty of statistics on the level of provision in terms of the number of hospital beds per 1,000 of the population, or the average size of doctors' patient lists, but the measures of health output are nearly all negative in that they mostly measure the amount of ill-health in society. It is true that if the number of cases of tuberculosis falls then there is a health improvement with respect to that disease, but if at the same time the incidence of heart disease and lung cancer is increasing, what can be said about the healthiness of the population in general? One might, for example, refer to the long-run rise in the life expectancy of Western man. But what is needed ideally is an index of healthiness which takes account of the statistics on death rates, illness and debility, all in relation to some index of normal health and well being, but there is no such index in use at present by the planners and adminstrators of our health services.

A further difficulty in assessing the output of the public and social services is that the effects of any public programme cannot easily be separated from the results of other public or private activities. If the reader refers back to the cycle of poverty described on p. 134, he will notice that poor housing and poor health are linked together and that both have an adverse effect on educational attainment. Hence, any measured change in educational output could be the result of a variety of factors quite unrelated to the education service itself, a point of great significance when we consider the growing problems facing educational institutions in the world's areas of urban deprivation and decline.

Given this background of considerable ignorance about the aims and objectives of public services and uncertainty about their actual outputs and effects, any assessment of the efficency and productivity of these services is bound to be very approximate. As the wealth and prosperity of our economy has improved, so higher standards have been set for existing services and new forms of provision started. This 'ratchet' effect is one explanation of the continuous growth of public spending, but as was hinted earlier in this section, in the face of accelerating demands for resources and also perhaps slower rates of economic growth, a more rational examination of the objectives of governmental services and of the means of paying for them is bound to be called for.

Some Attempts at Rational Decision-Making in the Public Sector

We have looked briefly at some of the complexities that must be faced when dealing with various forms of collective consumption and investment, and it has been suggested that public sector behaviour is rather different from private enterprise market behaviour. Furthermore, there is no model of governmental behaviour that can be compared with the free-market model in its comprehensiveness and predictiveness. What have evolved however, mainly since World War II, are some systematic management procedures for public authority use and various techniques of analysis to assist in their decision-making. There is space in this book only to indicate the fundamentals of two of the most important developments in these fields.

The Management of Public Expenditures Traditional methods for controlling public spending tend to rely on annual budget authorisations followed by audits to check that public money has been used solely for the authorised purposes. A number of governments and public authorities are introducing more systematic controls over their spending and the most widely accepted of these procedures is known as Planning, Programming and Budgeting Systems — PPBS. The titles given to this type of control system tend to change over time as do details of operation, but there are common themes and ideas that emerge in all versions.

The essential elements in a PPB system are as follows:

1. A clarification and specification of the aims and purposes of the expenditure, and if possible the expression of these in terms of output targets on a certain time scale.
2. The organisation of 'production' units or programmes of action to achieve these targets.
3. An accurate assessment of the costs of the programmes in both financial and economic terms.
4. A projection of estimated future costs for the programmes set against the expected availability of resources.
5. The measurement and assessment of the output or performance of the programmes which is then compared with the targets set.
6. Regular reviews of aims and targets to ensure their continued desirability; the consideration of alternative programmes to meet agreed ends; special studies of needs, means and methods of analysis.

The reader should recognise those elements which pose most problems for the bodies that are attempting a PPBS approach.

Social Cost-Benefit Analysis Decisions on public expenditure have been made on a variety of criteria in the past from perhaps a sheer reaction to a crisis, to the recognition of a social need, to plain political dogma. 'Social cost-benefit analysis' is a technique that tries to step back from the political arena and instead attempts to measure the value or otherwise to society of particular decisions or projects. The discussion on pp.141-142 established that there could be important divergences between the private and wider social values attaching to any act, especially if externalities are present on any scale. In the context of the housepainting example given on p.141, a cost-benefit analysis would attempt to add together *all* the direct gains and losses associated with that action, whether public or private, and assess whether there is an overall cost or benefit to society arising from it.

As another example, consider a situation where a Government may be trying to decide whether to pass a law compelling the fitting and wearing of safety harnesses on all car seats. The immediate costs to the car owner are the charges for fitting and buying the harnesses (which are easily estimated) and perhaps the loss of personal freedom for the owner and his passengers at being compelled to do something (which is difficult to measure in money terms). Left to the market mechanism and an individual assessment by the car owner, we know that relatively few seat belts would be fitted and fewer actually worn. And yet the car driver may consistently underestimate the risk of accident, while passengers are not usually in a position to express an effective view about the matter and hence their interests tend to be ignored. The costs facing a driver and owner in the event of accident are such items as vehicle repairs, personal pain and injury, interruption and loss of earnings and even of life. The public authorities must in addition bear the costs of police, rescue and hospital services, increased social security charges and perhaps repairs to roads and equipment. Society in general bears the cost of lost potential output and increased worry and stress. A cost-benefit analysis must try to express as many of these items as possible in money terms so that it can arrive at an overall evaluation of net benefit or cost. One of the most difficult problems facing the analyst is of course that of placing money prices and values on non-marketable intangibles such as pain, loss of life, stress, time and convenience.

In the UK, the greatest amount of experience of cost-benefit analysis has so far been gained in transportation studies ranging from motorway and underground railway studies to the analysis of the Channel tunnel and third London airport schemes. Two of the most common problems concerning intangibles that have arisen with these are concerned with the valuation of time and of human life. As regards time, the most widely used procedure is to assume that an employee's working time, if saved, is worth per hour the same as the wages paid to him. More difficult problems arise when attempts are made to evaluate leisure time, and since this is a more subjective issue, analysts tend to try a variety of values (always so far below working time values) leaving the final choice to the decision-taker.

Human life has been valued in various educational, health and transportation studies by estimating the value of any lost output arising from death or injury. One distasteful outcome of this procedure is of course that old and handicapped people are given low values. The reader will note that even in these difficult cases, the analyst will try to relate back to market valuations to gain some point of reference. Where this proves too difficult or inappropriate, as in the case of visual amenity and appreciation, there is no alternative but to confess defeat and allow judgement and opinion to take over.

THE TOTAL WELL-BEING OF SOCIETY

Management techniques may be able to help governments to spend their money so as to get more education, law and order or health per £1 spent, but they are of little help so far in weighing up the benefits of an extra £10 million spent on education rather than on the health services. At this level, we are looking across the whole complex of public policy and trying to decide the relative amounts to devote to all the various public functions. Some economists have taken the view that governments should be seen as the collective embodiment of the wishes and desires of the individual members of society. They then discuss the various voting strategies that could be adopted by electors to ensure that the Government looks after their interests. Given the nature of most Western democracies, governments' decisions can be only very crude approximations to the wishes of society. We might imagine a future population sitting comfortably in their own homes before an audio-visual console complete with computer terminal, and listening to the arguments for and against some proposal before simultaneously pressing their Yes, No, Don't Know, and Abstain buttons. Such a system of majority rule by instant referendum would have its dangers however, especially for those with minority interests. Minorities, whether of race, religion or income group, are still part of any society, and minority interests ought to have some influence on decisions — the problem is, how much influence? With this last question, we broach one of the fundamental issues facing any society. As we saw in Chapter 7, relative status or significance may be the result of political power or long-standing custom. In most democracies, there is a rule of one man one vote at the political level. At the economic level, however, those with the greatest purchasing power tend to have the greatest economic significance, and government action in the sphere of income distribution is an attempt to even out the balance of economic power. But as we have seen in this chapter, governments develop their own patterns of income and expenditure and may well develop their own aims and objectives, thus becoming an economic power in their own right not necessarily very responsive to society's demands.

This question of the relative weightings of significance or influence to be allowed to various sections of a population seems to be of more and more importance to developed countries, especially those in relative economic decline. The various attempts by UK governments since 1961 to introduce some kind of voluntary prices and incomes policy have all hit the major stumbling block of how to balance the claims of one group of workers against another, or the interests of shareholders against the consumer. Fundamental questions about the nature and purpose of society are raised as soon as one begins to discuss the relative values (of goods, services or groups of people) that may have evolved through history or the market place. Sometimes, as we have seen in this chapter, a society will try to adjust these relationships by governmental intervention in the market place or by direct public provision. Sometimes, the problem may appear to be soluble only by a complete change in the nature and purpose of the society and its economy. This theme is central to the next chapter on the socialist economy.

Chapter 9

The Socialist Economy

It was possible in Chapter 6 to describe the essential features of a capitalist economy both in terms of its institutional structure and of the economic relationships likely to rule in such an economy. It is much more difficult to describe a socialist economy with similar conviction. One fundamental problem is that there is no generally accepted and definitive model of a socialist economy and society, even though a high proportion of the world's population lives in economies dominated by versions of Marxist Communism. Any selection of socialist 'archetypes' is bound to offend the supporters of those variants excluded from the list, but we are only attempting here to suggest the flavour of the socialist approach to economics and society. We begin this chapter therefore with an outline of three concepts of socialism — Utopian soialism, Marxian socialism and communism, and what we shall call democratic socialism.

Utopian Socialism

Utopia is the imaginary island described in Sir Thomas More's famous book published in 1516. It was an island in which the benevolent rule of King Utopus combined with the democratic election of state and local officers to produce a nation living in freedom, peace, happiness and security. More's *Utopia* was not a mere updating of Plato's *Republic,* although there are many points of similarity; More was careful to describe not only the government of the island, but also the practical arrangements of everyday life as regards the role of family life, the organisation of work on the land and in the cities, the diet and clothing of the inhabitants, and the laws and rules of social behaviour. It is a blueprint for an ideal and perfect society in which man could live a full and happy life. In its emphasis on the socialised nature of such activities as the use of public property, farming, eating, the rearing of young and the standards of behaviour expected, it is socialistic in flavour.

However, 'Utopia' comes from the Greek meaning 'nowhere', and this reminds us that the tradition of Utopian socialism that is found in France and Britain has tended to be personalised and idealistic rather than practical. In the first part of the nineteenth century, for example, Louis Blanc and Saint-Simon in France, Robert Owen in Britain and Charles Fourier in America, all took optimistic views of the potential for co-operative and collective forms of production within an industrialised state, and various (mainly short-lived) attempts were made by them or their followers to establish communities based on their principles. Perhaps inevitably, these experiments took place in generally hostile economic and social environments and they tended to lose their momentum when the dynamism of their leader or founder failed.

Although Saint-Simon anticipated a golden age of plenty based on modern technology and industrialisation, the excesses of rapid industrialisation and mass production so shocked many Utopian socialists that by the end of the last century they began to look back to a pre-industrial age for their inspiration. One such was the artist, writer and craftsman William Morris, whose vision of the ideal society was not unlike More's in its emphasis on the simple life, small-scale craft production and collective social responsibility. The Utopian approach has been criticised on many grounds (see p. 161), but perhaps the most damaging criticism is that perfect Utopias seem to be inhabited by near-perfect people and that rarely do their creators tell us in what manner a society can progress from its present imperfections to the state of bliss.

Marxian Socialism and Communism

Historical Materialism   The writings of Karl Marx (1818-83), when taken together, present an integrated view of such basic human concerns as ethics, sociology, politics and economics. This view of mankind, unique in its time in its comprehensiveness, evolved from Marx's attempt to understand and explain what was happening to nineteenth-century Europe as it went through the throes of rapid industrialisation. His studies of past and contemporary societies convinced him that a society can be understood only when the pattern of its production, consumption and exchange has been exposed. Marx attacked earlier philosophical and religious traditions because they began by exploring possible universal and heavenly attributes and then tried to impose them on earth-bound mankind. Man is the only true measure of man according to Marx. The nature of his society, its political and social order, its morality and ethics, are all determined by what production takes place, how it is organised, and by what process its fruits are distributed. This is the materialist basis of what Marx called 'scientific socialism' to distinguish it from the kind of stargazing socialism that was described in the previous section.

Another dimension to be added to this materialist view of history is its determinism. The opening passages of the *Manifesto of the Communist Party,* written in 1848 by Marx and Frederick Engels, use examples drawn from ancient Rome, feudal Europe, and the industrial might of Great Britain to outline the historical development of Europe in terms of a constant struggle between economic classes for supremacy. As soon as any particular class gained economic and political power, it inevitably generated an opposing class which would in turn seek control. What Marx saw as especially significant about nineteenth-century industrial societies was that the class struggle had become simplified into two great diametrically opposed factions, the bourgeoisie and the proletariat. The bourgeoisie were the owners of capital and the means of production, the hirers of wage labour, while the proletariat were those with no capital of their own, able to survive only by selling their labour to the bourgeoisie. As we shall see later, Marx believed that the interests of these two classs were inevitably in conflict.

The Inevitable Collapse of Capitalism Das Kapital, Marx's major three-volume work published between 1864 and 1890, is an analysis of the process of capitalist production and accumulation. In the course of this exposition of the nature of capitalism, the scenario for the inevitable collapse of capitalism is set out and what follows is an attempt to suggest the chief characters, relationships and events Marx expected to appear.

The value of a good is determined by the amount of 'socially necessary' labour that it contains. The concept of socially necessary labour can be thought of as a uniform measure of labour input based on the normally prevailing conditions of production and requiring an average degree of skill and intensity of effort. Production requires the combination of labour input with capital goods and services in the form of raw materials, plant, machinery, etc. Capital, in the form of buildings, machines and materials, was in turn produced as a result of labour input and is no more than the physical embodiment of past labour services.

The bourgeoisie own and control the capital stock, but can only put it to use by hiring labour services from the proletariat for wages. The wages paid are barely sufficient for subsistence, but the exchange values[1] of the goods produced are much greater than the wages paid and the resulting surplus accrues to the capitalist. Part of this surplus is used by the bourgeoisie for consumption, but the rest is invested in the accumulation of more capital. The competitive nature of capitalism encourages capital accumulation and the growing stock of capital allows increasing amounts of production (Marx accepted that capitalism had lead to a spectacular rise in productive potential).

The inevitability of capitalist crisis now becomes clear. The proletariat is exploited because the surplus product of its labour is taken by the capitalist. The increasing capital stock per worker that comes with rapid accumulation, together with improvements in technology, increases labour productivity and therefore the rate of exploitation, i.e. the ratio of the surplus to subsistence wages. The low level of purchasing power available to the workers will mean that total consumption will not keep pace with the potential for increased output. Under-consumption or over-production leads to unemployment and the failure of most small businesses. The surviving capitalists combine for their own protection into a shrinking class of powerful monopolists while the proletariat is swollen by the influx of the 'reserve army' of dispossessed bourgeois and the unemployed. The conflict between the interests of capitalist and worker deepens until the inevitable overthrow of the capitalist class occurs.

Alienation and Dehumanisation under Capitalism In the early writings of Marx it is clear that he hates capitalism because he sees man as enslaved under the capitalist mode of production. The work performed by the wage earner under conditions of capitalist division of labour tends to be dehumanised and repetitive; the worker can derive no satisfaction from his work — it is the mere use of labour power as a means of subsistence rather than as an extension of his creative force and personality. The competitive nature of capitalism and its dependence on private property and accumulation places a barrier between men which damages the humanity of both capitalist and worker alike. The State is merely an extension of the power of the dominant class and hence there is a divorce betwen man and society. Commodities are produced not because they are useful but because they can be bought and sold at a profit, and the result is commodity 'fetishism', or production and consumption for their own sake.

[1]This is the market price of a good, but it can be quite different from 'true' value based on its content of socially necessary labour. Marx also considered that if a thing had no utility, it had no value however much labour input it embodied. The reader may guess that Marx's theory of value was very complex!

All these divisions between man and man, man and society, man and his work, Marx called 'alienation', and it is an important concept if we are to grasp something of the kind of socialist society Marx had in mind.

The Socialist Economy and its Transition to Communism The reader might wonder why we have spent so much of the last few sections in discussing Marx's analysis of capitalism rather than his views on the proper organisation of a socialist state. The fact is that Marx and most of his followers were more interested in hastening the downfall of the capitalist regime by political action and analysis than in preparing detailed plans for the post-capitalist phase. Indeed, in terms of Marxian logic, since socialism would inevitably replace capitalism and since the forms, rules, production processes, structure, etc. of the new classless society would be determined by the natural evolution of the revolutionary situation, it would be inappropriate to engage in visionary activities. Nevertheless, there is something that can be said about the nature of the expected post-revolutionary society.

According to Marx, there would be two main stages in the evolution of a fully communist society. In the first, or socialist, stage, the abolition of private property and the establishment of a classless society would immediately remove the basic cause of class conflict in society. Incomes would be more equally distributed but the methods of payment would probably still be on the basis of 'bourgeois' differentials and incentives. Greater opportunities for individual development would be provided alongside a major extension in the public provision of goods and services. Initially, the new society would be under threat from old bourgeois tendencies within and from hostile capitalist regimes without society, and the gains of the revolution would need to be preserved by the establishment of a 'dictatorship of the proletariat' which would be lead by the Communist Party. It is significant that none of the socialist countries of the world claims to have progressed beyond this stage to the ultimate of the 'true' communist society.

The next, 'higher', form of socialism or true communism would be brought about by two fundamental changes:
1. An expected tremendous leap in the productive potential of the socialist economy as a result of freeing man from the wastes of alienation and the monopoly restriction of capitalist production, and
2. The evolution of a truly free and social man.

In the true communist society there would be no criminals, no conflict, no coercion and no state or authority because clearly there would be no need for them to exist. Man would voluntarily and freely give his labour to socially useful work, would feel no desire for private property, and would behave in a naturally social, co-operative and creative manner. He would not attempt to take from the common stores anything that he was not clearly entitled to. Then the principle of 'from each according to his ability, to each according to his needs' would become fully operational.

Democratic Liberal Socialism

As a contrast to the 'ideological' approach of Marxian socialism, a brief look at what we have here called democratic liberal socialism may be of value. This title does not represent any particular socialist party or group, but is meant to indicate a pragmatic style of socialism that would include some or all of the following principles:

1. A commitment to parliamentary democracy (even if that means that anti-socialist parties can gain control).
2. A rejection of the 'inevitability' of capitalist collapse, especially in the light of modern experience of steadily rising living standards under capitalism.
3. A concern about the use to which the economic power derived from private property ownership is put, rather than concern about ownership as such. There will often, however, be a commitment to take into public ownership certain key industries and utilities such as energy supply, communications and transport.
4. A willingness to accept and use the free enterprise capitalist market allocation system over much or most of the economy, as well as a preparedness to intervene in or to manipulate markets whenever this is felt to be in the public interest.

In broad terms, most European democratic socialist and labour parties would follow this general line, and its practical manifestation is the 'mixed' economy and the welfare state. Much of the discussion in Chapter 8 is therefore relevant for this approach to socialism, but the practical nature of democratic socialism implies a problem-solving orientation rather than the building of a society on predetermined lines. There is further discussion of governmental intervention and regulation in the mixed economy in the next chapter.

Some Common Socialist Themes

It would appear that the search for a basic blueprint for a socialist economy that would gain the approval of all the various shades of socialist opinion is a vain one. From what has gone before, however, it is possible to suggest some recurring themes.

There is always some vision of mankind living in a society displaying the features of equality, brotherhood and personal freedom. The principle of equality does not usually mean (even in the higher form of communism) treating every citizen exactly equally. On the contrary, it implies that economic and social resources will be bestowed where they will lead to the greatest social and private benefit, that is, according to 'need'.

There is a belief in the predominance of social values over private values, of co-operative over competitive effort, of public over private property, and a shift in the balance from private to public consumption. Creative work rather than idleness or useless production is to be the basis of social recognition and prestige. All this is supposed to lead to an equality of opportunity for all citizens to develop their own personalities and individualism as far as possible. It is generally assumed that this free development of the individual will be consistent with the collective needs of society. This ties in with an optimistic belief in the fundamental 'goodness' of social man once the right social and economic environment is created.

Until this ideal is obtained, there will be a need for some form of central guidance and control to ensure that development is along the 'right' lines. Any authorities should be democratically elected and be publicly accountable. An atmosphere of public and private responsibility should prevail. This sense of brotherhood and responsibility is expected to extend beyond national boundaries, and strong international bonds of co-operation and mutual assistance should be developed.

SOME ORGANISATIONAL AND DECISION PROBLEMS TO BE SOLVED IN A SOCIALIST ECONOMY

We must now broach some of the critical problems to be faced in an attempt to set up and run a socialist or collectivist economy. The various Utopias are the personal visions of individual writers and thinkers and this means that the crucial questions have been answered in accordance with that individual's ideals. Marxian scientific socialism and communism deliberately avoids providing answers, while the democratic socialist approach tends towards the solution of problems on a piecemeal basis. And yet socialistic states and economies exist and they run, although they have usually evolved as a result of pragmatic solutions to pressing problems rather than being built according to a predetermined plan.

The Basic Economic Problems

The obvious economic questions to be decided are those that face any economy and have been fully covered in Chapters 2 to 8. These are the questions of what to produce and in what quantities; where and by which technology will production take place; how is transportation and distribution to be handled. In the pure capitalist economy, all these problems are dealt with by the price system and the market mechanism. In the democratic liberal socialist state or mixed economy, the market system copes with most questions and the public authorities intervene to correct faults or fill gaps. For the fully socialist collectivist economy, with no significant private property, there is no obvious mechanism for solving these problems.

One possibility that has been considered is to decentralise the economy and for the managers of the socialist enterprises and farms to operate the price and market mechanism as if conditions of perfect competition prevailed. The public authorities would then purchase out of tax revenues whatever was needed for the supply of collective or social consumption and investment. It is unlikely that all markets would be free of intervention since we might expect that wage and salary levels would be centrally determined in accordance with some generally accepted social criteria (see Chapter 8, p. 158). Similarly, the supply of investment funds might be closely regulated, and the production of socially undesirable goods and services prohibited or curbed. Overall, however, a market form of socialism is theoretically feasible, and in countries such as Yugoslavia we have a rough approximation to this model.

At the other extreme would be a complete rejection of market processes and reliance instead on detailed administrative decision-making subject to a degree of democratic regulation and control. There are all manner of possible variants between these two, and one variant widely used in the past will be described on pp. 167-176.

Centralisation or Decentralisation — A Problem of Scale and Co-ordination

The essential problem here is one of scale. Small independent societies living at a fairly basic and primitive level have been described in earlier chapters of this book (especially Chapters 2 and 8) and they often have, perforce, communistic structures. Marx took the view, based on his analysis of the Paris Commune of 1871, that a series of small, dispersed communes and co-operatives would not be able to carry through the building of the new socialist society and that some degree of centralisation was essential. He was anxious, however, to ensure the destruction of the earlier 'bourgeois' forms of centralised power which were seen as exerting an oppressive power from above, and to establish in their place a national unity of communes in which power came from below.

There is probably a fundamental incompatibility between the modern industrialised economy based on large-scale production and an attempt to use the same technology organised by voluntary groupings of small independent communes. Modern capitalism is large-scale, bureaucratic, and increasingly concentrated, and it is more than likely that a socialist economy using a similar technology would have to be centralised and bureaucratic also. Those who long for a return to small-scale community life based on a non-mechanical or non-chemical agriculture and a craft-based industry are looking for a very hard and simple way of life indeed, and must be prepared to give up the levels of productivity and consumption associated with the economies of scale and of modern technology.

THE ECONOMICS OF THE CENTRALISED COMMAND ECONOMY

For most of the rest of this chapter, the characteristics of a completely centralised economy will be discussed. The essential features of the economy to be described are similar to those that prevailed in most of the European countries under Communist Party rule until the mid 1960s. Similar features have appeared in capitalist countries at times of crisis, especially in the world wars, and also in those developing countries that have gone through a socialist revolution, such as Cuba and China.

The Planned Economy

The centralised socialist economy operates under the guidance of an economic plan enforced by the issue of instructions which permeate downwards through the economy via a complex administrative structure. For this reason it is often call a 'command' economy. At the top of the hierarchy is the highest political authority in the State, which in effect will be the Central Executive Committee of the Socialist or Communist Party (see Figure 9.1). The Central Committee, presumably after consultations with the populace in general and the rank and file of the Party in particular, determines the major priorities for the economy in terms of growth, investment, consumption, technological development and social need. The Committee is assisted by a Central Planning Bureau which will translate the broad objectives of the Central Committee into quantified targets with specified time scales. The time horizons of the plans will depend on the purpose of the exercise, e.g. if long-term developments are in issue, then a strategic plan of fifteen to twenty years' length may be prepared, but normally, detailed planning is possible only with the greater certainty of the medium and short term, and hence five- to seven-year plans are most likely.

Having discussed the implications of a set of variants, the targets will be finalised by the Planning Bureau and then incorporated by the National Assembly into a state law. This legalisation of the plan emphasises that it is both a political and an economic document, and in addition gives the necessary authority to require, under the threat of penalty, general adherence to it.

Figure 9.1   The Command Economy

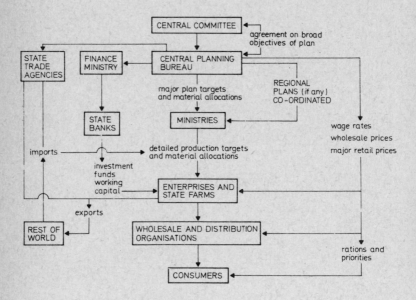

The Allocation of Material Inputs

The five- or seven-year plan must be made operational, and this means the preparation of detailed annual plans consistent with the targets and objectives of the medium-term plan. The Planning Bureau draws up annual production targets for the key sectors of the economy, and these are passed on to industry or regionally based ministries which interpret the main targets into more detailed schedules of commodity and service output. What has to be done is to prepare a complete list of all the final goods and services that the society will need plus a schedule of all the raw materials, components, machinery and plant, transport facilities, etc., that are necessary to produce that list of final demands. An enlightening exercise would be for the reader to note down all the different goods in just one room of his home together with all the possible variations in terms of style, colour, size, etc. An instruction has to be issued by a central authority for each such good before they will be produced in a command economy. Instructions will in a sense have to be given in a competitive capitalist economy of course, but in that case the instructions will have originated in hundreds and thousands of independent offices, factories and shops using the information made available by the price and market mechanisms.

A crucial problem is to ensure that it is physically possible to meet the planned outputs, and this involves a detailed study of all input requirements. (The reader may find it useful here to refer back to Table 5.1). The planners need to known the pattern of inter-industry flows for their economy. Table 5.1 shows input/output flows in money terms, and this is of use in a market economy, but the planners in our command economy need to know the flows of materials and components between industries in quantity terms. They need to know how much coal is required to produce a ton of steel, how much steel and of what types goes into making tractors, how many tractors are needed per hectare of cultivated land, etc. The planners also need to have some idea about whether these technical relationships are changing over time, and if so, how fast and in what direction.

It should be obvious that a much bigger and more detailed matrix than that given in Table 5.1 is needed, ideally with one row and column for each product. The biggest input/output matrices in current use in Eastern Europe have about 150 to 200 rows and columns, but in the early 1960s some 19,000 products[2] were being planned and specified by the Russian Central Planning Bureau and so it is clear that input/output techniques are hardly refined enough yet to be used for detailed planning purposes although they can be used for testing the broad features of a plan. In practice, the ministries would use various rules of thumb based on past experience of enterprise outputs and inputs to work out what was feasible. State enterprises and farms would be informed of their provisional production targets and there would then follow a period of negotiation between enterprise managers and the ministries until reasonable and possible targets had

[2]For comparison, even in the 1920s the American mail-order company, Sears, Roebuck, was listing some 35,000 items in its catalogue.

been agreed. The production units would then receive their final production targets for the year, a list of constraints on such things as labour costs and quality limits, and a set of authorisations to take delivery of the necessary materials, parts, machinery, etc., from other named enterprises. Delivery instructions would also be included. The state banks would have been alerted by the Finance Ministry to allow funds to the enterprises in accordance with their planned needs. Foreign trade would be organised mainly to fill gaps in the material supply position that could not be met from internal resources, but the enterprises would merely take delivey from or send output to the centralised import and export agencies.

It is essential that all these material flows balance out with the minimum of waste. The necessity for every production unit to get close to its target is obvious, because any breakdown or failure in supply will have repercussions on other enterprises. Using an earlier example, a failure to meet steel output targets will affect tractor production and in turn the size of the harvest. Breakdowns and failures, especially if caused by the vagaries of natural forces such as weather, are bound to occur, but they put a strain on the administrative machine that it may not be capable of coping with in a satisfactory manner.

The Allocation and Distribution of Goods and Services

If the reader refers once more to the input/output table, he will see that the planner has to determine the destination of each amount of output. As we saw in the last section, some of the output will be allocated to other enterprises to enable them, in turn, to produce. Some output will be commandeered by the public authorities for their own use as collective consumption and investment, while yet more will go to the state export agencies. The remainder is allocated to the general public as private consumption. In an economy operated entirely by command, private consumption would be regulated by the issue (according to some scale of 'need' or entitlement) of coupons or vouchers which are surrendered in exchange for goods and services. This form of rationing to final consumers has often been used in time of national crisis even in market economies, especially in time of war, but it has not found favour for long in times of peace. The allocation of materials to enterprises is in effect a form of rationing, but it is much simpler and easier to allocate thousands of commodities to millions of people by the use of a money system with consumer choice. Workers are therefore normally paid mainly in cash and they are free to spend that money as they wish on the goods made available in the shops.

When comparing the allocation of goods and services in socialist and capitalist economies, there are two important points to be kept in mind:

1. A socialist state might be expected to devote a rather larger proportion of total output to collective consumption than a capitalist state, and the public provision of facilities for education, health, sport, cultural activities, transport and housing, etc., will generally have a high priority. Not all of these services will necessarily be available free of charge, but where charges are made they are likely to be well below cost (as is usually the case with housing and public transport in Eastern Europe). Some observers of Eastern Europe do not, however, detect big differences between East and West in the share of GNP going to stage budgets, but such figures may well overlook the lower level of development of the communist world and the wide range of semi-public facilities and services provided by the state enterprises.

2. The preference for present as against future consumption in a free enterprise market economy is a matter for individual and private choice and is indicated by the level of interest rates ruling in the money and capital markets. Market interest rates are in turn linked to the rate of return on capital investment. In a socialist state where individuals cannot invest in productive assets, where investment takes place as a result of administrative decision and where wages and purchasing power are regulated, there is no way for a market rate of interest to appear. As we shall see in Chapter 10, many socialist economies have recently introduced interest payments for the use of state-owned capital and finance, but in essence, the situation remains one where the authorities decide on the balance between present and future demands.

For example, the first Russian five-year plan, covering the period 1929 to 1932, gave overriding priority to the development of heavy industry — a priority, incidentally, that was to feature in most of the subsequent plans also. This meant that the population had to be 'persuaded' to accept a slow improvement in their consumption levels in return for the promise of more rapid improvements in their standard of living when the economy had been provivided with a solid industrial base. This is equivalent to the setting of a very low interest rate.

Indicators and Motivators

Socialist ideologists trust and believe that the mere existence of the socialist economy will remove the necessity for personal and private gain as an incentive for productive effort; but since a command economy is very far from Marx's true communist economy, we may assume that individuals are motivated by a certain degree of self-interest as well as some commitment to the welfare of the society in general. In the next three sections, we shall consider how people are likely to react, given that they are working in a command environment.

The Decision-Making Units   There are four main decision-making units to consider: the Central Planning Bureau and its branches; the managements of the productive enterprises; the managements of the various wholesale and retail distributive units; and the consumer.

The management of a production enterprise will have very little room to manoeuvre. It is given specific instructions concerning what to produce and from where to obtain supplies. The manager's attention is focused on the production plan targets and on their fulfilment. Not surprisingly, he is likely to adopt certain strategies in these circumstances. Although he was a party to the negotiation of the plan targets as agreed, he will normally have tried to obtain a target that can be hit without too much effort. He knows that non-achievement of the target will significantly affect the bonuses that he will be allowed to pay his workers and himself. On the other hand, the planners will be trying to squeeze the maximum out of the economy and will tend to go for targets that require some effort to reach. A kind of game can then develop with the manager trying to deceive the planners about the capacity of his enterprise, while the planners retaliate by forcing higher targets.

Once the targets are set and agreed, the manager may see himself in a 'make or break' situation in which he will go all out for plan fulfilment as long as this looks possible, but will slacken off his effort if the target should appear beyond reach. The slackening off occurs partly because there is no point in working so hard if the bonuses are already lost, and partly because lower output may lead to a reduced target next time round. In his effort to fulfil his plan, the manager will have to deal with many problems that arise from factors beyond his control. If important raw materials and components do not arrive at the proper time, if machinery breaks down and spare parts are not available, if labour proves to be inadequate in some way, then output is lost and the target in jeopardy. The official links for dealing with such problems will be with the ministries, but the bureaucratic structure may involve delays in getting corrective action. The manager can then be expected to establish unofficial contacts with other manufacturers and suppliers. Unofficial and generally illegal arrangements for the barter of materials and plant have tended to develop in the communist economies as enterprise managers struggled to deal with the bottlenecks and failures of the administrative machine.[3]

The managers of the wholesale and retail enterprises have a rather different set of problems. Their job is to see that goods are distributed rapidly and efficiently and that proper stocks are maintained. They do not place orders with the production enterprises, but receive allocations of goods in accordance with the plan. Not only will the range of goods supplied be determined by the planners, but so will the prices to be charged. Some prices will be fixed in furtherance of some social aim, as when key foodstuffs are given low prices and alcohol a high price. Most prices will be set at a level which just ensures that everything is sold, i.e. market clearing prices. This is done to avoid queues, black-market dealing, and the accumulation of unwanted stocks.

The consumer's purchasing power is also subject to the influence of the planner. Basic wage and salary levels for the various occupations will be predetermined although there can be boosts to income from bonuses and premiums for special effort. There will be a wide range of social security payments or, more likely, some minimum state income for non-workers, but there will be no unearned income in the form of rent, interest or profits. In times of crisis, workers may be directed to particular jobs, but in general a relatively free labour market can be expected. This will entail some response of wage differentials to the relative scarcities of types of labour, but there will normally be equal pay for women, so incomes can be expected to be relatively more equally distributed than in most of the capitalist world.

Although the consumer has the freedom to choose from among the goods and services available in the shops, this does not necessarily imply that the consumer has any direct influence on the selection of that range. The reasons for this lack of consumer control are explored in the next two sections.

Information Exchange and the Channels of Communication One way to illustrate the links and interactions between the management and other decision units is to follow through the impact of some change in consumer demand. Assume that consumers, in the course of a year, come to prefer a particular type of record player that is available in the shops. The retail enterprises notice that their stocks of this model start to go down unusually rapidly and may even be exhausted so that queues tend to form whenever it is known that a delivery of this model

[3]This section should be compared with the analysis in Chapters 4 and 5.

has taken place. On the other hand, the stocks of the less favoured models start to build up. If the consumer preferences revealed by this situation are to be acted upon, the relevant planning authorities must be informed. There is no incentive, however, for the retail managers to act quickly to pass on the information, since they will receive no reward for doing so — but let us assume that they report back to the appropriate ministry if only to reduce the number of complaints they get from dissatisfied customers.

The ministry planners will not be very willing to tinker with the production targets and material allocations already laboriously agreed with the production enterprises, and they may well respond in the short run by ordering a rise in the price of the favoured record player to discourage demand and a cut in the price of the others to give their sales a boost. This may ease the stock position of the retailers and the value of their total sales may rise as a result of these price adjustments, but there is as yet no move to change the pattern of production in accordance with consumer preferences. The planners must decide how significant and permanent this change of taste is, but in any event they are not likely to make significant revisions in production targets until the next annual plan. It should also be remembered that in the case of some product types or groups, the authorities may decide to deliberately ignore consumer preferences either because those preferences are officially regarded as undesirable in themselves, or because meeting them would involve a significant departure from the objectives of the five-year plan. In the meantime, the production of an unwanted (and perhaps unsaleable) good continues while the availability of a much wanted good is restricted.

Now in *any* economy, the consumer can only express a practical interest or lack of interest in products that are actually produced and available to him, and in a competitive market economy, part of the competitive process is the constant search for new products and technologies or more appealing variants of existing products. There is little incentive for the planners and producers in a command economy to search for and try out new ideas, styles, products and processes since these tend initially to create extra problems with production and greater uncertainty about consumer demand. There will be a natural preference for 'playing safe' with well-tried and tested products and a dislike of pandering to the vagaries of fashion or consumer taste. It is not therefore surprising that planners prefer to deal with only a few types of car or TV set rather than offering a vast range, and in any case they would probably argue that such a variety was unnecessary and wasteful.

The Role of Prices and Profits in a Command Economy In the competitive market economy, prices are the key economic indicators and profit the key motivator, but what is their role in the centralised command economy? At the production enterprise and material supply level, prices are likely to be little more than administrative accounting units used in official book-keeping. The social ownership of the means of production together with the administration of material balances is likely to downgrade the significance of prices. There will be a tendency to regard land, buildings and capital funds as social goods that should not carry a 'price', an attitude that will be fostered by an ideological and psychological dislike of rent and interest payments which will be associated with forms of capitalist exploitation. Prices may be deliberately manipulated for political, social and economic reasons — for example, the setting of very low prices for coal and steel and high prices for light engineering goods is one way of expressing the planner's preference for heavy industry over consumption goods production. In general, however, it is likely that producer prices will be based on the average costs of production for each industry branch, which will mean that in accounting terms, many enterprises will make profits while others make losses. We have already seen that consumer prices will be adjusted according to consumer demand so as to clear stocks. Given, in addition, that many basic material prices are aritrarily fixed by the authorities, that wage rates are controlled, and that both profit margins and losses are to a great extent 'planned', then the final prices of goods as they appear to consumers and producers will probably bear little relation to comparable free market prices and costs.

Whether or not this is regarded as a serious problem depends on how far one accepts the pricing decisions of the planners as an accurate reflection of the society's 'true' costs. In Chapter 8 we saw that social cost-benefit analysis is difficult because so many costs and benefits have no unambiguous market price. In a socialist economy, we really need a social cost-benefit approach to all pricing and supply problems, but we may have very little in the way of a logical valuation system to use as a pricing base. The Marxian labour theory of value (pp. 161) has not proved to be operational concept in the socialist countries and it is interesting that Eastern European countries are not above using Western capitalist prices to set standards, especially in foreign trade deals.

Profits are as ambiguous in a command economy as are prices. There must be surpluses in a command economy to enable it to invest, develop and grow. The planners may prefer to acquire the necessary surpluses by the manipulation of costs, wages and prices rather than by levying taxes on incomes since incomes are already supposed to reflect the workers' 'share' in the national product. If prices are arbitrary in an economy, then so will the profits that result be largely arbitrary. The major point to keep in mind is that in a centralised command economy of the kind described in this chapter, profits are accounting residues that do not provide a motivation or incentive for action. High profit rates in an industry or trade will not necessarily lead to more resources being allocated to that activity, nor will low profits lead to a cut back in allocations. The productive and retail enterprise managers and their fellow workers will not get a share of the profits that arise from their work and will have their eyes instead on bonuses for plan fulfillment.

A SUMMARY OF THE POTENTIAL STRENGTHS AND WEAKNESSES OF THE SOCIALIST COMMAND ECONOMY

There has been a tendency in the last few sections to emphasise the illogicalities and inefficiencies of a command economy, but we must now attempt a more balanced assessment of the merits and demerits of such a system.

The Strengths

Motivation   The public ownership of the means of production greatly reduces class divisions and antagonisms arising from worker/capitalist relationships, while the motivation of private profit is replaced by some expression of the collective interests of society. Workers are encouraged to display a collective pride and responsibility in their work, and trade unions — if they exist — are expected to foster the idea of mutual dependence and assistance between workers and managers. Work, whether by hand or by brain, becomes an expression of social responsibility and confers dignity and status on the worker — alienation is expected to disappear.

Equality   Incomes are probably more evenly distributed, the economic power of wealth eliminated, and extremes of poverty abolished. Educational and economic opportunities are widened and the rewards go to ability and effort.

The use of Economic Resources   The economy is so planned that full employment can be maintained and economic fluctuations largely avoided.

Economic Growth   The planners' stress on more output, the ability to determine high levels of investment, the marshalling of special cadres in association with the organisation of crash programmes to eliminate bottlenecks in the economy, all, it is argued, enable a high rate of growth to be sustained. From 1950 to the late 1960s when Eastern European socialist countries were essentially command economies, their average annual rates of growth compared favourably with most of Western Europe even after the downward adjustment of their official figures so as to bring them more into line with Western methods of measurement.

The Avoidance of Waste and the Failures of Competition   The socialist regime may be expected to pay attention to the balance between private and social interests. There will be a tendency to avoid or discourage the over-rapid obsolescence of goods, the production of 'frivolous' forms of consumption, and the use of non-informational advertising and marketing.

The Weaknesses

Ideological and Bureaucratic Inflexibility   For the command economy to even exist, there must be a powerful political leadership, and this political leadership will usually be sustained by a body of ideas — in this case a socialist ideology — that may act as a straitjacket on new thought. This, together with the sheer complexity of the bureaucratic organisation that such an economy entails, is likely to lead to cautiousness, defensiveness, the over-rigid application of rules, and a general slowness to adjust to new situations. Private initiative, where it does occur, may be confined to socially undesirable areas, e.g. output target cheating and black-market activities.

Consumer Neglect   High investment levels, high levels of collective provision, and the absence of effective ways for the consumer to pass on his preferences at the retail stage will probably mean that the range of consumer goods produced by the economy is felt to be unnecessarily restricted.

Errors   The length of planning periods, the inflexibility of targets, and the use of 'crash' programmes can lead to a magnification of the effects of decision errors.

Irrational Prices   It will be impossible to calculate the 'true' costs and benefits of any decision in the absence of a 'rational' valuation system. Similarly, the measurement of efficiency and cost-effectiveness is made very difficult.

Alienation Can Return   The longer that a command economy imposes consumer austerity, rigid labour discipline and sustained high levels of effort, the more likely it is that the population will begin to feel 'put upon' or even oppressed by the regime. New class divisions based on party or other elites can appear. In these circumstances, unless the Party is able to regenerate the necessary ideological zeal, the motivational strengths of the economy will weaken and there could be a widespread return to the preservation of private interests. Once this happens, a worker in a state enterprise or farm can feel just as alienated as the capitalist worker is supposed to feel.

Freedom   Many of those who support the concept of a competitive capitalist economy for its economic efficiency also argue that it fosters personal freedoms. There is no doubt that the command economy imposes severe limitations on personal freedoms of all kinds, but this is done in the name of the social or collective will of the people. The reader must use his own judgement about the ability of the ruling party to reflect that will.

IS CAPITALISM 'BETTER' THAN SOCIALISM?

There is no simple, rational way to answer this question in purely economic terms, and in any case, the political aspects are of crucial importance. The meaning of 'better' in this context must be clearly defined first. This must involve a specification of the aims and objectives of a society, the allocation of relative degrees of importance to these aims, and then testing which economic regime would most nearly allow their attainment. It is possible to compare American technology with Russian, or the range of goods in Parisian shops with that in Prague, or the relative rates of growth in Japan and Albania, but individual comparisons of this kind cannot give an assessment of the overall well-being of the populations in each of these societies. Indeed, we may well question whether such comparisons made between economies with quite different histories, cultures, stages of development, natural resources, etc., are really very meaningful.

What can be more usefully attempted is the examination of how far an economy meets the needs of society as currently expressed. The socialist economies of Europe have been undergoing some agonising self-appraisals during the last ten years or so, during which criticisms of the command-type structure came more and more into the open. These economies were seen as being not well adapted to the growing sophistication of their peoples and problems. Specific weaknesses in the fields of economic growth, consumer choice and bureaucratic inflexibility were to lead to considerable changes or 'reforms' in the command structure described in this chapter, although the economies were to remain firmly in the socialist camp. The significance of these reforms will be discussed in the next chapter along with recent developments in capitalist economies. The command economy format may still have its place, however, and tends to appear in modified forms during times of great national emergency such as all-out war or in the period of reconstruction following revolutions led by Marxist groups or parties, usually involving, these days, an attempt by a backward or underdeveloped economy to pull itself out of its own circle of poverty.

Chapter 10

Is There a Future for Free Market Economics?

INTRODUCTION

We have been ranging widely in this book over societies and economies past and present, primitive and advanced, capitalist and socialist, in an attempt to bring out essential economic charcteristics and relationships. In this chapter, a broad view of contemporary trends in the world's major economies will be taken and many matters opened up in earlier chapters brought together so as to take stock of our present stage of advanced economic evolution.

PART I

ASPECTS OF MODERN PRIVATE ENTERPRISE

Some Significant Trends

The danger with simply presenting a string of 'significant' trends in modern private enterprise is not only that the order in which they are presented may be interpreted as implying their relative importance, but also that a casual link or sequence may be suggested there none is known to exist. Most of the trends to be discussed appeared broadly simultaneously, and are often closely interconnected. For example, J. K. Galbraith in his book *The New Industrial State* interprets many of these trends as 'the imperatives of technology', suggesting a degree of deterministic inevitability that we would hesitate to adopt. Nevertheless, the approach does provide a possible point of departure.

One has only to compare stereo record players with 'wind-up' gramophones, automatic washing machines with scrubbing boards, and colour TV sets with pianos to emphasise the greater degree of sophistication in the technology of present-day consumer goods over those of the comparatively recent past. Consumers benefit as technical change improves the performance of old-style products, but are in addition introduced to new products and services unthinkable under old-fashioned technology. An example of the latter is the current rapid increase in the sales of pocket electronic calculators to the domestic market, a change that represents a massive leap from sums worked laboriously with pen and paper to what is effectively a mini computer operation. Over recent decades, consumers in modern capitalist economies have come to enjoy and demand not only improved performance from their goods but also the thrill of consuming up-to-date technological advance.

In the absence of genuine price competition in the markets for mass-produced goods, a firm will seek to preserve the share it holds of its current market or attempt to break into a new market by developing and exploiting a degree of technological superiority (see Chapters 4 and 5). The steady growth in the big firms of long-term research and development (R&D) programmes is a manifestation of the attempt to keep one jump ahead of rivals (as is, of course, the appearance of industrial espionage the result of a desire to prevent competitors from gaining a technical advantage).

In these circumstances, the time-lag between having an idea for a product and its final display in the shops becomes extended. Apart from the necessary R&D activity, a great deal of time and money can go into the design and construction of the new production facilities required. Production processes are themselves subject to technological change and there are often important economies to be gained from large-scale installations. All this tends to raise the level of the fixed costs that have to be recovered, and mass sales then become essential if the required return on capital is to be achieved. Since most firms in this kind of market will be engaged in the same race for supremacy, any product is likely to have a fairly short sales life. [1] In such circumstances, the losses arising from error in production and marketing decisions can be very high indeed. A firm must be expected to adopt strategies that will reduce these risks as far as possible. Certainly the quality and complexity of organisational effort required in such a firm will be of a high order and beyond the long-run capabilities of the 'one man boss' type of management.

Some Ways to Reduce Risk and Uncertainty

The trends outlined above imply that modern businessmen face risks

[1] Patents are intended to give legal protection for genuine technical improvements and new inventions for at least a limited period of time, but there is nothing to stop rival firms from trying to develop an alternative way of doing the same thing.

and uncertainties on a much larger scale than they ever did in the past when product and market changes took place relatively slowly and when most products could be developed and manufactured on the strength of quite small capital investments and in 'back-yard' factories. A foreseeable response to this situation has been the effort to gain more control over the market environment and to minimise the effects of unexpected occurrences. One of the earliest strategies adopted for this purpose and which became widespread in the USA at the end of the last century is the extension of the firm's control to the production stages before and after that originally occupied by the firm. An early example in both Europe and America was the attempt by iron and steel makers to own and control not only the producers and suppliers of raw materials such as coal mines, iron ore and limestone quarries, but also some of the ultimate users of their product in the metal manufacturing industry. This development of ownership and control up and down the production and distribution chain (vertical integration) was the most common form of industrial combination in the period from 1900 to 1939 and could develop from any point in the chain — as illustrated by the widespread phenomenon of large retail organisations moving into the manufacture of the goods they sell.

Another well-established strategy is to take over or eliminate rivals at the same stage of production, as when a firm engaged in textile finishing and dyeing attempts to control or acquire other firms in the same trade; this is called 'horizontal integration'. Both vertical and horizontal integration give rise to public fears about the possible misuse of monopoly powers arising from these strategies and they lead to the kind of governmental controls described in Chapter 6.

The great business depression of the early 1930s demonstrated to capitalists the dangers of being totally committed to one particular industry or product area. The trend that dominated industrial combinations from the 1940s to the 1960s was the move by large firms into different but related areas to their home business. A typical example from both sides of the Atlantic was when vertically integrated firms in the film-making and distribution industry began to look for a hedge against the decline in cinema attendances that accompanied the rise of television viewing. These firms decided that they were really in the 'entertainment' business and so they moved into the entertainment and leisure areas such as dance halls, bowling alleys, bingo, television film and pop record manufacture. This process is appropriately labelled 'diversification' and as far as the firms were concerned had the merit of spreading risks and opening up new market opportunities and also allowed expertise and experience in a particular trade to be applied in different but related areas.

In the second half of the 1960s another form of extension of influence for the firm came to the fore. This time the aim was not primarily to consolidate market shares or to make use of specialised skills related to particular areas of business, but rather to allow successful managements to apply their general management and financial skill wherever it might produce significant gain. Any firm, no matter what its line of business, that was not making the most profitable use of its assets or which was lagging because of ineffective or inept management and control could find itself captured and absorbed by another, but not necessarily larger, firm. There would then follow a rigorous investigation into the firm's potential and probably a major reorganisation (perhaps even the winding up of the firm). The new type of firm that emerges from this process is probably one where a parent or 'holding' company manages, via a variety of financial and managerial controls, a collection of disparate firms. The firms making up such a 'conglomerate', as they are called, are linked by common ownership and managerial tutelage, but each may in fact operate with a high degree of autonomy as a result of the decentralisation of detailed decision-making. One more organisational development that should be mentioned here is the firm which has a large part of its operation based overseas in subsidiaries and associated companies. The biggest of these can span the world and are known as multinationals. These companies raise special problems which we will deal with in Chapter 12.

The New Dimensions of Management

The developments in technology, in the scale of plant and in the complexity of business organisation that we have been examining, have required fundamental changes in the nature of the managerial function. The modern large, science- or technology-based company requires the skills of a wide range of specialists such as accountants, scientists, engineers, personnel managers, marketing men and lawyers. A striking feature of the pattern of employment in the twentieth-century industrialised economy has been the steady growth in the proportion of employees in non-manual or 'white-collar' jobs. The office staff of a large manufacturing company can often considerably outnumber those engaged in direct production. Decisions about the choice of production process, the siting of a factory, the nature of an advertising campaign or the pattern of distribution to be adopted will be made by the senior executives of such a firm only after they have received the reports and recommendations of the appropriate experts in the field. Galbraith argues that the co-ordination and combined influence of these 'management technicians' leads to a whole new style of company control where what he calls 'the managerial technostructure' acquires important new powers and objectives.

The rise of the 'technostructure' was made possible by the fact that very large companies are nearly always organised as 'joint stock' companies, i.e. the ownership of the company's assets is vested in stocks and shares which can be bought and sold on the open market. In the early days of the Industrial Revolution or in the case of small firms today, the man running the firm was usually the man who put up the necessary capital — he is the classic owner-entrepreneur of the traditional economic textbooks. But the steady advance of the very large joint stock company where the number of shareholders can run into many thousands has opened up a gulf between owners and managers.

It is possible today to find companies, whose shares are dealt in on the open market, where some individuals hold a significant percentage of the voting ordinary shares. Such individuals are likely to be either recent founders of the firm (and their relations) or members of families that have had long-standing ownership and managerial connections with the company.

More typical individual shareholders however will hold only a tiny fraction of the total voting shares in a large public company. The number of individuals holding shares directly in such a company can run into hundreds of thousands. Ordinary shareholders can exert pressure on the company's directors in two main ways — they can refuse to reappoint them or can question and criticise them for their performance at the annual general meetings of the company, or they can simply sell their holdings and thereby perhaps affect share values. There is no lack of evidence to show (a) that attendances at AGMs are usually poor, (b) that individual shareholders find it difficult to organise any kind of revolt against directors mainly because so many individuals would have to co-operate before sufficient voting strength could be gathered, and (c) that shareholders are at a disadvantage in any question-and-answer session because of the lack of detailed information available to them. In such circumstances, it has been argued, the directors of large public companies may not be under the effective control of the shareholders and owners of the company.

Alongside these developments in manager/ownership relationships have been other changes in the nature of shareholdings in general. The individual investor in stocks and shares has realised the dangers of 'puting all his eggs in one basket', and he is increasingly spreading his risks by holding a diversified 'portfolio' of investments. The selection of the investments to make up his portfolio requires experience and expertise usually beyond the investor's capability. In these circumstances it is both convenient and profitable to hand one's wealth over to the 'expert' to invest and manage on one's behalf. In the UK, the rapid growth of investment and unit trusts[2] during the 1960s was a significant manifestation of the idea of hiring specialist skills.

More important still than the investment and unit trust holdings are the very large holdings in the hands of insurance and pension funds, which were estimated at over 20 per cent of all ordinary share holdings at the end of the 1960s. The member of the public who pays contributions to a pension fund in expectation of future benefits will not always realise that his money is being invested on his behalf on the Stock Exchange. In this case the links between the ultimate providers of investment funds and company managers are tenuous in the extreme.

The extent of the growth in the importance of these so-called 'institutional' investors is indicated by estimates[3] of the beneficial ownership of ordinary shares quoted on the London Stock Exchange. These show that the percentage of the market value of ordinary shares owned by persons, executors and trustees fell from 66 per cent in 1957 to 47 per cent in 1970, while over the same period the holdings of insurance and pension funds, investment and unit trusts, rose from 18 per cent to 32 per cent.

The overall effect of such developments is to give more and more people a stake in modern capitalism. On the other hand, the nature of this investment is such that the freedom of action of the technostructure may be increasing.

How Big is Modern Business?

The compounding of such influences as economies of scale, rapid technological change, diversification and the other forms of company merger leads to an increase in the size of business concerns. Size can be measured in various ways, for example by value of assets or of sales, or by numbers employed. By the end of the 1960s the largest 100 companies in the UK were estimated to control from 50 to 65 per

[2]*Investment trusts* are limited companies which reinvest the funds contributed by their own shareholders in a selected portfolio of shares.

Unit trusts are not limited companies but trusts operating under government regulations. They are aimed at the small investor who buys 'units' or sections of a block of investments selected by professional managers and they are held in trust on the investors' behalf.

[3]J. Moyle, *The Pattern of Ordinary Share Ownership 1957-1970* (CUP, 1971).

cent of manufacturing and distributive business, depending on the particular measure used. Not only is there a high degree of dominance by the biggest firms, but this dominance has been increasing steadily over the last twenty-five years, during which time it has almost doubled.

A similar degree of dominance has been observed in France, West Germany, Italy, Japan, the Netherlands and the USA. The potential importance of the top firms, many of which are multinational in the scale and scope of their operations, is suggested by the controversial prediction of one American researcher that if present trends continue, the bulk of the world's manufacturing output will, by 1985, be supplied by only 300 world-wide companies of which 200 will be based in the USA. There are already a number of vast corporations with sales revenues that exceed the Gross National Product of some of the smaller European countries.

Great size, the diversification of interests and the divorce of ownership from the management of capital has greatly enhanced the modern corporation's capacity to survive. The jobs and career prospects of the technostructure depend on both survival and growth. One of the tasks that the management can be expected to set itself, therefore, is to prepare a plan or set of programmes for investment, product development, market penetration, etc., that will keep the 'juggernaut' rolling. The corporate plan or strategy that evolves will try to forestall dangers to company development and will specify the tactics for dealing with them. These corporations are unlikely to wither and die in the way that family and one-man concerns do, since even if the present management fails to maintain the necessary momentum, a rival management or even, as we shall see later, a Government may step in to revitalise the company's assets.

Consumer Power or Management Manipulation

The separation of ownership from control in the modern corporation leads, as we have seen, to a reduction in the effective power of the shareholder. The average investor is too small on his own to have any chance of getting rid of a board of directors and an organised revolt is difficult and costly to mount. The large institutional investors, represented by the managers of the insurance and pensions funds prefer not to intervene in the running of a company unless it is clearly getting into difficulties. Hence it has been suggested that as long as the company's executives can keep the shareholders moderately happy by paying adequate dividends and by maintaining share valuations, then the technostructure will be able to busy itself with its own goals and aims. The usual assumption is that companies will try to maximise profits, but a number of economists over the last decade or so have proposed a variety of other possible goals. These alternative goals include the maximisation of sales and asset growth, the avoidance of takeover, maintaining stock market valuations, and setting profit targets that will keep the shareholders happy but also allow scope for various managerial perks and benefits, empire building, etc. All these goals are easier to achieve if the corporation is growing.

We shall consider in the next section whether these goals are necessarily in conflict with profit maximisation, but at this point we raise an issue concerning the setting of managerial goals and their relation to the role of the consumer in modern economies. It is alleged by some economists that the modern corporation as depicted so far in this chapter is capable of 'revising the sequence', as Galbraith calls it, of market forces. In the traditional sequence as broadly outlined in Chapter 4, the consumer decides what shall be produced by exercising his purchasing power either for or against various products. The producer can only respond to the price and profit information coming to him via the market process and is therefore dictated to by the strength of consumer preferences. The consumer is said to be 'sovereign'. Now it has been argued that this sequence can be reversed by the modern corporation as follows. The technostructure in setting up its corporate plan will put a high priority on the continuous growth of the company. Market and technical research is carried out in order to discover (a) gaps in the existing trading environment that could be filled by existing or modified products, and (b) new products for which a market does not at present exist. It is the latter strategy that is seen as crucial. Since the costs of new product failure are frequently very great, the corporation takes steps to render failure most unlikely. This is done by conducting, via the mass media, an intensive advertising and sales campaign exploiting all the psychological and other techniques now available to the marketing executive. The consumer will have been steadily 'softened up' by all the advertisements across the economy portraying the 'good life' as consisting of the opportunity to consume more and more goods of an increasingly exotic nature.

The revised sequence now has the corporation deciding what shall be produced and then setting out to ensure that the consumer buys it — the consumer is no longer sovereign, but is rather a puppet performer in a consumption game in which the corporation makes the rules and pulls the strings. It is difficult to know how seriously to take these ideas; there is after all a general presumption in economic theory that an increase in consumption leads to an increase in total satisfaction. In addition, if the basic necessities of life are already provided, is there any reason why people should not be allowed to take part in some kind of consumption game? It is possible to withdraw from participation to a large extent if one so wishes.

And yet, as we shall see in Chapters 11 and 12, the constant stress on more and more production and consumption does have global consequences of very great significance.

A Cause for Concern?

A simple projection of the trends discussed in Chapter 8 and so far in this chapter would seem to lead to an economy characterised not by competitive market structures but by two dominant power groups, the State on one hand and the big corporations on the other. The critics of the broadly Galbraithian assessment so far presented in this chapter, however, would argue that the case has been overstated. They agree that the largest firms have been growing rapidly, but so has the size of the markets that they operate in. The big corporation in the big market may be less dominant in that market than the smaller firm in a much smaller market, so sheer size alone is not necessarily of significance.

One measure of the degree of market domination is the 'concentration ratio' which usually measures the sales of the four ⁴largest companies as a percentage of the total sales of all companies in that industry. One some interpretations of the USA ratios, the conclusion can be drawn that there is only a slow, or in some industries a zero, rate of growth in the degree of concentration, but this is not true of UK manufacturing industry where a sharp rise in concentration took place in the 1950s and 1960s. If one looks at the the shares in *total* manufacturing industry sales, employment or net output of the top 100 or 200 firms, on the other hand, then the evidence in both countries is clear — that an increasing share of total business is in the hands of the few hundred biggest corporations.

Complications arise in the discussion of individual industry concentration ratios however, because of the problem of deciding to which industry a firm belongs when only part of its total activities falls into one industry group. In this case, total sales may be lumped into the home industry group, thus overstating the degree of concentration. Similar problems arise when a firm has a high proportion of overseas sales in its total, although the overall total goes into the ratio calculation. With these points in mind, we should be cautious

⁴Most concentration ratios available are for the top four firms, and although some have been constructed for larger numbers, up to the top eight firms for example, the trends observed are broadly the same.

when using concentration ratios to measure the degree of competition within an industry. This 'degree of competition' problem is clearly shown in the rapid growth of diversified conglomerate companies which may have very little effect on the level of concentration within an industry, although it will certainly increase the control of all industry in fewer hands, namely, of the managers.

Another aspect to be kept in mind is that in most Western developed economies, the highest concentration ratios tend to occur in industries such as petroleum, transport equipment (especially cars and aircraft), rubber and chemicals — mainly the fast-growing industries with a technological base. Concentration is generally low in a wide range of industries including timber, furniture, clothing and footwear, and food processing. To keep things in perspective, it should also be remembered that manufacturing industries account for only about one-third of GNP in the UK.

If the worries about the 'big business corporation' are therefore primarily concerned with a reduction in the degree of competition in various markets and industries, then fears about the size of modern corporations may be misplaced. It has even been suggested that competition may be intensified. In Chapters 4 and 6, we discussed various barriers to entry to an industry including economies of scale, minimum efficient plant size, the need for big capital outlays, and product differentiation backed by massive advertising expenditures. Now while such barriers may prove insurmountable by small firms, they are nearly all vulnerable to the resources and skills available to the modern corporate technostructure.

Let us consider again the question of motivation. The Galbraithian type analysis suggests that the directors and executives of a large company are almost free of any external control and responsibility as a result of the feeble power of the shareholders, and can therefore pursue their own goals. We need to ask, however, whether goals like growth, security, big R&D budgets and diversified opportunities are necessarily in conflict with the traditional goal of profit maximisation. If profits are to be maximised over the company's normal planning horizon rather than in the short term, then all these goals can be reconciled. The highest possible long-run profits can only assist the aims of the technostructure.

Furthermore, even though directors and executives may hold only a very small percentage of the company's total issued share capital, these holdings will often form a high percentage of the executive's total personal wealth. He will thus be directly interested in both good dividends and stable growth. He will also be careful not to disturb the flocks of vulture-like conglomerates on the look-out for poorly run, i.e. low profit, companies, or the managers of the trusts and funds who could reduce share prices by selling off their holdings in companies with below average performance. Another factor which will probably grow in importance is the widespread adoption of modern management accounting and other techniques, computerised financial analysis, etc., a trend reinforced and fostered by the steady recruitment into the technostructure of business school graduates trained from the start on the assumption of profit maximisation as the only proper goal. As one writer has suggested, whereas the old-style tycoon and the family heirarchies could wield their power with autocratic eccentricity if they wished, the modern company man must make money to survive.

Even so, there may well be something to fear from a highly competitive struggle which takes the form of a battle between giants. The bigger they are, the harder they fall, and the aftermath of such a conflict could endanger thousands of jobs and perhaps even national economies. When a few groups of men, backed up by however many experts, can make decisions which affect huge amounts of capital, vast quantities of materials, and armies of work people, then perhaps we are more in the world of politics than of economics. After all, what is to stop such corporations tiring of the competitive struggle and simply carving up their markets in much the same way that governments have made territorial divisions? What can a national government do when a multinational corporation, with even more resources than that government, uses its control over resources against the interests of that government? The United Nations has begun to investigate these problems, but it is unlikely that economists have spent enough time and effort in investigating them as yet, to make confident predictions.

PART II

THE STATE IN THE MIXED ECONOMY

The expansion in the role of the State was explained in broad terms in Chapter 8 as a response to the stresses, strains and needs arising from the evolution of the modern capitalist economy. Galbraith's interpretation of growing governmental involvement in the American economy would suggest that public services and commercial and economic policy are manipulated so as to serve the interests of the corporate technostructure. It is true, of course, that there are powerful industrial (and agricultural) pressure groups at work in Western economies, but this does not necessarily mean that governments can be dictated to by them. Better education and better roads, for example, do help the business community but they are also demanded by the electorate at large.

The rise in the significance of public expenditure this century has helped to sustain and stabilise high consumption levels in the developed economies. Their populations have come to expect a continuous improvement in their living standards. The trade union movement has been an enthusiastic supporter of economic growth and full employment. Hence, the general economic and political environment, especially since World War II, has been favourable to the interests of the corporate managements.

Much of the governmental intervention in the workings of free enterprise market systems has however been aimed at dealing with apparent weaknesses and failures in those systems, and has been justified on three main grounds:

1. A belief that the market system is not working properly and is being distorted by private monopoly power or any other agreement or practice that restricts the degree of competition in the market.

2. An acceptance that the market mechanism is incapable of handling certain choices in a satisfactory manner, i.e. public goods and social costs.

3. A belief that the results of the competitive free market process are in some respects unsatisfactory and need correction.

As regards the first group, the nature of typical governmental intervention to ensure a competitive market environment was dealt with in Chapter 6, while Chapter 8 covered activities in the second group. It is to the problems of the third group that we now turn.

We begin by examining state intervention at the macro level by looking at aspects of national economic planning, regional problems and inflation, and then go on to consider some more detailed forms of intervention at the industry and firm level.

The Rise (and Decline) of Indicative Planning

In Chapter 9 we considered aspects of economic planning within a socialist command economy, but there are many other possible styles and degrees of economic planning. One version that has been tried by a number of European governments during the post-war period, notably in France, the Netherlands, Norway and the UK, is what is called 'indicative planning'. This type of planning activity is set within a predominantly free enterprise market economy and cannot therefore be based on detailed administrative instructions but must rather take the form of a set of agreed strategies and targets to which free market agents are encouraged to adhere. The plan can 'point the way' but it can only be carried out if the participants are prepared to co-operate. Governments have had many motives for attempting this type of voluntary collectivism, but in most cases the aims have been to,

1. raise the rate of economic growth of the country,
2. increase the rate of investment and to improve its quality,
3. avoid the wastes and disruption caused by fluctuations and instabilities in the economy whether these be in the form of unemployment, price rises, balance of payments problems or regional imbalances.
4. systematically isolate and deal with structural weaknesses in the economy, barriers to growth, restrictions on competition, etc., all with the aim of improving its general efficiency.

For a government to launch into indicative planning there must first be a presumption that market forces, if left to their own devices, will either not deal with these problems at all, or do so too slowly and ineffectually for the government's liking.

French Planning   Indicative planning in France began as a practical response to a pressing problem, but it was helped from the beginning by a long-established centralist approach to governmental administration. The first French economic plan covering the period 1946 to 1952 was an attempt to make rational and effective use of American economic aid during the period of recovery and reconstruction after World War II. As Europe moved into the prosperous '50s and '60s, the nature and aims of French planning changed. Heavy industry and then manufacturing industry gradually became less important target areas, so that by the end of the 1960s, the fifth plan was mainly concerned with social and community services, cultural matters and special regional problems.

Since the very practical first plan, the philosophy of French planning has evolved into something like the following: Before faster economic growth and steadily rising living standards can be achieved, there has to be a high and sustained level of investment by the commercial, industrial and public sectors. High investment rates will be encouraged if business uncertainties can be reduced and economic fluctuations avoided. A generally agreed set of economic targets reinforced by governmental intervention in key areas would engender a feeling of confidence in the business community and encourage firms to take a longer term and more favourable view of the economic environment, and so invest accordingly.

The experts in the central Commisariat du Plan begin by mapping out some feasible growth targets and plan priorities. These are submitted to Parliament and the Conseil Economique et Social (a watchdog council made up of selected interest groups) after initial cabinet vetting, so that the preferred plan variants can be isolated. Various modernisation commissions, covering both national and industry-wide areas and made up of representatives from business, trade unions, the civil service and academics, then get down to details. The commissions, in consultation with the Commisariat, attempt to discover, analyse and prepare solutions to any blockages or hindrances to the desired growth pattern. As in socialist planning, inconsistencies in the various industry and regional plans must be eliminated as far as possible, so that achieveable industry targets can be agreed upon.

Unlike socialist planning, the plan itself is in no real sense compulsory, although the ministries and public authorities must act in accordance with the final plan targets. Similarly, the major financial institutions (large publicly owned) will be expected to use their control of capital and credit in furtherance of the plan. Some ministries, especially finance, can influence the investment and pricing policies of individual private enterprises by the use of special planning agreements, loans, and various other forms of financial and taxation inducements. But in the last analysis, the plan can only be binding on the private sector if the business community wishes it to be. Business interests are widely represented on the various planning bodies, and will have contributed to the generally agreed conclusions, so they will have some commitment to the final version. The business community is also aware that a general adhereance to the industry targets will increase the value of the plan document as a forecast of future economic trends. In fact, French planning can be seen as a major exercise in co-operative forecasting.

Although this voluntary co-operation is regarded by many as the real strength of French planning, others see dangers in the possibly excessive influence it places in the hands of the big corporations. It is perhaps inevitable that the biggest companies are well represented on the various commissions, since they will account for a large share of the hoped-for investment and growth. It is certainly easier for the ministries and financial institutions to deal with a few very large companies which are able to make a real impact, than to deal with thousands of small firms. The French authorities have even declared themselves in favour of larger business units as preferable to the fragmentation more typical of French industry. The planning system has been under increasing strain in recent years, especially with threats of trade union non-cooperation. It has probably slipped from being the 'grand affaire' that it was once called, and is best seen today as providing channels through which major public, social and economic issues can be debated.

The British Planning Experiments   It was a traditionally anti-planning Conservative Government that looked to the French for planning inspiration at the end of the 1950s. The UK economy had by then already established its typical post-war characteristics of slow growth relative to most European countries, poor investment rates, and a weak balance of payments. The UK Government favoured co-operative forecasting in 1961, but was ideologically opposed to detailed economic planning and state intervention. The compromise was to create the National Economic Development Council (NEDC) on which representatives of the business and trade union communities were present as well as officials from the Government and the public enterprises. Within a year or so, over twenty Economic Development Committees (EDCs) representing various industry groups were also in existence. Work went ahead to study the bottlenecks and weaknesses in the UK economy that might prevent it from attaining a faster rate of growth, and a number of interesting and useful pamphlets were published. Following the election of a Labour Government in 1964, a new but short-lived ministry, the Department of Economic Affairs, took over the planning function of the NEDC. Regional planning bodies were also set up and work began on the preparation of regional economic development plans which were meant to be (but never were) fully integrated into the national planning exercise.

The UK now had an institutional structure which had a number of similarities with that operated by the French, but events following the publication of the hurriedly prepared 'National Plan' in 1965 demonstrated that the British model was of a quite different nature to the French. Firstly, there was never a high degree of commitment to the National Plan by the business community, a large section of which was opposed to the idea of planning in principle. Secondly, the network of detailed and discretionary administrative controls used by the French was largely absent in the UK, and in any event there was a strong resistance to the kind of selective intervention and bargaining with individual companies so successfully used by the French. Thirdly, unlike France, the UK had a well-developed capital and money market which granted greater freedom and independence to the private sector. Lastly, Britain's economic health was so susceptible to balance of payments and foreign exchange disequilibria that it proved impossible to create a period of comparative stability to allow a 'feel' for economic planning of the indicative kind to develop. Within two years of its appearance, the National Plan was submerged by short-run economic crises, and in spite of attempts to keep the idea alive by the issue of discussion documents, neither Labour nor Conservative governments have shown much interest since.

Indicative planning requires a favourable environment both economically and politically for its essential elements of voluntary co-operation to work. The same might be said for attempts to introduce and operate a system of voluntary prices and incomes control. An economic plan launched as a way out of acute economic crisis might therefore gain the necessary commitment for its success.

Regional Economic Problems

The relatively early date (the end of the eighteenth century) of Britain's Industrial Revolution, together with its initial dependence on coal as the main source of energy, meant that heavy industry was concentrated in a few major locations. The penalties of being 'first' meant that outdated technology combined with industrial inertia to create pockets of traditional industry which were very vulnerable to changes in the level of business activity and the pressures of foreign competition. Ever since the mid-1930s, UK governments have attempted to ameliorate the resulting problems of high regional unemployment by an increasingly complex battery of controls and subsidies. These have taken many forms, from the power to refuse planning and building permissions to industry and commerce in areas of high employment, to the provision of cheap or free factory space in the assisted areas, from special loans and grants to aid private investment in the afflicted regions, to the payment of wage subsidies. Instead of concentrating on increasing labour mobility, the general aim has been to take work to the workers by the use of persuasion, financial inducements and the prevention of undesired development. The compulsory 'direction' of labour and capital has been regarded as intolerable except in times of national emergency such as wartime.

Inflation

Unfortunately, the generally full employment situation experienced by the capitalist world since the Second World War has been accompanied by persistent inflation. Inflation in the UK has caused problems in two main directions: (*a*) the fact that over recent decades, the UK has frequently suffered rates of inflation higher than those ruling in her major trading rivals' economies. During the period 1947 to 1967, when the exchange rate for sterling was fixed and rigidly adhered to, inflation led to a continual strain on the balance of payments as British goods suffered from price competition in the world markets. Sterling devaluation has become a common feature of the early 1970s, and fears about inflation have turned more towards (*b*) the damaging effects of inflation in itself. The very rapid and accelerating rise in world and domestic prices from about 1970 reinforced by the oil and commodity price crises are subjecting many economies to severe strains. These strains are mainly associated with the problem of ensuring that the burdens of very rapid inflation are shared as 'fairly' as possible across the population, and with the threat that inflation brings to economic and political stability.

Now the various possible causes of inflation are well known, although there is controversy about which are the most important at any one time and hence about the best cure. That debate is outside the scope of this book. Post-war UK governments have tried most of the more orthodox cures at one time or another, such as restricting aggregate demand and controlling the money supply, but there has been an increasing tendency to act directly on wage and price levels.

There have been, for example, several attempts at achieving a system of voluntary wage and price controls. Sometimes an independent board or panel would be set up to scrutinise proposed price and wage increases so as to determine whether they are 'justified'. The State has also used its direct power as an employer of civil servants and as the sponsor of nationalised industries to hold down the level of wage settlements and price increases in these sectors.

In the 1960s and '70s the introduction of statutory controls such as wage freezes became more common, mainly because voluntary systems proved to be very unreliable. There were also attempts to use legislation to limit trade union militancy since a link between the rate of inflation and the frequency and seriousness of strikes and industrial disputes was believed to be established. A discernable trend in the early 1970s was in the use of direct and more specific controls over such things as company dividends and profit margins. This development is likely to be taken further if the Labour Party's proposed 'planning agreements' between the Government and selected key companies are put into full operation. These aggreements may include investment, development and locational matters as well as prices, wages and profits, and have similar characteristics to the selective agreements already mentioned as part of the French planning mechanism.

The Protection and Encouragement of National Economic Assets

The protection and subsidisation of the British agricultural industry is long established and, especially in relation to the European Common Market, increasingly controversial. The steady decline in Britain's relative position in such things as economic growth, living standards and share of world exports of manufactures has led governments into more and more interventionalist industrial policies. The relatively low proportion of Britain's GNP going into investment was pinpointed as a key area of weakness, and a variety of inducements to investment has been tried. These have mainly taken the form of tax and depreciation concessions available to industry in general (the special regional assistance mentioned on pp. 195, is in addition to this). For a time, in the late 1960s and early '70s, direct cash grants were made to firms that carried out approved investments. Financial assistance was also made available to specific industries and companies where this seemed to be in the 'national interest'. Sometimes this aid was linked to regional problems, but often the aim appeared to be to ensure the survival of a British company in a field where foreign dominance might otherwise be complete. This is most obvious in industries where large R&D budgets and heavy capital expenditure are required but are unlikely to be financed from private sources. Prime examples in the UK are the computer and aircraft industries. Both are struggling in a world market dominated by giant American companies and also have sensitive links with the defence industry.

Governments have encouraged and helped to finance mergers and combinations of firms in industries where it was believed that the larger units so created would gain significant economies of scale or be able to mount more effective R&D programmes. The Labour Government's ill-fated Industrial Reorganisation Corporation was set up for this purpose in the late 1960s and concentrated on what were regarded as key industrial areas such as machine tool manufacture. Significantly, the IRC not only organised mergers in private industry, but also took a stake in the equity of the companies concerned. The declared intention was to resell these holdings to the public when the reorganisation had been successfully completed, but it did set a kind of precedent. British government shareholdings in the private sector are not new, of course, but as in the case of the old Suez Canal Company or British Petroleum, they had in the past arisen almost by accident. In the second half of the 1960s and the early '70s, the range of shareholdings increased as a result of 'rescue' operations mounted to prevent the collapse of important companies. One of the most significant of these to date was concerned with the Clydeside shipbuilding industry. Another was the aero-engine division of Rolls Royce. In these cases the motives for public rescue included the need to preserve employment, the preservation of technological superiority in a key defence area, and simple national pride.

Further developments can be expected from the Labour Government elected in 1974 which is pledged to set up a National Enterprise Board. The proposed Board has the dual functions of acting as a holding company for existing state shareholdings, and of extending public ownership into any area of commerce or industry where the 'national interest' requires it. The controversy over the manner in which North Sea oil should be exploited illustrates the concern felt by many politicians about the need to protect national rights in the face of international commercial interests.

Industrial Co-operation and Social Responsilibity

The concentration in the hands of a few hundred big corporations of economic power over men, money and materials was likely to bring these corporations into the arena of public debate and controversy. Meanwhile, a series of amalgamations in the trade union movement meant that by the early 1970s, over three-quarters of Britain's 11 million trade unionists belonged to the biggest 23 out of a national total of 470 unions. Inevitably, the leaders of these great national unions became powerful figures with a considerable responsibility for the industrial peace of the country. Although the complex and highly integrated nature of much of modern industry can give a handful of militant workers the power to shut down a whole plant, there is no doubt that the disruption to production and sales that a nationally organised strike can bring, especially in key sectors of the economy, is a major bargaining counter. The anxiety of the corporate technostructure to keep the production process in continuous operation is alleged to have led managements into a policy of appeasement with the unions. The willingness of the corporations to give way to wage demands has been bolstered by the knowledge that so long as the Government could be relied on to maintain full employment, increased wage costs could be passed on to the consumer in the form of higher prices without any significant loss of sales.

Government intervention in the industrial relations scene has usually been as a mediator, but increasingly, action has been justified by governments as in the role of 'protector of the general public interest'. Tripartite co-operation between private enterprise, trade unions and the Government has been tried in many forms, as we saw with the NEDC and voluntary prices and incomes policies. Perversely, the preference by both sides of industry for compromise rather than confrontation can lead to the intervention of governments in this relationship being resented by both sides of industry.

The State has demanded a degree of public and social responsibility at the company as well as at the national level. The public concern over the problems of industrial pollution and the 'waste' of resources in unnecessary packaging requires that the private enterprise corporation should foster a wider duty to society than that of profit-

making. Managements that lead companies into large-scale bankrupt-
cies or failures are now condemned for 'irresponsibility', and
governments find themselves involved, as we have seen, in rescue
operations. Such failures can also lead to the provision of financial aid
to those who suffer (e.g. the 1974 holiday trade collapses), or the
closer scrutiny and supervision of company operations as happened
following the collapse of certain insurance companies.

Some writers on management problems have so accepted the social
and public duties of the modern corporation that they have
recommended that companies build them into their corporate plans.
This could involve companies in providing, in addition to a balance
sheet and profit and loss account, some kind of social cost-benefit
analysis or 'social audit' of their activities. For the present, such moves
may be interpreted as useful public relations exercises, but an increasing awareness of the social environment could eventually mean
changes in company goals and strategies. It is only fair to add that
many company chairmen have expressed great doubts about how far
they can or should subordinate the interests of their shareholders to
the possibly conflicting interests of other groups in society.

The Role of Public Enterprise

A major area of state intervention in the UK and in a number of other
Western countries, notably France and Italy, is the direct public
ownership and operation of major industries and services. The circumstances leading up to the nationalisation of an industry are often
complex. Most of those enterprises that came into public ownership
before 1945 were operating in industries where competition was
wasteful and where monopoly was technically and economically the
most efficient organisational form, as in the case of telephone services
and the national electricity grid. On the other hand, the major exten-
sions in public ownership in Britain's transport and energy industries
that were introduced by the 1945-51 Labour Government were mainly politically inspired. Even so, many of the industries nationalised at
this time, such as coal and railways, were not the centre of great controversy. Most business and political resistance has been concentrated
on preventing the takeover by the State of profitable private utilities
and of manufacturing industry. If there was felt to be some risk to the
public, however, in letting private enterprise have complete freedom
of action, even a Conservative Government has been prepared to
hand over to a public body, as witnessed by the Atomic Energy
Authority and the old Independent (commericial) Television
Authority.

Whatever the arguments for or against the public ownership of particular industries, we are still left with the need to lay down general guidelines for their management. The UK practice has usually been to hand the industry over to a 'public corporation', a statutory body created individually by Act of Parliament, the latter also specifying the general powers and duties of the managing board. Important powers over such things as appointments to the board of the corporation and the borrowing and investment plans of the industry have been reserved to the relevant ministry, while the day-to-day running of the corporation has been left in the hands of the board. The corporations were expected to operate in 'the public interest' and to conform to any general policy directives issued by the Government. Unfortunately, no really satisfactory or operational definition of what the 'public interest' might be has ever been produced, and the boards have therefore tended to follow their own particular interpretations of the phrase except where they have been subject to ministerial intervention.

Continual difficulty has arisen over the problem of reconciling concepts of 'public service' with 'commercial' behaviour. During the 1960s, general guidelines on pricing policy, profitability and investment criteria were evolved, but these still left great scope for variation by boards or ministers. The industries have sometimes been used in furtherance of policies to aid areas of high unemployment. The ambivalence of their position was emphasised in the early 1970s when their prices were severely restricted as part of the attempt to control inflation, athough one inevitable result was a serious deterioration in their general financial position. As we saw in Chapter 9, there are great problems within an industrialised socialist economy in devising rational and consistent criteria for the guidance of managers, so we should not be surprised that these problems are probably more complex still for public enterprises operating within a mixed economy. In Part III of this chapter we turn to some of the efforts being made to deal with the conflicts that have developed between managements and planners in the socialist economies.

PART III

'ECONOMIC REFORM' UNDER SOCIALISM

The Need for Reform

At the end of Chapter 9 we summarised some of the weaknesses likely to be inherent in a rigorously centralised command economy. These weaknesses become more obvious as an economy develops and becomes more sophisticated. Poor quality, low-level technology and the subordination of consumers' wishes are all tolerable when a country is engaged in a massive national effort to meet a few basic priorities. The socialist economies in Europe were mostly beyond that stage by the early 1960s and were finding that the 'command'-type structure was failing in a number of important respects. With the sole exception of Yugoslavia, the European socialist economies experienced a significantly slower rate of economic growth in the 1960s. Slower growth rates are not in themselves a cause for alarm, as we shall suggest in the next chapter, but the communist regimes had put a great deal of political emphasis on this index of their own economic performance.

Since the death of Stalin in 1953, there has been a fitful but noticeable relaxation of tensions inside the communist bloc which, among other things, has permitted workers and consumers to be more outspoken in expressing their dissatisfactions. There has also been great interest in developing new economic principles and techniques, ostens'' iy still within the Marxist-Leninist framework, to deal with serious weaknesses in the pricing system and the flow of economic information. The increasingly influential mathematical school of Soviet economists was able to demonstrate both at the practical level (for example with computerised techniques for solving problems in the efficient organisation of production and distribution) and at the theoretical level that the command economy could and should be 'rationalised'.

The basic needs were for (a) greater flexibility and speed of adjustment in production schedules, (b) information that was better both in quality and speed of availability, (c) prices that more accurately reflected society costs, and (d) incentives systems that would encourage maximum production from given resources rather than reward under performance, i.e. reduce the amount of slack in the economy. It was in this last area especially that considerable gains were expected.

The Nature of the 'Reforms'

The argument for economic reforms was developed at the public level during the first half of the 1960s. The Soviet economist E. G. Liberman had neatly summarised the basic task in 1962, when he said that it was to ensure that ' . . . what is profitable for society must be profitable for each enterprise'. The debate on Liberman's proposals culminated in a report by A. N. Kosygin to the Central Committee in September 1965 which outlined what was to be done. The chief elements in these and later proposals are now dealt with.

Motivation and Incentives   First there was a considerable reduction in the long list of output targets, labour norms and financial limits, etc., set for each enterprise. Important new targets were set however, notably one for total profits and another for the rate of profit in relation to capital employed. Bonuses would be paid to managers and workers out of an enterprise fund to be created out of any surpluses left over from profits after compulsory payments to the State. Further amounts from the enterprise fund could be used for social and cultural amenities for the workers and for the finance of new technologies and product developments.

The new profit motive was to be reinforced by the setting of targets in the form of sales volume and value rather than output volumes. It was hoped that the combination of these two major innovations would make managers both cost-conscious, and sensitive to consumer wishes. Wholesale and retail organisations were eventually to have full powers to refuse the acceptance of goods that they considered to be inferior in quality or design. State agencies would meanwhile endeavour to set higher quality and technical standards and specifications for industry.

Price Reforms   As we have already seen in Chapter 9, the old pattern of 'accounting' prices meant that many enterprises had planned financial losses. For the profit incentive to make much sense, prices would have to be raised so as to enable each enterprise to cover its costs of production. It was decided to fix prices in line with the costs of production of the average, 'normally functioning', enterprise in each industry branch. The major price revision that followed in 1967 considerably reduced the number of loss-making enterprises, but it still left many complexities for the planners, such as setting 'fair' profit targets for enterprises with especially favourable or adverse production conditions. In addition to adjusting existing prices, a price was also attached to various resources hitherto regarded by enterprises as 'free' goods. Hence, capital funds supplied by the State either as fixed or working capital would in future carry an interest charge, while land used by enterprises would carry a rental payment. The aim of these payments was to discourage the wasteful use of resources, and although the interest rates and rent levels fixed by the State are low by comparison with Western Europe, they do seem to have made managers more receptive to the concept of economic efficiency.

Longer time Horizons In spite of the five- and seven-year plans typically prepared at the Central Bureau level, most enterprises had become excessively dependent on their detailed annual plan targets. They were therefore likely to be taken unawares by developments and trends that ought to have been foreseen. Enterprises are now expected to prepare five-year corporate plans which are to be in conformity with the national plan targets. it is hoped that this practice will give greater stability and coherence to planning and will discourage the manipulation of annual plans by managers for short-term advantages. The parallels with company corporate planning in the West are obvious.

Industrial Concentration A very significant development in the Russian economic structure that was not contemplated in the 1965 reforms was the announcement in 1973 that many of the planning functions exercised by the central industry branch ministries will be gradually handed over to 'associations' of enterprises. The typical Soviet enterprise is the single plant or factory unit, but this proposal could lead to multiplant groupings carrying out their own research and product development with a high degree of autonomy from the central authorities. This particular development followed initiatives taken elsewhere in the communist bloc. By the late 1960s, for example, there were already concentrations of production units into large 'trusts' or corporations in East Germany, Hungary and Romania. Poland began to set up large units with a unified financial and control structure in the early 1970s. All these moves have been accompanied by some devolution of power from central planning bodies to profit-motivated managements — a new technostructure?

Just How Real are the Reforms?

The economic reforms of 1965 did not herald a dramatic and fundamental change in the way Eastern European economies work. In the USSR, the new ideas were introduced cautiously and then only over certain sections of industry. Countries with moderately advanced industrial economies and with only post-war experience of communist rule, such as East German, Czechoslovakia and Poland, were rather more adventurous. Starting in 1968, Hungary began a series of very significant changes in the traditional command structure of her economy, but broadly similar moves in Czechoslovakia were brought to an abrupt end by the invasion by the armies of the Warsaw Pact. Yugoslavia had already evolved a new-style economy by the end of the 1960s and will be treated separately later. The rather less developed economies of Bulgaria and Albania showed market reluctance to give up the traditional Soviet model. Leaving aside Yugoslavia and Hungary then, it seems that the reforms have so far had only limited effect. Some of the reasons for this are as follows:

1. The central allocation of supplies via the 'material balance' procedure has been largely preserved under the new regime.

2. Many important indices concerning finance, major new investment, labour costs and product mix are still issued by the ministries.

3. Although prices have been revised, they are still not determined by, or very responsive to, market pressures at the various stages of production. Only in Hungary have major price sectors been allowed to adjust to market demands and supply, and this has meant that the material balancing of supplies, raw materials, etc., has had to be abandoned.

4. The administrative hierarchy has been very reluctant to give up its jobs and its influence. habit, fear, inertia and self-interest frequently hamper effective change. Indeed, when problems started to be generated by the working of the reforms, the bureaucracy was happy to use these problems as an excuse for going back to the traditional methods.

5. It was hoped that enterprise managers would be weaned from plan juggling to interest in cost reduction and efficiency criteria by the profit-linked bonus schemes, but since the plan sales, product mix and profit levels are still set by the central planners, the old game of bluff and counter-bluff over feasible targets described on p. 172 has tended to appear again.

Some Awkward Implications of the 'Reforms'

The movement towards the use of market forces, the introduction of the profit motive and of payments for the use of capital and land, inevitably met resistance from the 'old guard' of the Communist Party. This resistance was based partly on a deep distrust of such devices as 'capitalistic' in flavour, and partly on a realisation that any greater freedom of action for enterprise managers would be likely to lead to less influence and power for party officials. The problem facing the party leadership was that although freer market relationships with decentralised decision-making might raise growth rates and reduce the 'slack' in the economy, it also made economic planning much more difficult. If consumers are to exercise their choice in the market and enterprises are to try to meet those choices at the lowest possible cost, how can their activities be made consistent with the centralised planning of major prices, wage allocations, material supplies and new investment? In other words, once decentralised market decision-making is allowed to develop, where, in a socialist State, does it logically end?

Economists such as Oskar Lange and A. P. Lerner have drawn up sets of theoretical rules and procedures which they claimed would lead to the efficient allocation of resources under a decentralised liberal-socialist economy. The State would still own the means of production and the central authorities would have a major role in investment decisions. The key production decisions would, however, be made by industry and enterprise managers who would behave as if they were profit maximisers in a perfectly competitive market environment. Where they were in an actual or near monopoly position, of course, managers would be expected to avoid monopoly profits and to charge prices which reflected the value to society of the factors and materials used. There have been no attempts so far to put such a system (and the above has perforce given only the barest outline) into practice, but one country has evolved an economy that has some of its characteristics — Yugoslavia.

Yugoslavia still has national and regional economic plans, but they are in some ways more like the French indicative plans than those of the USSR. Yugoslavia followed its own 'road to socialism' from the early 1950s, and has evolved a system that combines the state ownership of enterprise assets with managements controlled by elected workers' councils, small-scale private enterprise with large organisations owned jointly by the State and by foreign capitalist corporations, all within the framework of an essentially free market environment. If the roads opened by the economic 'reforms' were to lead to this kind of result for the communist world in general, then the orthordox parties are bound to be very cautious. It seems likely that the major reasons why the Czech reforms led to invasion and subsequent economic 'regression' whereas Hungary was, at the same time, permitted to decentralise to a very considerable degree, are to be found in the extent to which hard-line party leaders felt that they could retain authority and control.

We ought to keep in mind also that there is increasing evidence that 'capitalistic' practices will lead to 'capitalistic' attitudes and behaviour. Nearly all the socialist countries that carried through even limited economic reforms began to experience an unaccustomed degree of inflation, leading in Poland, for example, to unrest among the workers. Slight business fluctuations have begun to appear in Yugoslavia and Hungary, creating pockets of unemployment. Big bonuses to managers and higher payments to workers in very profitable enterprises are tending to increase income differentials. It becomes easier for people to accumulate considerable wealth during their lifetime (inheritance is still of negligible significance), often in the form of houses or flats which have been known to be let to fellow workers at exorbitant rents! Consumer 'fetishism' can appear, and official newspapers carry moralistic articles condemning ostentatious living and conspicuous consumption. All these deviations from the collectivist ideal can be seized upon as the first escapees from the Pandora's box opened by the economic reforms. The socialist baby, it might be argued, runs the risk of being thrown out with the bureaucratic bath water.

GREATER CONVERGENCE OR INCREASING DIVERSITY?

One link between the Marxian and the Galbraithian views of world economic development is that both see the modes of production and the prevailing technology as major determinants of a society's economic, social and political structure. Hence, the appearance in capitalist and socialist economies of very large autonomous corporate organisations based on the economics of large-scale production and complex technology and requiring the services of a powerful managerial/technical elite could be interpreted as a confirmation of this view. For Galbraith, the trend towards decentralisation in socialist economies and the manipulation of public authorities in the USA are both manifestations of the technostructure's need to establish an independent but secure status in society.

Another area of supposed convergence might be in the evolution of broadly similar roles for the market mechanism in both East and West. In capitalist and mixed economies, the unfortunate effects of an over-reliance on private commercial interests has led to more demands for the provision of social goods and services and the curbing of unbridled market individualism. In the socialist world there is a more widespread awareness of the improved efficiency that can be gained from a judicious use of the market mechanism driven by private profit. While the profit motive is gaining ground in the East, it is being tempered by demands for social responsibility in the West. The capitalist consumer is perhaps subject to more manipulation by advertisers and marketeers while the socialist consumer is being gradually set free from bureaucratic constraint. The State is more active in administering prices in the West, while freer market pricing appears in the East. Economic planning becomes less detailed and domineering in the socialist camp, while the other camp is subject to an increasing degree of governmental direction and intervention. Multinational corporations span the Iron Curtain, East German Wartburg cars are driven in Bonn, while Fiats and Renaults are built in Poland, Yugoslavia and Romania — even Pepsi Cola is bottled in Novorossisk.

Surely, one might argue, in a decade or so more, the similarities between the socialist and capitalist economies will be greater than the differences. And yet the evidence really is that there is much greater diversity amongst the members of the communist bloc than ever before. There is no longer a 'typical' socialist economy since the range is spread between highly centralised and planned Albania and highly market-orientated Yugoslavia. Unfortunately, lack of space does not allow discussion of the other socialist variants in the developing or 'third' world, such as China and Cuba. Although the pop cultures and the consumer goods of the industrialised capitalist world become more universal, there remain very considerable differences of national 'style'. The steady incursion of public purchasing power and governmental intervention takes place in nearly all Western economies, but the degree to which those economies can be called 'mixed' is far from uniform. In Germany and the USA, private enterprise operating within a market environment is still dominant. In France, Italy and the UK, on the other hand, the degree of state intervention into the private sector has reached a level where, according to some writers, they are no longer 'mixed' but 'corporatist' economies. 'Corporatist' here means that the big corporations have accepted general political control in return for economic stability and security.

From the global point of view, it is possible to argue that the highly industrialised nations, whether East or West, do look more and more alike when compared with the developing countries. At this level, the widening gap between rich and poor, developed and developing countries, must appear to be more important than ideological differences in Europe. This issue is taken up in the next chapter, but we can attempt to answer now the question posed at the start of this chapter: Is there a future for free market economics? If this refers to an economy entirely organised on a market basis, then the answer must be, No. On the other hand, there is almost certain to be a continuing future for free market *activity* in substantial sections of the world's diversity of economies, whether mainly collectivist or individualist, developed or developing.

Chapter 11

The View from the Bridge

In this chapter we shall examine the forces which divide the poor from the rich nations, and give some consideration to the outlook for global improvements in consumption and production. There can be no doubt that at present the gap between rich and poor countries is widening. The developed economies we were discussing in the last chapter generate incomes per head of the population many times the levels found in poor countries. In West Germany and the USA, income per head is something like thirty times that in India. Yet the annual growth of incomes in the former is more than three times the rate of the latter. Only if the growth of income and output per head is greater in poor than in rich countries, however, will the poor ever catch up. If West Germany and the USA are examples of developed economies, to term societies with low and sluggish income levels as 'developing' must be a resort to euphemism. 'Underdeveloped' is more appropriate word.

WHAT IS UNDERDEVELOPMENT?

There is no precise definition of this term, although all who use it mean roughly the same thing. The reader may gauge something of the nature of the phenomenon if we describe its salient characteristics. Apart from low income levels, an underdeveloped economy will be predominantly a primary producer; its techniques of production will be primitive; it may suffer from population pressures and foreign domination; its resources will be meagre and its social organisation circumscribed by custom and tradition; internal communications may be poor and there may be no truly 'national' economy. Not all of the countries we think of as underdeveloped possess these characteristics to the same degree — there are wide variations in income levels, for example — and some of the features may be quite lacking. A national economy can exist yet be held back by other components of underdevelopment.

Development, Underdevelopment, and Economic Growth

The terms 'economic growth' and 'economic development' are often used synonymously. The growth of a society's consumption and production year by year, however, is actually the consequence of economic development. Those systems which achieve substantial levels of consumption in the long terms will have become 'developed', since we understand the process of development to include changes in society which make growth possible. In Chapter 3 we suggested that such changes involved the way in which society was organised. While society is reorganising — or 'modernising' — itself, there may be little overall growth in output, just as a growth in output is not by itself a sufficient indication that development has taken place. The slow changes in the output of the USSR in the 1920s and 1930s disguised substantial changes in Russian society. During the First World War the output of the Indian economy grew with the demands of the belligerent nations for war materials, but this growth was not sustained. This was partly because of the unfavourable economic circumstances of the period, but partly because little 'development' had taken place. In other words, the necessary changes to secure continued growth of output had not been made, and the economy remained 'underdeveloped'. The changes necessary to produce 'development' will emerge as we look more closely at the characteristics of underdevelopment.

The Characteristics of Underdevelopment

The Predominance of Primary Production For some writers, a feature of the changes which constitute 'development' is the declining importance of primary production, particularly agriculture. In the UK and in most other other industrialised countries the proportion of the working population employed in agriculture is minute. From about a quarter in the mid nineteenth century, the proportion of the workforce in primary production, which includes mining and quarrying, is now about 3.5 per cent. This decline indicates one of the structural changes which are part of the development process. Professor Colin Clark has emphasised the importance of the decline of agriculture relative to industry, and then that of industry and agriculture together relative to the service sectors. The decline of agriculture as development proceeds is a consequence of rising agricultural productivity. High levels of output per man release labour for factory production, and eventually the resultant rising incomes leads to demands for labour-intensive service industries. In the UK the proportions employed in primary, secondary, and tertiary industry in 1970 were respectively 3.5 per cent, 39.0 per cent and 57.5 per cent.

A comparison of the UK with, say, India, Mexico, or Egypt is striking. In the decade or so following the Second World War. the proportions of workers employed in agriculture in each of these countries was roughly 69 per cent, 67 per cent and 52 per cent respectively. If a small agricultural sector is a feature of a developed economy, this term cannot apply to the countries last mentioned. It is not, however, the mere predominance of agriculture that is the important feature of underdevelopment. After all, the USA has a higher proportion employed on the land than does the UK, and in Australia agricultural output is about 12 per cent of the total output of goods and services. The significance of agriculture for the third world is not just that it is the main employer but that its productivity is low. The bulk of farming will be at subsistence level, which means that the production *per capita* in the US and Northern Europe tends to be ten to twenty times greater than in the Far East and Latin America. The causes of this poor performance are interrelated but can be summarised as follows:

1. *Land starvation:* In countries such as India and Egypt the amount of cultivated land per head of the population can be calculated in fractions of an acre. We have already observed that there are technical limitations to factor substitution, and by any account the proportions of people to land in undeveloped countries is excessive.

2. *Land fragmentation:* The manner of land-ownership is a factor in low productivity. Successive subdivision can lead to holdings too small to be worked effectively by the owner, and so he becomes 'underemployed'. Where one man owns a workable acreage, it can consist, as the result of inheritance customs, of dispersed plots which thwart the introduction of new techniques and the economies of scale.

3. *Primitive technology:* Biblical farming methods go hand-in-hand with small acreage per worker to keep farming at subsistence levels. Draught animals, for example, take precedence over tractors, although fragmented holdings may limit energy inputs to manual labour. The introduction of new methods requires knowledge and understanding and even when this hurdle can be crossed, the incentive to innovate can be stifled by the vagaries of landlord-tenant relationships. This will be the case if improvements carried out accrue to the landlord and not the tenant. It is not just the small size of holdings which makes improvement difficult. Holdings may also vary considerably in size, from plantation-sized estates down to patches of a fraction of an acre. And if cultivators are too poor or too ignorant to use fertilisers and irrigation, natural variations in soil fertility are likely to persist, resulting in a wide range of yields per acre.

Low Income Per Head   To say that underdeveloped countries are poor is to proffer a tautology. Yet a salient point of comparison betwen industrialised countries and underdeveloped countries is the huge disparity in income and consumption. The USA enjoyed in 1970 a *per capita* income in excess of $3,000, while in Ethiopia, India and Malawi, the level was less than $100. The reason is not hard to find. With the majority of the population of the latter employed in backward subsistence agriculture, it is hardly surprising that income levels compare abysmally with an economy which has managed to utilise its enormous natural resources.

Underdeveloped Resources   It is not that underdeveloped countries have no natural resources, but rather they do not make the best use of the resources they have. Underdeveloped countries may well be poor because they lack mineral reserves, etc., but most have water supplies, for example, which are not fully used. Irrigation schemes require the organisation of capital and labour and if there are factors which inhibit such development, resources are likely to remain undeveloped. Yet an increase in the flow of resources may be an essential precondition to the raising of productivity, and thereby incomes. Irrigation is a particularly good example of this feature of underdevelopment, since it is so obviously related to the agricultural sector on which so many poor countries depend.

Capital Deficiency   We have already said that resources can be human as well as natural. Ethiopia may lack the land and mineral reserves of the USA, but what is to stop it creating man-made capital assets? It is the fact that capital must be created out of consumption. With average income of less than $100 per head there will not be much scope for curtailing consumption levels still further. Not surprisingly, the rates of saving in underdeveloped countries are low in comparison with the first world. In India and Pakistan the proportion of total incomes which are spent per year on investment goods is only 6-7 per cent, while in the industrial countries of the northern hemisphere it ranges from 15-18 per cent. Investment goods, however, are only the measurable aspects of investment. If we were to consider expenditures on health and education which improve the characteristics of a country's human resources and which can also be regarded as a form of investment, then the disparity would become even greater.

Low income per head gives rise to capital deficiency, but it is only an average for the whole economy. Related to the difficulty of reducing consumption to release resources for investment is the fact that consumption is not spread evenly. This might be beneficial for capital accumulation if the average were not so low. The rich are only relatively richer in poor countries and thus the number of incomes large enough to save can be very small. There are suggestions, however, that the inequality of income distribution may actually be greater in poor countries than in rich. Simon Kuznets has produced (now disputed) figures showing that in the late 1940s the percentage of total income received by the poorest 60 per cent of the population was 28 per cent for India but 36 per cent in the UK. The share of total income received by the richest 20 per cent was 55 per cent for India and 45 per cent for the UK. This may be no more than an indication that poor countries are at an added disadvantage. Moreover, the saving habits of the higher incomes in underdeveloped countries are not always favourable to capital formation. For social rather than economic reasons, savings are more likely to go into land and property than industrial investment. In Cyprus the social need to provide marriageable daughters with a dowry house has forced on even humble families a compulsion to acquire property. The amount of saving the rich may wish to undertake, however, may be adversely affected by some of the consumption habits we referred to in Chapter 2. Conspicuous consumption is frequently characteristic of the affluent, and the 'demonstrtion effect' operates particularly for expensive imported goods.

Vicious Circles

Many of the characteristics of underdeveloped countries are interrelated. Populations which are large in relation to land keep farms small and inefficient. This keeps incomes low, which in turn makes it difficult to raise capital which might improve efficiency. Poor countries are prey to vicious circles of this kind. There are many variations but essentially they reduce to the notion that poverty breeds poverty breeds poverty. (Compare with the poverty cycle in Chapter 7.) An important component of the poverty circles is a phenomenon we call 'backwardness'. This operates at two levels.

Firstly, the population as a whole can be said to be backward. A physical consequence of poverty is malnutrition. Malnutrition reduces the ability to work or to work effectively, and output per head remains poor and falling, so that malnutrition increases. Malnutrition, moreover, increases the incidence of endemic and debilitating diseases and measurably impairs brain development. A crude correlation exists, for example, between literacy and nutrition. Average *per capita* calorie intake is around 1,800 and 3,000 in India and the UK respectively, while the illiteracy rates (per cent of population over ten years) are about 80 per cent and 5 per cent (figures for 1955 — UN demographic year book). Low educational attainment creates difficulties in the propagation of methods and skills to improve efficiency. There is, of course, much more to illiteracy than malnutrition alone. Societies with traditional values have little need for literacy, nor for numeracy, if, for example, the currency is not on a money basis. Traditional values, moreover, may limit consumption horizons. Status, for example, may be reflected in family size, and children may consequently be 'consumed' instead of goods. Occupational patterns which restrict labour mobility, even if educational standards were raised, may similarly be dictated by traditional values. We are not saying that traditional values are good or bad, but merely pointing out that if economic development — particularly the reduction of the importance of rural employment — is a goal, then traditional values will stand in the way.

Secondly, backwardness can permeate a system's institutions, and here again traditional values may play a part. The middle class, for example, which has been instrumental in so many countries in easing the structural changes necessary to achieve growth in total output, is often small or lacking in an underdeveloped country. A middle class may have little vested interest in land ownership and must seek wealth or status in other directions. If the acquisition of wealth is socially acceptable only through the ownership of land, the opportunities for a middle class will be few. Backward institutions, however, need not be the result of traditional values alone. They can be the result of capital deficiency. Inability to raise money for road building, etc., for example, keeps markets local rather than national, and inhibits the use of money in exchange. This in turn will keep banking institutions primitive, with the further result that even if there were the desire to save and to use savings productively, there may be no outlets for saving other than direct production. There is no reason to suppose that those with incomes high enough to save will also have the willingness and the ability to run a business. In saying this we are implicitly accepting the values of a capitalistic society, and we would remind readers that this is again a value judgement. But in the European experience the existence of a 'rentier' class has allowed those with entrepreneurial flair to exercise their talents unencumbered by inadequate personal wealth.

Again, institutions may be backward because the government is backward. Inefficiency of government is an all too frequent feature of underdeveloped countries. This can be because those who exercise political power, e.g. a landed aristocracy or a military junta, have no inherent administrative ability or integrity, and/or because the execution of administrative directives is ineffective because of the lack of the necessary skills. An effective civil service depends, for example, on educational standards. Where there are the required skills, customary values may render them inoperative through graft and corruption. Thus roads, for example, may be unbuilt because those with power do not see the need for them, because there is no machinery for collecting the necessary funds, or because taxes are so maladminstered that they are invariably insufficient. Backwardness results in the failure to develop existing resources, and thus feeds into a further vicious circle. We can trace these relationships in Figure 11.1. The diagram emphasises that backwardness is both the cause and the result of underdeveloped resources. These two characteristics together with capital scarcity produce a fourth, low productivity, which in turn leads to low incomes. Most of these incomes are consumed in basic survival, and there is little left over for either saving or for consumption of non-agricultural goods. Thus there is little reason to initiate industrial production of consumer goods, and the resources for industrial, social and agricultural investment are limited by low incomes. With low levels of investment, productivity remains low, and low productivity feeds into low incomes, and so on.

Figure 11.1   Vicious Circles which keep countries poor

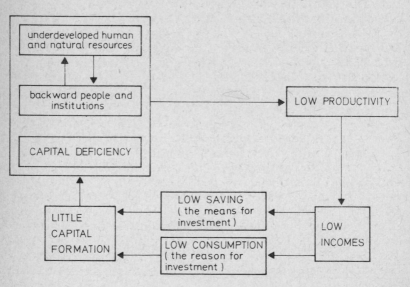

UNDERDEVELOPMENT IS A CONSEQUENCE OF DEVELOPMENT

In the next chapter we shall be dealing with international interrelationships, but an important facet of poor countries is the particular role which foreign interests play. This role can be summarised
by saying that underdevelopment in some countries is a consequence
of development in others. When we describe the features of an underdeveloped economy we are not describing the features of an alternative economic system. As the industrial upheavals of eighteenth-
and nineteenth-century Europe produced capitalist and then socialist
societies, they also set in motion forces which produced underdevelopment. In that economic growth stems from changes in
organisation, particularly industrialisation, and in that industrialisation
in turn promotes international interdependence, the rise of industry in
Europe created an imbalance which worked to the disadvantage of
areas of established settlement such as Asia and, until recently, the
Middle East. Areas of recent settlement — North America, Australia
— which possessed imported European populations and considerable
natural resources were able to benefit from, and to copy, industrialisation in Europe. This was not the case with the older areas.
While they may have possessed natural resources, they had societies
which were less amenable to the changes which industrialisation required. What industrial sectors they could develop were not strong
enough, with the exception of Japan, to compete with those in
Europe. Instead they succumbed to the superior economic and the
resultant military strength of European cultures, and became suppliers
of raw materials. Industrialisation in Europe had there been the means
by which economic development had resulted in economic growth.
But economic development in Europe sometimes made industrialisation more difficult for others. There are some specific circumstances in which this can be so.

'Enclave' economies

Primary production in underdeveloped countries is not all subsistence
agriculture. It can consist of cash crops such as jute, cotton, coffee,
etc., or of minerals produced by plantation methods, and production
can be highly developed. A developed 'enclave', usually of a
capitalistic nature, is thus formed in an otherwise backward economy.
Within the enclave social overhead capital, such as roads and port
facilities, will exist on a scale beyond such provision for the economy
as a whole, but it will exist only to serve the production of a single output. Oil production until recently has been a good example. Technical
requirements were unavailable locally and had to be imported in the

form of labour skills and capital equipment. Such enclaves will place no demands on the rest of the economy and do not therefore provide much stimulus for the changes necessary for development.

Export Orientation

Needless to say, the main markets for the product of the enclave will be overseas, and are likely to be the main if not the only source of foreign exchange. This need not be a bad thing. Exports finance imports, and industrial imports are badly needed. In practice, however, it is not a satisfactory state of affairs. If exports are made up of a single product the revenues from it can be very volatile. Frequent changes in world demand and in local supply conditions cause even greater fluctuations in export earnings, since an adverse shift in demand will cause both the price of the product and the amount bought to fall.

Foreign Domination

Aside from the dangers of dependence on a limited range of exports, by no means all foreign exchange earned is available to the 'host' country. The enclave will most likely have been established by foreign interests who will have provided the capital and could constitute a drain of foreign exchange in the form of repatriated profits. Foreign interests in themselves are not necessarily harmful. Foreign capital can remedy capital deficiency, etc. It is the narrow range of the interests which limits the impact on the economy as a whole. Foreign capital will tend to stay in the enclave. Even where there is some 'spill-over', the bargaining power the foreign presence exerts can be considerable. A single foreign company may deal with a large number of small near-subsistence farmers and thereby obtain the product for export very advantageously. At one time a single buyer dealt with nearly half of Nigeria's commercial exports. Economic domination, however, cannot be separated from political. There are many examples of enclave being imposed by military and political pressures, and of rigid separation from the rest of the enclave, e.g. nineteenth-century India.

Dependence on Imports

If a poor country is importing capital goods it cannot produce itself, reliance of imports is not necessarily harmful. This is not so if such imports go exclusively to the enclave or if, as is not infrequently the case, if foreign exchange is used to finance the conspicuous consumption of luxury imports.

THE POPULATION PROBLEM

Population pressures are associated with underdevelopment. For the world as a whole populations are indeed growing more rapidly in poor rather than in rich countries. In 1970 the growth of the world's population was at the rate of about 2 per cent per annum. Yet for the rich, developed countries, growth was between 1 per cent and $1\frac{1}{2}$ per cent, while the peoples of the poor nations were increasing at about twice that rate. Migration apart, population growth is a matter of the balance between births and deaths. If the rate at which people are born is the same as the rate at which they die, the size of the population will remain largely unchanged. We say largely, because if life expectancy is low, as it is in many underdeveloped countries, a drop in the death rate may allow many more women to survive up to the limits of child-bearing age, i.e. up to say forty-five years of age, thereby increasing the potential number of births.

If the number of births exceeds the number of deaths, then the population will grow. Growth, however, will not be a simple increase. In Trinidad the number of births per thousand in the 1950s was about forty, the number of deaths ten. So the net increase per thousand of the population was about thirty. Today those thirty are now of child-bearing age, and they represent part of an extra thousand of the population. If they repeat the habits of their parents, breed and die at the same rate, they will have added an accumulating addition to the population. It is not just that populations increase by so many per thousand, but that the numbers of thousands, i.e. the size of the populations themselves, also increase. If births consistently exceed deaths, populations will increase exponentially.

Population Growth in Underdeveloped Countries

The consequences of population increase have particular relevance for poor countries, and not because it is a visible indicator of their poverty. Alcohol was thought to be a major cause of urban poverty in nineteenth-century Britain, yet it was even more a consequence. Similarly population growth is both cause and effect of underdevelopment. It has really only been in the last two or three decades that exponential population growth has been a dramatic feature of poor countries. Throughout the nineteenth century and into the twentieth, world population increase came from the industrialised countries and the populations of the third world remained stagnant, kept in check by high infant mortality and low life expectancy, as well as by periodic catastrophies, such as the Bengal famine of 1943 which killed possibly up to 3.5 million people.

A change in mortality, particularly in infant mortality, has been one of the most common ways of changing the balance between births and deaths, since only small changes in hygiene, medicine and diet are required. These were the principle causes of improving infant mortality in Europe in the nineteenth century, and mortality in general in the underdeveloped countries since the Second World War. But a dramatic contrast has been the speed at which this change has occurred. The drop in the death rate in British Guiana between 1940 and 1950, for example, was of a similar magnitude to that in Northern Europe between 1850 and the First World War. The reason for this acceleration has been the cheapening and the increasing effectiveness of the means to control diseases such as malaria. But if declining mortality is not matched by a similar decline in the birth rate, by a decrease in 'fertility' — the number of births per household — an exponential growth in poulation will result. In Europe and the New World a decrease in the birth rate did, within a generation of two, follow reductions in mortality: in the third world this does not appear to be happening as yet. The reasons are partly social and partly economic. On the one hand raising of children in Europe became increasingly expensive. Child labour became socially unacceptable and with compulsory education, opportunities for children to contribute to household income were delayed. With the growth of mass consumption, children additionally came to represent a cost in terms of forgone goods and services. On the other hand, average incomes in poor countries are often too low for consumption beyond subsistence to be contemplated, and the 'demonstration effect' (see Chapter 2) does not operate. In primitive agriculture children can contribute to family income, and so there appears a point to large families. Perhaps more importantly, an extended family spanning three generations where the young care for the old takes the place of a social security system, and family size can reflect virility and therefore status. In poor countries this last aspect of family size must be some compensation for miserably low consumption.

That birth rates in underdeveloped countries have not fallen with death rates is a consequence of poverty. It is also a cause. In a population growting because birth rates are high and death rates are low, the numbers of the dependent population below working age will be increasing. Children will be born in numbers greater than those entering the working population, which must thus feed a larger number of mouths. This might be possible if productivity were to be increased, but this in turn requires an increase in capital per head. But if the population is growing faster than productivity, output and therefore income per head must also decline. If income per head falls, capital per head must also fall. We are back in a vicious circle. It is a sad comment on human ingenuity that advancing medical knowledge has (so far) kept growing numbers of people alive at ever lowering standards of living.

We are not suggesting that population growth is undesirable in itself. A growing population carries with it an inbuilt demand for housing, schools, roads, etc., which collectively increase the level of economic activity. The notion that with every mouth goes a pair of hands has been a justification for population growth in the western hemisphere where it provided a stimulus for industrialisation. Demographic change and its relationship to economic change is an enormously complicated subject, but an important difference between population growth in rich and poor countries stands out. In the former, populations have always been much smaller in relation to natural resources than in the latter. Indeed, we have seen that the presence of undeveloped resources is a characteristic of an underdeveloped economy. We attribute the first observations of the relationship between population and resources to Thomas Malthus, in his *Essay on the Principle of Population* (1798).

The Ghost of Malthus

Malthus saw population rising in a geometric progression, i.e. exponentially, while the means to support it increases only arithmetically. The difference, in other words, between compound and simple interest. The consequence of population outstripping resources must be, according to Malthus, an eventual check to population growth by a rising incidence of famine and disease. In the short term — in the century and three quarters since Malthus first wrote — he was proved wrong. He did not foresee industrial and technical change which enabled mankind to open up new areas of food production, and to improve the productivity of the old. We have now reached a stage, however, at which we can no longer take the continuance of such development for granted. Indeed the contrary is the case. A recent revival of Malthus's ideas is contained in a report directed by Dr D. L. Meadows — 'The Limits to Growth' (1972). This report is the result of a brief to extrapolate current world trends of production and consumption, and it starkly revealed the significance of exponential growth. If world population is growing at a current rate of about 2 per cent per annum it is effectively doubling itself roughly three times in a century. In 100 years' time world population will be eight times its present size, if nothing happens to stop it. How will this population feed itself?

World Population and Food Supplies

In the last resort, the capacity of the world to feed itself depends upon three things. It depends on the size of the world's population, the supply of suitable land, and the productivity of agriculture. The amount of land available for food production is greater than that in use today, but since we are already using the most readily available land, additions can only be made by the expensive irrigation and cultivation of inferior land such as desert, etc. Nevertheless, assuming that such land will eventually be put to use, Figure 11.2 shows the relationship between land resources and the need for food. The amount of land is shown at about twice the area in cultivation today, and the land needed for food production is shown to be increasing exponentially, based on a similar increase in population. Land has other uses than for food production, however, and the demands for land for industrial and urban use must reduce the area available for food. Thus arable land available for agriculture is shown to be greater than at present, but decreasing over time.

Figure 11.2   The growing need for food production

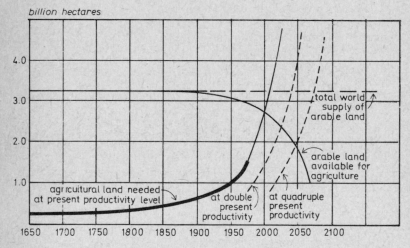

Total world supply of arable land is about 3.2 billion hectares. About 0.4 hectares per person of arable land are needed at present productivity. The curve of land needed thus reflects the population growth curve. The light line after 1970 shows the projected need for land, assuming that world population continues to grow at its present rate. Arable land available decreases because arable land is removed for urban-industrial use as population grows. The dotted curves show land needed if present productivity is doubled or quadrupled. (Taken from Dennis L. Meadows, et al, 'The Limits to Growth').

The extrapolations shows that such is the nature of exponential growth that the two curves cross in the relatively near future, around the year 2000. The reader will notice that even if no land were required for agricultural purposes, there would be no appreciable delay of the time when food consumption will be drastically curtailed. Neither does it make much difference if agricultural productivity can be increased by shifting the land-need curve to the right. At four times present productivity, Armageddon is pushed only into the twenty-first century. All this, of course, is on the assumption that arable land can be increased. Resources to do so much come from incomes, which empirically can be increased rapidly only by industrial development.

Industrial Growth and Natural Resources

The outlook for global industrial production is also one of exponential growth pushing on ultimately finite resources. At present the growth of industrial output is even faster than that of population. Growing at about 7 per cent, industrial production will double every ten years or so. With population growth the exponential quality was due to the reproductive properties of each addition to the population. With industrial growth the exponential element is the creation of productive capital in excess of that required for replacement. If in any one year more capital is created than is used up, in the next year productive capacity will have increased. The current rate of increase means that the world is fast using up its stocks of non-renewable natural resources, mineral ores, etc., which once mined cannot be replaced. For some minerals such as aluminium, copper and mercury, known resoures will be used up in one or two decades. Of course, mineral reserves may be greater than we think. Oil is continually being discovered in the North Sea. On the other hand, the rate at which resources are being used up is not itself constant. A decade ago the rate of world industrial growth was nearer 5 per cent than 7 per cent. Unless the pattern of human activity changes, in a decade's time it will be greater than 7 per cent. Just the population growth will be checked by the limited supply of arable land, so will industrial growth be checked by finite reserves of raw material.

Industrial Growth and Technology

If agricultural productivity can be improved, then so too can the use of raw materials. If the total world reserves of a raw material are finite this does not mean that the raw material must be used up as industrialisation proceeds. Metals in particular can be recycled. Recycling does not increase the total availability of resources, but reduces the rate at which they are used. Recycling, however, is at present expensive, and the cost can be expressed in terms of the industrial output which cannot be used for consumption. A parochial example is that of municipal refuse disposal. The technology for separating out the raw materials — paper, class, metals, etc. — from domestic refuse is available, but the plant is expensive. A local authority which spends money on such equipment cannot also spend the same money on education, etc. As raw materials become more expensive, recovery costs will become more bearable. Even when recovery costs are acceptable, and 100 per cent of all material used is recoverable, the amount of material in existence is limited and must eventually limit further industrial growth.

Industrial Growth and Pollution

We have only in the past decade or so become aware of the consequences of growing pollution associated with industrial growth. Pollution will have two effects on long-term growth. It will decrease agricultural productivity directly, by lowering yields, and indirectly by making food unsafe to eat. It will also directly check population growth by increasing the death rate through industrial diseases and the cumulative effects of the consumption of toxic compounds such as mercury. Pollution can be controlled, but as with recycling this is at a cost of final industrial output. As with recycling, at the present level of technology the more effective anti-pollution devices are, the more expensive they will be.

Vicious Circles Again

Interdependences between developed and underdeveloped countries make it difficult for the development process to begin in the latter. There are also vicious circles operating to ensure the eventual ending of global economic growth. World economic growth *per capita* can only be maintained if industrial and agricultural output grow with population. Growth of agricultural output depends upon industrial growth to provide the means for bringing marginal land into cultivation, as well as improving the productivity of that already in use. But industry also uses arable land. Moreover, as industry grows, so does pollution and the demand for industrial materials. Thus industrial growth must also create resources for solving these problems. If pollution is not checked it will reduce agricultural productivity and thus offset the use of industry for this end.

It seems that we have again reached the stage where we can see that population growth will ultimately be checked by the limitation of land and other resources. Just when that ceiling is reached, however, will depend upon man's willingness and ability to change some of the relationships that we have outlined. To say that such a chain of events can be regulated if mankind voluntarily reduces the growth of his population is to overlook two factors. First, the growth of the world's industrial output comes largely from the rich countries, and the rate of growth of industry will be greatly increased if there is any mass escape from the 'underdevelopment trap'. Second, the world's consumption of foodstuffs is extremely uneven from one country to another. The period in which population size is beyond the capacity to feed it has already arrived for many nations.

We may have given the impression that the limitations to growth will be imposed simulataneously. This is not the case, as the current discussions on world food supplies would indicate, and we are already beginning to feel, very painfully in areas like the southern Sahara, the effects of resource limitation. When we spoke of exponential growth we may have implied that it was smooth growth. This is also not the case. The experience of South-East Asia shows that food shortages may last for a year or two and then be relieved by the vagaries of the earth's climate. Increasing limitation of food supplies is more likely to be indicated by the increasing frequency of bad years relative to good.

Similarly with the limitations to industrial growth. Technology may allow for the production of synthetic raw materials and for the arresting of a serious pollutant. But even synthetic materials have to be produced out of something, and since matter is indestructible, unless the final product can be designed to contain all the matter required for its production, there will always be pollution.

The solution to these problems facing the human race may seem crashingly obvious. The rates of growth of population and industry will have to be checked. How this can come about is quite another matter. In our view, peaceful and humane solutions to these problems depend on international co-operation, and the 1974 UN World Food Conference in Rome is an indication that this prospect is being seriously considered. But there are powerful conflicts of interest which will have to be resolved. Poor countries legitimately want to increase their standards of living, but as world resources are limited this can only happen in the long run if the rich countries are prepared to curb theirs. This presents rich countries with a problem of 'social engineering' — of how to persuade the populations of the affluent societies to accept cuts in consumption. If such problems are not solved voluntarily by mankind, however, they will be solved for us through the kind of checks which Malthus envisaged — war, pestilence, famine, and disease. In the next chapter we shall look more closely at the economic relationships between countries, relationships which will determine the prospects of essential international co-operation.

Chapter 12

Economic Interdependence

Towards the end of the last chapter we referred to the prospects for long-term world growth within the framework of a global system. Inputs of industrial investment and natural resources are to produce the outputs which enable the human race to survive. The means to produce this global output, however, come from individual countries. An individual country can be regarded as one of many sub-systems which make up the international economy just as households and firms are sub-systems of a national economy. The capacity to produce varies greatly, as we have observed in the last chapter, from one system to another. So great is this variation that it is rarely possible for a single country to produce the outputs required for its survival entirely from its own resources. We turn now to consider the nature of the environment in which an individual system operates and some of the consequences of the growth of world trade. We shall examine these relationships with a particular objective in mind, namely to consider whether there is anything in the way economic systems interact which enhances or diminishes the prospects of the co-operation necessary to harbour the planet's resources for the common good.

DIFFERING RESOURCE ALLOCATION IS THE BASIS FOR TRADE BETWEEN COUNTRIES

The antithesis of trade is self-sufficiency. We have seen that in the remote past the self-sufficient household was the basic economic unit. With the passing of time the unit of self-sufficiency became ever larger until now few national economies can exist in isolation. The fundamental reason for this change has been technology. Man has learned how to utilise resources other than just land for agriculture. He has created human resources by acquiring skills. In doing so he has learned to adjust to the imbalances in the distribution of natural resources. Industrial countries, such as the UK, support a population greater than could be fed from that country's own food resources alone. This has been made possible by trading production based on inputs which are plentiful for products of those which are scarce for the country in question. Thus a country with large amounts of land, but relatively small amounts of capital and labour, will find it advantageous to trade agricultural products for goods which are labour or capital intensive. Since a choice of production techniques is possible, the permutations of potential input combinations are endless. Some combinations are more satisfactory than others, however, and trade between economic systems will be beneficial as long as each economic system is endowed with a different allocation of production inputs. The differing resource allocations between countries allow specilisation, and even though such differences may be slight, as long as they exist there will be potential gains from trade over self-sufficiency.

Comparative Costs of Production

International specialisation is only an extension of the principle of the division of labour within countries, and it is obvious why specialisation must be beneficial. Why invest time and effort in making something yourself when you can buy the same thing more cheaply elsewhere? It is only obvious, however, when differences in costs between systems are absolute. Bananas can be grown in greenhouses, but they can be grown much more easily in a sub-tropical climate. A country which wants to consume bananas but has a temperate climate could more beneficially sell greenhouses and buy bananas with the income. Banana producers here have an absolute advantage. But trade between systems does not follow only absolute cost differences. West Germany may be a better producer of machine tools than the UK, yet she imports as well as exports such products. This is because there is a difference in comparative costs as well as absolute costs. The comparison is not between the manufacture of machine tools in Germany and the UK, but between the costs in Germany of making machine tools and the costs of making other products, such as textiles.

The Principle of Comparative Cost Advantage

Germany and the UK both produce machine tools and textiles. The input required to produce a unit of output of each commodity differs in the two countries. In Germany, say, a unit of machine tool output can be produced by 100 hours of labour inputs, and a unit of textiles by 50 hours. In the UK the inputs required are greater in each case. A unit of machine tools requires 150 man-hours and a unit of textiles 60 man-hours. As a more efficient producer of both machine tools and textiles, it would seem that Germany would have no reason to trade with the UK. But for each country, production of one of the goods is at the cost of not producing the other. Labour that Germany uses for textile production is not being used to produce machine tools. We have postulated differences in inputs so that each unit of machine tools Germany produces is at the cost of two units of textiles, since it takes twice the labour input to produce machine tools that it takes to produce textiles. If, however, Germany were able to trade machine tools with another country, and get more than two units of textiles in exchange, it would pay her to specialise in machine-tool production. Production relationships in the UK offer just such opportunities. For every unit of machine tools she produces, she is losing the production of two and a half units of textiles. Morever, it takes two and a half times the labour to produce machine tools than it does textiles. If the UK were able to trade textiles with Germany, and pay *less* than two and half a units of textiles for a unit of machine tools, then it would pay her to specialise in textiles. As it happens from our simple example, with Germany requiring anything *more* than two units of textiles for a unit of machine tools, and the UK willing to pay *up to* two and a half units of textiles, the basis for trade exists.

If German and UK producers of both commodities were free to choose the country in which they sold their products, we could summarise the benefits arising from comparative cost advantage as follows:

	In Germany	*In UK*
1 unit of German machine tools buys	2.0 units textiles	2.5 units textiles
1 unit of UK textiles buys	0.5 units machine tools	0.4 units machine tools

Trade Flows

As economic systems have developed over the past century world trade has followed a pattern which is, in the main, consistent with the structural changes associated with the economic development process and with changes in comparative cost advantage. The decline of agriculture relative to industry, for example, has been reflected, but so too have changes within each of these broad groups. In the USA in the forty years from 1913 to 1953, food and agricultural products declined from over a half to about two-fifths of exports, and in the same period, US food imports increased as a proportion of total imports. The declining importance of such primary products indicates the growing importance of manufacturing industry. The increasing percentage of food imports suggests specialisation. Similarly, primary products remained a large if somewhat declining (76 per cent to 69 per cent) part of India's exports while she too remained both an exporter and importer of food. The intra-European trade in manufactures since the Second World War seems a particularly striking example of comparative cost advantage in action.

Does Comparative Cost Advantage Adequately Explain the Pattern of World Trade?

Our hypothetical example is highly simplified and it ignores some very important features of international economic relationships.

The Rate of Currency Exchange   In a perfectly competitive world, the prices which a country's goods fetch on the global market will be determined by the countervailing pressures of buyers and sellers. An increase in world demand for German machine tools will increase their price. If the units of output are measured in money terms, this will be tantamount to an increase in the units produced (or a reduction in man-hours required to produce a single unit). The exchangeability of machine tools in terms of textiles will be enhanced — more textiles will be required per unit of machine tools — and resources diverted into the machine-tool industry. In practice, however, the picture is complicated by the fact that the price of a country's exports depends only partly upon the world demand for them. It also depends upon the rate of exchange between the exporting country's currency and that of the rest of the world. In a world of perfect markets the rate of currency exchange should also depend upon the demand for a country's goods. An increased demand for German goods should lead to an increased price for German currency. The rate of currency exchange, however, can be artificially altered by government action. This does not in itself alter comparative costs, since they are an internal matter. If a country's exports are made artificially expensive or cheap, however, trade can be prevented from following comparative costs.

Political Factors   Exchange rate manipulation may be motivated by a desire to change trade balances, but there are other, and sometimes stronger, political forces at work. Particularly since the Second World War, trade flows have become bound up with the ideological struggle between East and West which has replaced the more blatant imperialism of an earlier epoch. US industrial involvement in Europe after 1945 is one example of this struggle and the competitive attentions paid to the third world is another. Some trade goods can take the form of an offer which cannot be refused if the 'assisted' country is to continue to receive aid.

Nationalism Nationalism is clearly a political factor, yet it deserves a separate heading. The manifestations of nationalism are often economic in character and are usually a response to such adverse economic circumstances as operated in the inter-war period. In its economic form it is an attempt to distort the international environment to the advantage of a particular economic system. This is done by raising tariffs, giving subsidies, imposing import quotas, and by arranging a variety of preferences for that country's own products. When we examine the nature of such obstacles to international trade and the reasons for them, we shall see that they are frequently self-defeating.

THE INTERNATIONAL ENVIRONMENT

A single country has three sets of contacts with the wider world environment: (*a*) there is trad~~e~~ ~~in~~ goods, (*b*) an economy can buy or sell services such as transport and insurance in much the same way that it trades in goods, and (*c*) factors of production can move between countries. The movement of goods in the international economy is in fact a surrogate for the movement of factors. Countries have different factor endowment, and unless factors of production can be moved across frontiers, this difference is the basis for the trade in finished products. Some production inputs are indeed immobile, particularly land. Some, such as labour, are not. Mobility, of course, is a relative term and at any one time the actual amounts of migrant labour, temporary or permanent, are likely to be small in comparison with the size of indigenous populations. Yet it is possible for a country like Switzerland to depend for its standard of living upon large amounts of migrant labour in much the same way as the UK depends upon the imports of food and raw materials. The term 'goods' in world trade indicates capital goods as well as consumer goods, and thus an economy can import real capital goods as easily as it can import finished consumer products. The kind of services a country can buy includes the use, by borrowing, of money capital as well as consumer-orientated services such as tourism. (When a country sends its nationals abroad on holiday, and when it borrows money from other countries, it is 'importing' these services, since they must be paid for outside that country.)

A single economic system thus draws from the international environment inputs for both production and consumption. These inputs

Figure 12.1 The UK Economy in its 19th century world environment

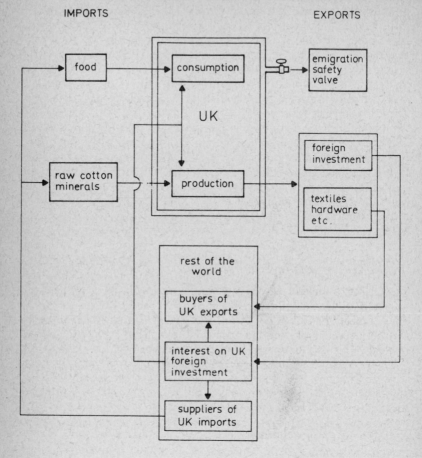

Note: The value of imports of food and raw materials continually exceeded the value of exports of industrial goods, but the difference was more than covered by net incomes from services such as the interest on foreign investments indicated above. Such investments were often spent directly on UK exports. Migration added to the interrelationships by stimulating the demand abroad for both UK capital and consumer goods and by the practice of remitting foreign currencies to relatives in the home country.

can take both a tangible and intangible form — they can be either goods or services. If a country draws on its environment it must return an output, whether of goods or services, for production or consumption. Inputs into a national system will be the outputs from one or more other systems. We will set aside for the moment the possibility that inputs can be in the form of a gift — i.e. foreign aid. If just one system requires imports, other systems become involved. If the international environment were comprised of only two countries, and one of the two imported goods and services from the other, the second would be obliged to import in return from the first. The alternatives would be for the first country to export without payment, or refuse to export in the first place. Experience shows that this latter event is improbable. (It is not impossible, however. Western merchants in the last century had great difficulty in persuading Imperial China that they had anything China wanted.) The point is belaboured because it is an important one. The international environment is such that it is extremely difficult, as we shall see, for any individual system to remain aloof from it.

An Economy in the World Environment

The points of contact between an economy and its environment are very numerous and the range of potential exports and imports will be considerable. To illustrate external relationships, a suitable example is the UK economy at some point in the second half of the nineteenth century. This economy was in many respects a highly efficient and specialised one. It imported a limited range of raw materials, raw textiles, and mineral ores. Endowed with relatively plentiful capital and labour, it converted these imports into a narrow range of widely consumed exports — textiles, hardwear, and engineering products. The profits from this exchange were exported as money capital to other countries, often to enable them to finance the purchase of exports of capital goods from the UK. The interest on these loans paid for further imports of foodstuffs required for the large industrial population. Since she was poorly endowed with land relative to labour and capital, comparative cost advantage for the UK lay in industrial production. If those relationships occasionally did not work smoothly, if, for example, there occurred a bottleneck in import supplies which forced up the cost of living, there was always the possibility of emigration. Figure 12.1 sets out these relationships diagrammatically.

The Balance of Payments

The total trade of a country is made up of a host of transactions. These transactions change as a country's relationships with the international environment change. Information that changes are taking place is provided by changes in the demand for a country currency. If a country is selling more than it is buying, the price of its currency in terms of the currencies of other countries — the exchange rate — will rise. German machine tools must be paid for in German currency, and the trader who buys from Germany must also buy currency. If more German currency is bought than is sold, if more goods and services are bought than are sold, then the price of that currency will rise. Changes in exchange rates are, however, imperfect indicators of a country's progress through its environment. They are certainly immediate indicators of change, since they vary from day to day, even from hour to hour. But they can conceal more than they reveal and they have to be carefully interpreted and analysed. One way to do this is to summarise a country's transactions into a balance of the payments made to it and by it.

Current Account and Capital Account

The balance of payments is divided into two parts. On the one hand the balance of payments on current account summarises transactions in goods and services, while capital account summarises the assets and liabilities acquired from trade. Capital account includes a country's loans and debts, and holdings of foreign currencies. Current account is further divided between trade in goods, i.e. the balance of trade, and trade in services or the 'invisibles' balance.

These divisions are set out in Table 12.1 in a brief summary of the UK balance of payments for 1972.

Table 12.1   The UK Balance of Payments, 1972

CURRENT ACCOUNT	£ million
1. Balance of trade (exports minus imports)	— 685
2. Balance of invisible trade (interest, services, etc.)	+768
3. Balance on current account	+ 83
CAPITAL ACCOUNT	
4. Net capital movements (investments)	—1,348
Represented by:	
government borrowing	+ 573
drawing on reserves	+ 692
current account balance	+ 83

Source 'United Kingdom Balance of Payments 1973', Central Statistical Office.

An adverse UK balance of visible trade (1) has persisted since the nineteenth century, and indeed it has been regarded as in a sense 'normal' for imports of foodstuffs and raw materials into the UK to exceed exports of manufacture. It has also been regarded as normal for this adverse balance to be covered by invisible earnings. (2) The current and capital account relationships for the economy shown in Figure 12.1 were such that invisible earnings were large enough to sustain a large annual transfer from current to capital account, i.e. an export of money capital. Item (4) above would thus grow by the amount of the current account balance (3), generating higher invisible earnings year by year. The adverse balance of trade assisted this accumulation. Had the UK not bought more goods from other countries than she supplied to the international economy, those countries which had borrowed from the UK could not have earned the sterling currency to pay interest on and make repayments of the money they had borrowed. Since the nineteenth century international relationships have changed, and these changes have been reflected in the UK balance of payments. Two world wars necessitated borrowing by the UK on a scale which reduced her invisible earnings from interest payments. At the same time changes in comparative cost advantage and in political relationships have made exports, visible and invisible, more dificult to sell, which in no way reduces dependence upon imports. The balance of payments is thus more than a summary of transactions, it is a statement of interdependence. This point is well shown in the current energy crisis. Oil-producing countries sell oil and buy other goods and services. Oil revenues are greater than the small populations of oil-producing countries can spend. Oil producers can only export oil at their present scale if they lend their balance of payments surpluses abroad. Whereas the UK in our example had to import more than she exported to allow other countries to borrow money, the oil producers have to lend money in order to export their oil.

The Balance of Payments Problem

The phrase 'the balance of payments problem' is often used in a way which suggests that the balance of payments is some malignant organism and if it would only go away our lives would be easier. The balance of payments is, in fact, only a statement of a country's external relationships, and it is in these that problems, if any, lie. It is only possible for one country to consume more than it produces if, at the same time, others produce more than they consume. One country's surplus is another country's deficit. If, over time, a single country's deficits and surpluses even out, there will be no balance of payments problem. A problem only arises if there is persistent deficit or surplus. The country which consumes more than it produces can only do so by capital account transfers, and it can only do this as long as it has capital assets, or can borrow on the prospects of them. Conversely, surplus countries cannot accumulate capital account reserves indefinitely. In spite of nationalistic arguments to the contrary, there is no point in saving for a rainy day which never arrives. Yet if surplus countries do not pass on their excess purchasing power, the surpluses will fade anyway as importing countries lose their ability to buy.

CONTROL OF THE INTERNATIONAL ENVIRONMENT

To remedy the tendency to overproduce and to underconsume, a country must adjust its productive patterns. The economic structure of a society cannot be altered overnight, however, and in the meanwhile the international environment cannot be assumed to be unchanging. Some form of control over the environment would seem to be required. There are, in fact, many ways in which countries, and groups within countries, seek to control the international environment. We shall see that if the objective is economic advantage, attempts at control can be damaging in general, as well as self-defeating for the country concerned.

A Country Acting on its Own

There are two broad ways in which a country acting by itself may seek to change its relationships with other countries: (*a*) it can interfere with the prices at which goods and services are traded, and (*b*) it can place institutional obstacles in the path of trade flows. Prices can be changed by altering the price of the country's currency. This means that foreign currency has to be bought and sold to prevent the exchange rate from altering as it adjusts to changes in trade. The possibility is conditional upon adequate reserves of foreign curency, and exchange rate manipulation can only be a temporary expedient. Prices can also be changed by the use of tariffs and subsidies. Tariffs make imports more expensive than domestic production, and exports can be cheapened and thus encouraged by a subsidy. Such methods distort the pattern of comparative cost advantage, but then that is their purpose. In that they distort comparative cost advantage, they will also lessen the gains from trade. Such losses can be temporary since one benefit from a tariff is that it may allow a potential comparative cost advantage to be realised. This is the so-called 'infant industry' argument for protection. Highly organised production abroad may be sold at prices in the world market far below the costs of production of a home industry which is still in its infancy. A temporary tariff, it is argued, will allow a growth in output of the infant industry and a lowering of average costs to competitive levels. The argument has particular relevance for underdeveloped countries, but all too often tariffs and subsidies are self-defeating. Firstly exports and imports, as we have seen, are interdependent. If a tariff is successful and reduces imports, it will thereby be reducing another country's exports, and *its* ability to buy the tariff country's exports. Secondly, they can invite retaliation and can become competitive. In such a case the world's consumers are likely to be buying fewer and fewer goods at ever-increasing prices. Moreover, protection, once given, creates vested interests that will strongly resist its removal.

Control of the environment by physical and institutional, rather than monetary or fiscal, methods ranges from obvious quantitative restrictions on imports to more subtle forms of discrimination in the home market. Government agencies may, as a matter of policy, buy imports only from domestic sources, and legal restrictions — on safety standards for motor vehicles, for example — can similarly favour domestic products. To say that such attempts to control the environment must be self-defeating in the long run should be qualiffied by referring to the objectives of such policies. They may not be economic, but strategic, political and social. Domestic agriculture may be supported because of the danger of relying on foreign food supplies in times of war, and similar arguments can apply to the engineering industries which can supply munitions. In the past France and Germany have protected agriculture to maintain a large peasant class which before 1914 was the basis of their huge conscripted armies. In the UK, protection of agriculture by subsidy has been justified on strategic and social grounds. The removal of support might have led to drastic structural change with attendant rural unemployment, etc. Again, governments may be aware of the economic consequences of distorting comparative cost advantage, but may be unable to change their policies because of the political power of particular interest groups. Supersonic aviation and the more mundane sugar beet are both examples of products subject to the influence of well organised and powerful pressure groups.

Countries Acting in Concert

The international economy consists of a large number of interrelated elements which are continually changing. Changes in the environment make for uncertainty, and individual countries may be particularly vulnerable. The reduction of uncertainty in the international environment is the objective of many forms of collective activity. Such activity can be grouped into four main categories, bearing in mind that they are often related.

1   *Involuntary Associations*   Empires, past and present, have been established as the result of one country imposing its will on others weaker than itself, in order to make its own environment more secure. It is not within the scope of this book to enquire whether such security is political or economic. If the reader is of the opinion that the basis of all war is economic, then it will make no difference. The British Empire, for example, gave considerable economic security to the mother country. Membership of the Empire was on a complementary basis, with Britain securing markets for her manufactures and supplies of raw materials. It is worth noting that in the long run, such involuntary association worked to the advantage of neither the dependent countries, many of which are now underdeveoped countries, nor to the mother country herself. The former had patterns of specialisation forced upon them, while the latter was not forced to adjust to changes in comparative cost advantage. But, in the short run, from economic security came political security. A comparison can be drawn with COMECON, the association of Eastern Bloc countries. Membership is hardly voluntary, and the association has a dominant 'partner' in the USSR. The reasons for the formation of COMECON were political rather than economic, since membership was not determined by economic complementarity but by the existence of a common, if enforced, economic system. Yet the economic consequences for the weaker members have been similar. Trade patterns have developed which work more to the short-term advantage of the dominant partner, although the longer term consequences are likely to be harmful.

2   *Voluntary Regional Groupings*   These are characterised by economic similarities between members rather than differences, and perhaps COMECON compares more with the voluntary European Economic Community than with the British Empire. The objective, however, is similar. It is to create an area of self-sufficiency which can thus be isolated as far as possible from the rest of the world environment. The separation is initially brought about by the formation of a customs union — each member has a common tariff with the rest of the world, while tariffs between members are eliminated. Behind this barrier, common institutions are developed to create an integrated economic whole. Space prohibits discussion of the mechanics

of such communities, or all their advantages and disadvantages. Within the tariff area, however, opportunities for specialisation may arise from the removal of trade restrictions and from economies of scale offered by the size of the protected market. But potentially severe distortions may result for the international economy which work to the particular disadvantage of poorer countries. They will have little chance of realising potential comparative cost advantage if their exports cannot gain access to wider markets. For this reason some voluntary associations, the Organization of African Unity, and the Latin America Free Trade Association, are defensive in character and are reactions to associations between the industrialised economies of the world.

3 *Voluntary Associations for a Particular Purpose* Some associations between countries have the object of resolving a specific area of uncertainty they share in common. A country may belong to an international cartel designed to control the price of a particular product, or to pool research, etc. Cartels in industrial goods are not, since the inter-war period, regarded with favour, but services are another matter. Civil aviation and shipping services are subject to international agreement, although the consequences are by no means wholly beneficial. The cost of achieving a more certain environment is often borne by the poorer countries. In shipping, for example, the greatest gains accrue to the large maritime nations. Poorer countries may be prevented from competing for trade by prices which are fixed by richer countries, and as a result are unable to develop their own services. For primary products there is a great deal of uncertainty. Demand and supply can fluctuate violently, causing large changes in prices and incomes. It is theoretically possible to control prices, and thus incomes, by stabilising the amounts of the product coming on to the market even although output varies. There have been attempts to organise world-wide sales of wheat, tin, coffee, etc., but very few have succeeded for long. A central authority buys the output and sells only enough to keep prices stable, with short falls being made up from stocks accumulated during years of abundance. The problem has been to secure the co-operation of a large number of small producers. In years of rising prices they tend to opt out of the agreement and sell at higher prices to private buyers.

4 *Voluntary Associations on a Global Scale* Lastly, there are agreements and institutions which have developed, not between similar economies or producers of the same products, but to resolve

uncertainties which affect the world as a whole. Since the Second World War there has been generally accepted co-operation to create a stable trading environment. Tariff wars have given way to GATT, the General Agreement on Tariffs and Trade, and international borrowing and lending has been made more stable by the operations of the International Monetary Fund. We shall return to the issue of international co-operation at the end of the chapter.

The Firm and its International Environment

A business which sells abroad is subject to the same kinds of uncertainty affecting firms which operate nationally. It faces uncertainty from the action of its competitors, from the governments, and in the markets for factors and products both at home and overseas. It thus has strong motives for seeking control over its environment. A product of these motives has been the growth of the multinational company, a firm which not only sells abroad but sells from abroad. Tariffs and the development of trading blocs have given impetus to the establishment by companies of subsidiaries behind foreign tariff barriers, and supplies of raw materials can be made more secure if they are produced by the firm which uses them. Both such developments make sound commercial sense. Multinational companies follow the pattern of comparative cost advantage by directing capital investment to locations where labour and other factors are cheapest, and a recent development for many poor countries has been a shift to the production by foreign-based companies of goods previously produced in the industrial countries of the world. The different patterns of taxation and company law, and national prestige for the recipient country, are added reasons for a business to operate internationally.

While the reasons for the growth of multinationals may be consistent with comparative cost advantage, their very nature gives them monopoly powers which distort the international economy. We have already spoken in Chapter 11 of the effects that a foreign enclave can have on a poor country. Even for richer countries, the operations of multinationals can be undesirable. Their size and diversity make them difficult to control and national economic policies aimed at such companies can be neutralised. It might not be possible to tax them effectively if profits made in one country can be offset by losses made in another. Anti-monopoly policies might be blunted if the company cannot be made to disclose information on its foreign activities. Monetary policies and exchange controls can be rendered ineffective when the turnover of a single company is larger than the national income of the host country. The ability of multinatonal companies to operate independently of national governments adds another complication to the prospects for international co-operation.

CAN THE WORLD'S PROBLEMS BE SOLVED?

It would be presumptuous of us to pretend that we can answer this question. We hope that we have given the reader a sufficient understanding of the relationships involved for him to see where the answers *might* lie. The fundamental economic problem is that of scarcity, and the means for human survival are becoming scarce at a faster rate. This scarcity is already demonstrably affecting the poorer countries in the world. The overall problem would seem thus to divide into two separate but related questions. Firstly, how to increase consumption and production in underdeveloped countries, and secondly how to decrease consumption and production in the more affluent. Underdeveloped countries are poor for two sets of reasons, and there is no agreement on which is the more important. They are poor because of unfavourable internal circumstances which keep them backward, and they are poor because international forces operate against them.

It might be tempting to suggest that improving their international environment is the answer to the last problem, that removing obstacles to trade and giving favoured treatment within trading blocs will provide the stimulus to development needed to raise consumption levels per head. This may only be a partial solution. Poor countries are primary producers because this is where much of their comparative cost advantage already lies, and primary products are what industrial countries already buy. It may be possible for poor countries to develop export industries, but the developed world has a massive technological lead. Perhaps it is not mere trade the poor countries need, but a limited self-sufficiency based on low — or intermediate — technology production. This could be developed by assistance from the richer nations.

Assistance to Poor Countries

Foreign assistance is seen as an alternative to the stimulation of trade to relieve international poverty. Foreign aid can take three forms.
1. Private overseas investment is a means whereby the capital deficiency of poor countries can be remedied, but as we have seen earlier in the chapter private capital will flow towards the greater profit possibilities, which may not be consistent with the greatest benefit to the recipient country. In many cases private foreign in-

vestment, instead of taking the form of an alternative to trade, will actually reinforce it, since foreign private capital is often associated with the production of primary products. The governments of poor countries, however, can raise capital in foreign capital markets, and while this capital will be provided by private investors, its use will be determined by the borrowing government. The effectiveness of such borrowing depends upon the efficiency of the government concerned, and while the governments of poor countries have made beneficial use of foreign capital markets, there have been cases where loans have been raised for conspicuous, prestigious projects such as airlines and sports stadiums rather than more directly productive investment.

2. The governments of rich countries can themselves provide capital for the poorer nations either by gifts or loans at favourable rates of interest. On the surface the effect on development can appear more beneficial than private investment. Government aid is usually associated with specific, large-scale projects. Egypt's Aswan High Dam is an example. But here again there are reservations to be made. A foreign government may give aid for a project which it thinks *ought* to benefit the recipient country, and poorer countries may acquiesce in aid projects because this is the way to get aid, even if the project is not, perhaps, at the top of the indigenous government's priorities. The government giving the aid may have to justify its actions to a domestic population, and assistance may be in a form which is of benefit to the donating country. The aid, for example, may have to be spent in the country of origin.

3. Technical assistance can come from both private institutions and governments. It may complement the provision of capital, but it can be regarded as an alternative in that its purpose can be to enable the utilisation of existing resources. In a vacuum, this 'trade *v.* aid' controversy could be resolved, but in the imperfect real world, poor countries have to compete with the rich in world markets for the means for survival which are rising in price. In a sense the prices of foodstuffs, etc. on which the poor depend are irrelevant. They are only a rationing device which at the moment means that it is the richer countries which can afford to survive. The balance can only be redressed if prices fall, which means that the demands of rich countries will have to fall. This takes us back to the question of how richer countries can be persuaded to demand/consume less so that resources can be diverted to the underdeveloped countries (see Chapter 11).

International Co-operation?

We have seen something of the factors which govern the relationships between economic systems, and we have seen enough to realise that there is no automatic mechanism which is going to reverse this 'rationing' process. There are indeed developments which can reduce the consumption of the richer countries — the increasing price of oil for example — but they do not at the same time increase the consumption by the poor (unless they possess oil reserves, that is). Any diversion must come through international agreement to co-operate. So far, international agreement has not been encouraging. Certainly there have been comparative successes since 1945 such as the World Bank, but these must be set against a favourable economic climate. It is the rich countries who have the economic bargaining power, it is they who have contributed to the international accord, and it is they who have enjoyed considerable prosperity. The ill-fated League of Nations is an example of what happens to an international agreement when circumstances become unfavourable. The reason is not hard to find. Governments consist of individuals who, whatever the political system, ultimately depend for their power upon the goodwill of their nationals. Food riots can shake a government in socialist Poland just as disaffected voters can change governments in the West. In the last resort, the prospects for the necessary international co-operation rest in political rather than economic factors. How, in other words, to persuade consumers in the richer countries that it is in their interests to accept a lower standard of living.

Chapter 13

Economics and Economists

BASIC LESSONS

There are three main ideas that we would like to think this book has brought out. Firstly, economics is about the human relationships which arise from the demands made upon physical resources and the limited availability of those resources. The basic economic fact is that *all* demands cannot be met simultaneously. Secondly, there are many different ways of dealing with the basic problem of scarcity. Throughout history, and in the world of today, we observe that the allocation of the power to consume can be determined by methods ranging from religious decree, through co-operative rationing to free market processes. The way in which a particular society solves its economic problems may influence the particular demands it makes upon resources, but this does not detract from the notion that all economic systems have a common basis. Thirdly, we stress that economic systems do not and cannot exist in a vacuum. Whether the economic 'system' is a person, a family, or an entire nation, there is bound to be interaction with its environment. This is as true for a primitive tribe facing flood and drought as for an advanced industrial economy dependent upon international trade.

ECONOMISTS AND ECONOMIC PROBLEMS

Having reminded readers of the nature of the basic economic problems, we can ask how helpful the study of economics is in solving and understanding these problems. There has been little formal theory in this book, and this has been deliberate. We did, however, devote Chapter 4 to an examination of the fundamentals of supply and demand analysis, and the reader, armed with a grasp of a few simple relationships, might begin to see for himself the process of cause and effect at work in everyday economic activity. He could try to predict the direction of price and output changes, for example, following the extension of fishing limits into what were previously international waters; he could suggest the consequences of a rise in steel prices, or of a labour shortage in central London.

In general, economists have been quite successful at handling problems of this kind. They have observed patterns of economic behaviour, have suggested the relationships involved, and devised ways of measuring economic change. They have sometimes found it possible to make fairly accurate predictions of economic changes based on assumptions about the *probable* behaviour of the various factors involved. The emphasis on probability, however, suggests uncertainty, and uncertainty can only be reduced by acquiring information. Even where information is inadequate, economists can still make fair guesses at the probable effects of a particular course of action by careful observation and measurement of past reactions.

There are, however, two other important difficulties to consider — complexity and inconsistsistency. Firstly, for many economic problems, the relationships involved can be extremely complex and the number of relevant factors can be very large, while the means of measuring them are imperfect — if they can be measured at all! Unfortunately, the 'big' problems are in this category. Inflation, full employment, flows of international payments and currencies, and world population growth are examples. Secondly, there is the difficulty of pursuing a number of desirable, but incompatible, objectives of economic policy. Full employment, stable prices, and free wage bargaining are all desirable objectives, but they prove to be unattainable if all three are sought simultaneously. The importance that workers attach to free wage negotiation is not normally part of our economic calculus. Yet in the short term the ability to conduct wage bargaining is so important for the negotiators that it could arguably be included somehow in the wage payment, as if a wage payment freely bargained for was worth more than one for the same amount that had been imposed. Free wage bargaining, however, makes it extremely difficult to contain inflation and still maintain full employment. The economist is ill equipped to deal with issues of this kind since they involve subjective assessments which are therefore very difficult to quantify.

ECONOMICS AS A SOCIAL SCIENCE

The key immeasurable factor in our wage bargaining example was the strength of human attitudes and here we are treading on ground that is currently regarded as being on the borderline of economics. The major question raised in Chapters 11 and 12 was whether it was possible or likely that the peoples of the relatively affluent, developed countries would be prepared to accept voluntarily a reduction in their actual or potential living standards in order to assist the survival and advance of the third world. On the basis of past experience, given the powerful 'ratchet' effect by which people adjust to higher expectations much more readily than to lower, and a recognition of the general lack of understanding about the interdependences of global economics, one can only be sceptical about an answer in the affirmative. Before the necessary reductions can take place, attitudes must change. Perhaps we need a strong douche of harsh reality in the form of worldwide slump and famine before significant adjustment can take place, but it would be much less painful and more humane to accept some degree of social manipulation or 'social engineering'. One might argue that it is no longer sufficient simply to understand an economic problem, but that one also needs to know how to tackle it, perhaps by non-economic means.

ECONOMICS AND POLITICAL CHANGE

'Social engineering' is primarily a political matter, and economic objectives such as long-run economic growth may be attainable only with political change. The relationship between economic and political change is a very complex one. Consider, for example, the problems for the Western world of adjusting to the oil crisis: How to save oil without resort to unemployment, how to develop new energy sources, and how to cope with the huge flows of unspent oil revenues in the hands of the suppliers? The origin of the crisis is, of course, in part political — from such pressures as Arab exasperation with the developed world's attitude towards the Palestinian problem, a determination to end what was considered to be an imperialistic over-exploitation of Arab natural resources, and a realisation that primary producers in the third world could for once have the upper hand in the commodity markets. We infer from this that economists *qua* economists must be aware of, and take into consideration, a further group of relevant factors if the 'big' problems are to be solved.

THE POLITICAL ECONOMISTS

Economists have not always felt themselves to be ill equipped to deal with the 'big' problems. The 'classical' economists, of the late eighteenth and nineteenth centuries (i.e. from Adam Smith to, say, J. S. Mill), had characteristics in their approach to economists that would set them apart from most modern economics. They all had a passionate desire to understand the world about them. They were acute observers of the contemporary scene and moreover were active participants in that scene. They found it difficult to abstract themselves from their environment and with numerous pamphlets and polemics would frequently attempt to alter that environment to make it conform with some idealised version. This involved them in frequent judgements about the nature of society and its performance. Karl Marx is the paramount example of the political economist — first observing, then interpreting and finally recommending action. Marx makes dificult reading for the modern economist not least because his theoretical ideas intermingle with his comments on and condemnations of capitalism as he saw it, and his views on man and man's role in society in general. 'Economics' seemed to be not just about the way resources were distributed between sections of the economy, but also about the ethics of the process itself.

SCIENTIFIC ECONOMICS

The attitudes of the classical economists are in strong contrast to those of more recent schools. The value judgements explicitly and implicitly expressed in the work of the early writers set economics aside from the objectivity which coul be obtained by the natural scientists.

Economists still place great emphasis on observation, but the 'observation' tends to take the form of statistics which are then processed by standardised procedures. The widespread use of mathematical and statistical analysis in this century has encouraged the projection of economics as an exact science. Since the economist is not able to set up laboratory experiments on a society or economy, he compensates by constructing theories and 'models' of the real world and then conducts 'experiments' on these models or tests their predictions against statistical measurements of real world economic behaviour. The statistics and the mathematical models create an air of scientific respectability. The rigour with which the logic of the models is extended and refined is intellectually stimulating and carries with its academic esteem. A high degree of separation or isolation of the economist from his socio-political environment is seen as a confirmation of his 'scientific' approach and of his 'positivism' or lack of emotional and political entanglement which might cloud or colour his observations and interpretations.

Economics remains, however, a social and not a natural science, and its subject matter is as inconstant as society itself. Any theories or models are likely to be only very crude approximations to real life situations, no matter how elegant the mathematics used. The data available is itself subject to many deficiencies. This is not to argue that theoretical and statistical analysis can or ought to be abandoned. We would suggest rather that the economist's attention ought to be foscused more sharply on the world as it is in all its uncomfortable complexity.

FULL CIRCLE

Perhaps it is time that most economists came to accept that they cannot be 'outside observers' of economies and societies. Some, like Galbraith, Myrdal and Schumacher, have been saying this for some time. Social investigators are always an intimate part of the system they observe and bring their own or their derived prejudices and judgements to bear. Economics has fallen into some disrepute in recent years, mainly, we believe, because some major economic problems have proved to be so intractable. Society no doubt expected too much of the scientific positivist economist. If he were to be prepared to involve himself with an understanding of political wills as well as economic forces then his effectiveness might increase. Perhaps he should abandon his attempt to maintain a value-free position and instead try to enlighten, explain and suggest feasible solutions which are in keeping, not necessarily with theoretical abstractions, but rather with the needs and aspirations of the parties involved. There are encouraging signs that more and more economists are coming to accept this approach, especially in view of (and perhaps because of) the very great human and economic problems that the world is likely to face over the next few decades.

Further Reading

Chapter 2

Consumption patterns tell us a great deal about consumption behaviour, and readers will find much interesting detail in *A History of the Cost of Living* by John Burnett (Penguin, 1969) and in Peter Wilsher's *The Pound in Your Pocket* (Cassell, 1970). *South India, Yesterday, Today, and Tomorrow* by T. Scarlett Epstein (Macmillan, 1973) contains contrasting material on consumption standards in a poor country and highlights the social consequences of underdevelopment. Consumer motivations and behaviour in a rich country are discussed in *The Powerful Consumer* by George Katona (McGraw-Hill, 1960), while a more sceptical attitude is reflected in J. K. Galbraith's now classic *The Affluent Society* (Penguin, 1962).

Chapter 3

There is no single text which covers the content of this chapter, since it contains both an historical survey of production and a consideration of the relationships involved in the production process. *A Theory of Economic History* by John Hicks (Oxford University Press, 1969) is an excellent short treatment of the growth of economic organisation. Robert Heilbroner's *The Making of Economic Society* (Prentice-Hall, 1962) covers a long time span at a more elementary level, stressing the benefits of the capitalist system. For the Industrial Revolution itself, the literature is extensive. A suitable introduction is Phyllis Deane's *The First Industrial Revolution* (Cambridge University Press, 1965). The relationships of the production process take us into an area covered in standard texts on economic analysis. Again there is a wide choice, but the reader who continues the study of economics is likely to come across *An Introduction to Positive Economics* by Richard Lipsey (Weidenfeld, 1973).

Chapters 4 and 5

The treatment in this chapter is somewhat different from that found in the standard economic textbooks, but readers will find that *Demand and Supply* by Ralph Turvey (George Allen & Unwin, 1971) is a very useful supplement, while a more advanced textbook with a strong 'real world' bias is Frank Livesey's *Economics* (Polytech Publishers, 1972). A more difficult text is *An Introduction to Modern Economics* by Joan Robinson and John Eatwell (McGraw-Hill, 1973) but much of Book 2 of that volume is very relevant.

Chapter 6

Understandably, books on capitalist systems tend to be written by their critics. The development of capitalism from a Marxist point of view is in *Studies in the Development of Capitalism* by Maurice Dobb (Routledge & Kegan Paul, 1946). *Religion and the Rise of Capitalism* by R. H. Tawney (Pelican Books, 1938) discusses the emergence of the profit motive. A useful comparison of the salient features of contrasting economic systems, including nineteenth- and twentieth-century capitalism is George Dalton's *Economic Systems and Society* (Penguin Education, 1974), which is also useful reading for Chapters 8, 9 and 11. The chapter covers many separate topics which reappear elsewhere in the book, but one area in particular is covered by *Monopoly and Restrictive Practices* by G. C. Allen (George Allen & Unwin, 1969) which contains, besides a description of the UK machinery for handling this problem, an interesting discussion of the changing political attitudes towards monopoly.

Chapter 7

Books on labour economics and income distribution tend to be very technical, but *The Economics of Labour* by E. H. Phelps-Brown can be read by a beginner with profit. On income and wealth distribution, there is an excellent collection of readings in *Wealth, Income and Inequality* edited by A. B. Atkinson (Penguin Education, 1973), and *Poverty* by D. Jackson (Macmillan, 1972) gives a concise account of the dynamics of the poverty cycle. Up-to-date material on many of the topics in this chapter is given in Chapter 5 of *The U.K. Economy — A Manual of Applied Economics* edited by A. R. Prest and D. J. Coppock (Weidenfeld & Nicolson, latest ed.). 'Social Trends', published annually by the Central Statistical Office (HMSO), is another invaluable source of information relative to this book.

Chapter 8

A good survey of much of this material is C. T. Sandford's *Economics of Public Finance* (Pergamon Press, 1969). The theoretical aspects of this chapter are deal with in a readable fashion by the following: *Public Goods and the Public Sector* by M. Peston (Macmillan, 1972); *Cost Benefit Analysis* by D. W. Pearce (Macmillan, 1971); *Cost-Benefit Analysis and Public Expenditure* by G. H. Peters (Eaton Paper no 8, IEA 3rd Edition, 1973); *Elements of Cost-Benefit Analysis* by E. J. Mishan (George Allen & Unwin, 1972). 'Public Expenditure, Parliament and P.P.B.' by Peter Else (PEP Broadsheet no 522, 1970) is a simple introduction to programme budgeting.

Chapter 9

A book which surveys the characteristics of both free market and socialist economies is *Economic Systems* by G. N. Halm (Holt, Rinehart & Winston, 1970), but beginners may find some chapters difficult. Less thorough but quite comprehensive is George Dalton's *Economic Systems and Society* (Penguin Education, 1974). The literature on socialist and communist economics is voluminous and often difficult — a good point to begin would be some of the readings in *Socialist Economics* edited by A. Nove and D. M. Nuti (Penguin Education, 1972), especially the readings from Marx, Engels, *et al.* (reading no 1), Lange (no 4), and Montias (no. 10).

Chapter 10

The books by J. K. Galbraith on modern capitalism are both very readable and controversial, especially *The New Industrial State* (Hamish Hamilton, 1967) and *Economics and the Public Purpose* (Andre Deutsch, 1974). A thought-provoking collection of articles is contained in *Capitalism Today* edited by D. Bell and I. Kristol (New American Library, 1971).

There are many books giving the economic background to governmental policy in the post-war period, two of the most thorough being *Britain's Economic Prospects* by R. E. Caves *et al.* (1968) and its sequel *Britain's Economic Prospects Reconsidered* edited by Sir Cairncross (1971), both published by George Allen & Unwin. Chapter 4 of A. R. Prest and D. J. Coppock's *The U.K. Economy — A Manual of Applied Economics* (Weidenfeld & Nicolson, latest ed.) is also useful, as is the analysis and background material in *Case Studies in Economics — Economic Policy*, edited by C. T. Sandford and M. S. Bradbury (Macmillan, 1970). Various aspects of indicative planning are well covered by *Economic Planning and Policies in Britain, France and Germany* by Denton, Forsyth and Maclennan (PEP George Allen & Unwin, 1968). On the economic reforms in the socialist world, the reader might try any of the following: *Soviet-Type Economies* by R. W. Campbell (Macmillan, 1974); *The Economics of Socialism* by J. Wilczynski (George Allen & Unwin, 1970); readings nos. 14 to 16 by Liberman, Kosygin and Nove respectively in *Socialist Economics*, edited by A. Nove and D. M. Nuti (Penguin Education, 1972); *Economic Reform in the Soviet Union* by M. Ellman (PEP, 1969); and George Dalton's *Economic Systems and Society* (Penguin Education, 1974).

L. Tivey's survey *Nationalisation in British Industry* (Jonathan Cape, 1966) sets out the general background to public ownership in the UK, and D. Coombes in his *State Enterprise, Business or Politics?* (George Allen & Unwin and PEP, 1971) discusses contemporary problems of management and control.

Chapters 11 and 12

These chapters are to some extent interrelated, and the reading matter is often common to both. *Economic Development: Theory, History, Policy* by G. M. Meier and R. E. Baldwin (John Wiley, 1957) presents past and present economic development in a useful form, although it may be a little dated. It begins with a survey of economic ideas on the subject, discusses the experience of the UK, and goes on to consider the problems of initiating development in poor countries and of maintaining it in the rich. The longer-term issues are introduced in *The Limits to Growth* by D. L. Meadows (Earth Island, 1972) which we have referred to in the text. The reading on development topics is immense, however, and George Dalton's *Economic*

Systems and Society (Penguin Education, 1974) contains a useful bibliography. Books on international trade invariably contain a certain amount of theory, and there are again many to choose from. One which has been consistently popular is *The International Economy* by P. T. Ellsworth (Macmillan, 1964).

Chapter 13

The content of the brief final chapter is concerned with the nature of economic ideas and with how they relate to economic problems, and *Economic Philosophy* by Joan Robinson (Penguin, 1966) is recommended as a readable extension of this theme. The political economists have had their works summarised in a wide range of commentaries, but we feel that there is much to be gained from a reading of their original texts. We have already referred to Adam Smith and Karl Marx, but the works of J. S. Mill (for example *Utilitarianism, On Liberty; etc.*, Everyman's Library) are a good indication of the breadth of vision of the early writers. Much more recent but in the same vein are J. M. Keynes's *Essays in Persuasion* (Macmillan, 1972). Some of the arguments currently surrounding the role of the economists and his success in solving economic problems are rehearsed in the introductory chapter of Peter Donaldson's *Economics of the Real World* (Penguin, 1973). The works of J. K. Galbraith have been frequently referred to and in the text of this chapter we refer to Gunnar Myrdal and E. F. Schumacher as writers who point to the sterility of much 'scientific' economics — representative works of the latter authors are, respectively, *Asian Drama: an inquiry into the poverty of nations* (as abridged by S. S. King, Allen Lane, 1972), and *Small is Beautiful; a study of economics as if people mattered* (Bloud & Briggs, 1973).

Index